Fostering Resilience and Well-Being in Children and Families in Poverty

Fostering Resilience and Well-Being in Children and Families in Poverty

Why Hope Still Matters

VALERIE MAHOLMES

OXFORD
UNIVERSITY PRESS

OXFORD

UNIVERSITY PRESS

Oxford University Press is a department of the University of Oxford.
It furthers the University's objective of excellence in research, scholarship,
and education by publishing worldwide.

Oxford   New York

Auckland   Cape Town   Dar es Salaam   Hong Kong   Karachi
Kuala Lumpur   Madrid   Melbourne   Mexico City   Nairobi
New Delhi   Shanghai   Taipei   Toronto

With offices in

Argentina   Austria   Brazil   Chile   Czech Republic   France   Greece
Guatemala   Hungary   Italy   Japan   Poland   Portugal   Singapore
South Korea   Switzerland   Thailand   Turkey   Ukraine   Vietnam

Oxford is a registered trademark of Oxford University Press
in the UK and certain other countries.

Published in the United States of America by
Oxford University Press
198 Madison Avenue, New York, NY 10016

© Oxford University Press 2014

Library of Congress Cataloging-in-Publication Data
Maholmes, Valerie.
Fostering resilience and well-being in children and families in poverty :
why hope still matters / Valerie Maholmes.
pages cm
Includes bibliographical references and index.
ISBN 978–0–19–995952–5 (hardback)
1. Poor children.   2. Poor families.   3. Resilience (Personality trait)   4. Hope.   I. Title.
HV713.M26 2014
362.7′7569—dc23
2013042427

3 5 7 9 8 6 4 2
Printed in the United States of America
on acid-free paper

This book is dedicated to all the children and families who have risen above the difficult circumstances of life and have charted their own unique path toward well-being, and to hopeful families that are yet finding the strength and resolve to continue on their journey toward an optimistic future. I also dedicate this book to my parents, Spencer and Mary, whose love and support have always given me hope, and to my friends, who showered me with optimistic words of encouragement.

CONTENTS

PREFACE

Recently, a colleague and I edited a comprehensive text on children and poverty (Maholmes and King, 2012) that examines the deleterious outcomes of growing up in and experiencing adversities associated with economic disadvantage. While putting together that volume, I began to wonder about children who grew up in adversity but who appear to fare well despite those circumstances. I wondered about the factors that contribute to their success. I thought about people I know and families I've worked with who, despite humble beginnings, were managing their lives successfully. I also reflected on popular figures who shared stories in the media about the ways in which they overcame early adversity in their lives. As I reflected on these stories, it occurred to me that a common theme among these individuals was hope. I began to see the various ways in which hope is a highly influential and motivating force in their lives. This kind of hope is not passive—it is not merely wishing for a better life, but it is active. It involves thinking, planning, and acting on those thoughts and plans to achieve desired outcomes. It is the driving force that keeps us moving despite the adversity and allows us to adapt and to be resilient in the midst of these circumstances. In reflecting on these themes, I decided that I wanted to tell the stories of individuals striving to overcome adversity. I wanted to review literature that corresponds to the strengths and abilities these individuals displayed. To do this, I draw upon the conceptual frameworks and theories of hope articulated in the positive psychology literature and provide everyday examples to illuminate these theories of hope. My goal in doing so is to make the concepts and theories we discuss so freely in academic circles more accessible to policymakers and practitioners who work with poor children and families. When hope and resilience are understood in practical terms, perhaps we can help more children and families better manage their circumstances and chart pathways toward well-being.

I am eternally grateful to the individuals who allowed me to come to their homes, places of business, and other venues to hear their stories and learn about their lives.

I wanted to make their stories the centerpiece of this volume in an attempt to help bring to life the research and theories that I present in each chapter. I only hope I've done justice to their stories. In meeting these families, I learned about the complexity of some of their lives and the challenges they encounter daily. For example, when I went to meet with a family member, I found myself arriving at the venue on the edge of a drug deal that apparently had just been completed. Some of the other families I had hoped to interview didn't show up to meetings or they lost telephone service and for various reasons could not participate with me in this process. To me, these "absences" are a story in and of themselves, speaking volumes about the competing priorities and dimensions of their lives that remain misunderstood and underappreciated by those of us who make momentary appearances in the lives of these courageous individuals. Nevertheless, they keep their focus on the priorities in their lives—keeping their family together, staying sober, withdrawing from negative family influences, and pursuing higher education. These priorities are how they define success—why they have hope and why they continue to strive toward well-being.

This book covers a range of topics that I believe are important to the community of policy and practice professionals. After giving overviews of the research on resilience, hope, optimism, and related psychological assets in the first 2 chapters, I explore in each subsequent chapter an important factor that I contend helps promote hope and foster resilience in poor children and families. I invite the reader to reflect on policies and practices that can be informed by the research presented and inspired by the interviews with family members. Here I provide questions that I hope will encourage reflection on the themes presented in the book. For example, in Chapter 3, I review basic information about the brain and how it develops, and I explore whether various types of experiences promote changes in the brain that may allow for positive adaptation in adverse contexts. Practitioners may reflect on the following: *In what ways can knowledge about the brain and its capacity for renewal and recovery inform intervention strategies and efforts to promote hope and foster resilience in disadvantaged youth?*

In Chapter 4, I discuss the influential role of the family in the lives of poor children. Research shows that family functioning has far-reaching effects on children's development, and parenting shapes how children experience the world and how they see their place in it. I review these ideas from a strengths-based perspective and discuss assets—such as family support systems, mental health, cultural practices, and positive worldview—that may help a family manage the day-to-day complexities associated with material poverty. Reflection question: *The protective role of parents and parenting is a recurring theme throughout the book. What policies or practices help or hinder parents from engaging effectively with their children and extended family? In what ways can more resources be directed toward supporting and educating parents in positive parenting practices?*

Children spend the vast majority of their lives in school. In Chapter 5, I put forward the notion that, aside from the family, the school is perhaps one of the most influential organizations in the life of a child. School can be protective against the challenges experienced by children who live in impoverished communities and family environments. Reflection question: *What strategies can be implemented to promote greater opportunities to learn for children in low-resourced, underprivileged schools?*

Positive friendships and adult relationships have the potential to ameliorate early adversity in the lives of children. In Chapter 6, I explore the importance of engaging in positive peer relationships and forming meaningful friendships, as well as the role of mentoring in fostering resilience. Reflection question: *Quality friendships and positive adults can have an enduring impact on the lives of children. In what ways can existing programs be modified to promote effective mentoring and engagement with youth? Are there untapped resources in the community that can be drawn upon to cultivate meaningful and long-term relationships for economically disadvantaged children?*

In Chapter 7, I explore community and neighborhood assets and how these may promote hope and foster resilience. The places where children grow up, the resources available to them, the models of success and failure in adolescents and adults, businesses, community organizations, and places of worship play a role in shaping a child's future orientation. How these successes or failures are interpreted for and by children may have an impact on their own sense of hopefulness and optimism for their future. Reflection question: *What policies or practices are needed to foster collectively efficacy in neighborhoods and to promote empowerment among neighborhood residents to solve local problems?*

Like communities and neighborhoods, cultural frames of reference shape the way a child views him- or herself in the world and, most importantly, culture plays a central role in the identification and use of important coping mechanisms and adaptive processes. In Chapter 8, I explore the mechanisms by which cultural values, practices, and norms may be protective against aspects of adversity and how hope and resilience may be fostered. Reflection question: *How can we build upon valued cultural practices and beliefs to promote hope and foster resilience among economically disadvantaged families? To what extent do some policies help or hinder the use of culturally informed coping strategies?*

Chapter 9 provides case examples of the ways in which key indicators of hope and resilience have been applied to promote positive youth outcomes. Summaries of interviews with families are presented, as well as examples of how programs and interventions were implemented to yield positive developmental outcomes. Reflection question: *What can be learned from the experiences of the families interviewed for this volume to inform policies and practices supporting family cohesion, educational opportunity, youth development, and support for single-father-headed households?*

I close this volume in Chapter 10 by outlining a set of strategies and principles gleaned from the research and from the interviews with families that could inform an action agenda on behalf of children and families. I ask the reader to consider the critical importance of integrating into policies, practices, and interventions elements that will inspire hope in children and families living in poverty.

Earlier, I referred to the individuals I interviewed as courageous. Indeed they are. There are countless other courageous individuals who may never have the opportunity to tell their stories or to validate their experiences with concepts and theories discussed in the literature. I hope this volume will represent their lives as well and that those of us who work with these families, who advocate for or legislate on their behalf, will also have the courage to have hope and to allow that hope to be a motivating and unrelenting force in our efforts to foster resilience and well-being in these families.

FOREWORD

In *Fostering Resilience and Well-Being in Children and Families in Poverty: Why Hope Still Matters*, Dr. Valerie Maholmes offers policymakers, clinicians, and parents alike welcome insight into why some children are able to overcome almost relentless social adversity and succeed.

For an America beleaguered by a widening chasm between wealth and poverty that threatens our deepest social values and even our unity as a nation, *Why Hope Still Matters* is both thought-provoking and timely.

Research has taught us a great deal about why so many young people are failing to reach their potential. Yet our viewpoints about why some of our young succeed, apparently against the odds, is less well grounded in science and more a function of our own life experience and resulting patterns of belief.

Consider my own life story.

My parents left sharecropping in Clarenden County, SC, just after WWII to achieve education and greater opportunity for their children. As a result, I spent my earliest years living in a small, rented South Baltimore row house near Fort McHenry—where the Star Spangled Banner still waves.

Every morning, like American schoolchildren everywhere, I recited the Pledge of Allegiance to our flag, although I must tell you that I had to question whether those inspiring words, "liberty and justice for all," included my brothers, sisters, and me.

Our poorly equipped, eight-room elementary school didn't even have a lunch room, an auditorium, or a gymnasium. Because my parents had received little formal education themselves, they were not able to send me to elementary school ready to learn, so I was trying to learn in what was then called the "third group."

Today, we would call that class "special education."

One day, a counselor asked me what I wanted to become in my life. I answered that I wanted to be a lawyer like Ms. Juanita Jackson Mitchell, who had stood up for us children at the Riverside Swimming Pool we children had marched to integrate.

I told him that I wanted to become a lawyer so that I could help others.

I must tell you, though, that my counselor just looked at me, a poor kid in the "third group," and he exclaimed: "You want to be a lawyer…! Who do you think you are?"

I was crushed—and I almost lost faith in myself that day—but in the months to come, good teachers like Mr. Hollis Posey listened to my dreams. They believed in my potential, encouraged me, and taught to my strengths.

Meanwhile, outside of school, our local recreation leader, "Captain" Jim Smith, took me under his wing; and Dr. Albert Friedman, our neighborhood pharmacist, trusted me and gave me my first job.

Together with my parents, they lifted me up by the strength of their example. They took my dream and made it their own.

So I kept working hard, and the day finally came when I made it out of the third group.

I went on to study at and graduate from Baltimore's top academic high school. Later, I would earn a *Phi Beta Kappa* key at Howard University and then a law degree.

I worked hard to perfect my calling, helping other people whenever I could; as a result, I am honored and privileged today to represent my community in the Congress of the United States.

I share this personal recollection with you not to celebrate my own success in life, but to encourage everyone who reads these words to support our next generation on their own life journeys.

Genetics and what we like to call our individual natures may have had something to do with the hope and resilience that have encouraged me throughout my life. Yet I also know that those qualities had to be *nurtured*—or I could well have fallen by the wayside as did so many of my childhood friends.

When Juanita Jackson Mitchell of the NAACP stood up for us children as we were attacked there at Riverside Swimming Pool, she gave me something far more important than the ability to cool off on a hot summer day. She taught me that I was a person with rights that others had to respect.

That lesson transformed me.

When my parents, Mr. Hollis Posey, and those other key people in my early life encouraged me to have higher expectations for myself, they helped to set me on a course that led me to the Congress of the United States.

Yet I doubt that I would have succeeded in that journey without the expanding social consciousness and generous public support of 1960s America.

Today, for our nation to once again achieve that effective, uplifting national perspective that will help more of our young people build stable, productive lives, we must better understand *how* young people can succeed against the odds.

We must learn how to better nurture their hope-filled natures. I predict that *Why Hope Still Matters* will be an important contribution toward that end.

Elijah Cummings, Member of Congress

ACKNOWLEDGMENTS

I especially want to acknowledge the support of Dr. Jacquelyn Beals, whose thoughtful feedback and insightful critiques challenged me to work to my best ability. I especially want to thank the staffs at Hope and a Home and at The Family Place for their willingness to share their exceptional knowledge and wisdom with me. I am awed by the work you do to ensure the health and well-being of the children and families you serve. Finally, to the individuals who agreed to share their insights with me, I hope that the power of your stories will change the lives of those who read this book in the way my life was changed by listening to your hopeful experiences.

ABOUT THE AUTHOR

Dr. Valerie Maholmes has devoted her career to studying factors that affect child developmental outcomes. Low-income minority children have been a particular focus of her research, practical, and civic work. She has been a faculty member at the Yale Child Study Center in the Yale School of Medicine, where she held the Irving B. Harris Assistant Professorship of Child Psychiatry, an endowed professorial chair. While at Yale, Dr. Maholmes worked in numerous capacities, including Director of Research and Policy at the School Development Program. She has served on numerous professional boards and was also a member of the New Haven Board of Education, where she served as Vice President/Secretary. Notably, she was awarded the prestigious science-policy fellowship with the Society for Research in Child Development and the American Association for the Advancement of Sciences. Dr. Maholmes completed her bachelor's and master's degrees at Montclair State University in Montclair, NJ, and a doctoral degree from Howard University in Washington, DC. She also earned a sixth-year degree from Fairfield University in Fairfield, CT. She is currently employed at the National Institutes of Health in Bethesda, MD.

Fostering Resilience and Well-Being in Children and Families in Poverty

1

Hope

The Motivation to Overcome Adversity

Hope springs eternal in the human breast: Man never is, but always to be blest.

—Alexander Pope, *An Essay on Man, Epistle I* (1733)

The essence of humanity is the life-long journey toward self-actualization. In the process of achieving their highest potential, individuals follow different pathways and may reach vastly different endpoints, yet their underlying drive is the same. Researchers, philosophers, and practitioners alike have sought to define the inner quality that urges us to strive, motivates belief, and gives rise to resilience. Carl Rogers, the founder of humanistic psychology, believed that humans have a self-actualizing tendency—an innate drive pushing each person to fulfill their potentials. Rogers (1995) believed that this tendency moves us to develop our capacities in ways that enhance our being and humanness and move us toward autonomy. This drive is directional and constructive, and although it can be suppressed, it cannot be destroyed without the destruction of the organism (Rogers, 1977). Maddi, a personality theorist (1996), describes this tendency as a "biological pressure to fulfill the genetic blueprint" (p. 106), suggesting that every person has a fundamental mandate to fulfill their potential (Pescitelli, 1996).

These theories are compelling, but they raise a number of questions: What is at the heart of this natural tendency to strive? What circumstances suppress these natural tendencies, and can they have an impact on individuals' ability to achieve their potential? How is the fundamental mandate to fulfill potential achieved? Do some factors thwart our best efforts to fulfill this mandate? And, conversely, are there factors that facilitate and enhance our ability to fulfill this mandate? This book explores these questions by drawing on the everyday lives of families in difficult circumstances who are in the process of overcoming these challenges.

My premise is that *hope* lies at the heart of the energy that propels people toward self-actualization: achieving the highest vision of themselves for the good of their families, themselves, their communities, and the greater humanity. It is my contention that hope is the essential mindset that enables individuals to have resilience in the face of adverse circumstances.

In everyday terms, hope is thought of as the optimistic anticipation of a positive outcome despite evidence to the contrary. It is generally perceived as the ability to look beyond the current circumstance or situation and expect something different from whatever is currently presenting itself. Hopefulness is thought to foster perseverance, persistence, and resilience in uncertainty in many of the same ways as Rogers' self-actualizing tendencies. Therefore, hope is often thought of as a quality that resides within the human spirit and can be summoned as needed in times of difficulty or adversity. We rely heavily on hope as a source of encouragement and motivation to sustain our efforts or to strive toward our best and highest potential, even when all evidence points to a less favorable outcome. Hope is believed to play an important role in a variety of processes, including coping and recovery from illness and injury. Hope may be a protective mechanism that provides a buffer against the full impact of an adverse situation and gives the wherewithal to push beyond the prevailing risks and strive toward recovery. Hope, when grounded in realism about one's situation, may give strength to manage the complexities of an illness and the associated emotional challenges, facilitating at least psychological well-being and improved quality of life. For the families of recovering patients, hope derived from social and cultural support networks, faith, and spirituality facilitates coping and positive responsiveness to the needs of the loved one (Bland & Darlington, 2002).

Against-all-odds human interest stories resonate deeply within us and keep us mindful of the power of the human spirit to overcome challenges and adversity. Inspirational narratives of people who accomplish seemingly impossible feats through sheer willpower and determination give rise to notions that many obstacles can be overcome with effort and persistence. Most of us can recall a story told within our family or social network about someone who never gave up despite daunting circumstances. In the popular media, Goldschein and Eisenberg (2011) chronicled the life of Ursula Burns, now a businesswoman, who grew up in a housing project on Manhattan's Lower East Side—a hub for gangs. Burns was raised by her single mother, who ran a daycare center out of her home and ironed shirts so she could afford to send her daughter to Catholic school. Ursula went to NYU, from there became an intern at Xerox, and at the time of this writing is Xerox's CEO and chairwoman—the first African American woman to head a *Fortune* 500 company.

The story of Oprah Winfrey's success is well known. She spent the first six years of her life living with her grandmother and wearing dresses made out of potato sacks. During that time, she experienced a series of adverse events, including child molestation and teen pregnancy. Only after Oprah's mother sent her to live with her father did her life turn around. Oprah earned a full scholarship to college, where she was discovered by a radio station and began her successful career. Oprah's name became an empire, and she is reportedly now worth more than $2.7 billion (Goldschein & Eisenberg, 2011).

The story of Dr. Ben Carson illustrates motivation to achieve. Ben was also raised by a single mother and, for the greatest part of his early childhood, didn't believe he was capable of learning because he always scored at the bottom of the class. Envisioning a brighter future for her children, Ben's mother constantly reiterated to them that there was nothing they couldn't achieve if they put enough work into it. While working as a housekeeper for a professor, Ben's mother quickly recognized the role that books played in the man's success. Upon realizing this, she made her two sons borrow books from the library, read them, and write her book reports. This was the first time Ben had ever read a book from start to finish, and this was also the turning point in his life. Ben realized the potential of hard work—a quality that helped him throughout his rise to a prestigious career in medicine. Because of his determination and hard work, as well as the deep-rooted self-confidence instilled in him by his mother, Ben went on to excel in the world of neurosurgery, becoming the first surgeon ever to successfully separate conjoined twins attached at the head (Academy of Achievement, 2012).

Former President Bill Clinton has a similar story: When Bill was 4 years old, his mother left him with her parents while she trained as a nurse. Bill's stepfather was an alcoholic, and family life was frequently disrupted by domestic violence; yet despite his rocky relationship with his stepfather, Bill changed his last name to Clinton as a teenager. When Clinton was 17, he met then-President John F. Kennedy and, as a result, decided that he wanted a career in politics. Clinton entered Georgetown University in 1964, graduated, and was awarded a Rhodes scholarship, which allowed him to continue his studies for the next two years at Oxford University. After attending Yale Law School, Bill eventually began the political career he first aspired to during his youth and was the youngest-ever governor of Arkansas. Clinton entered the 1992 race for president and was elected to serve for two terms (Encyclopedia of World Biography, n.d.).

Common to every individual in these adversity-to-prosperity stories is a defining moment, marked by a dawning awareness of their own capability that changed the course of their life. For some, this awareness was fostered by the intervention of a parent or teacher. For others, it resulted from an experience that gave them insight into what their future could be. Nonetheless, in each of these examples awareness gave rise to hope, and hope led to action. To hope for a particular outcome is an active process. It allows one to move toward a particular goal by envisioning and articulating that goal and by identifying and securing resources and supports to bring that goal to fruition.

These well-known stories inspire us to believe that anyone can rise above their circumstances to achieve their goals and dreams. However, many stories of overcoming and achievement that begin in equally challenging contexts may end not with material wealth but rather with a sense of accomplishment in their striving toward self-actualization—whatever that entails for each individual. If hope does spring eternal, the contexts in which individuals call upon hope may determine how assertive their actions, how effortful their striving, how clearly articulated their goals.

Few contexts embody more adversity and uncertainty than does poverty. Children and families living in and affected by poverty are often referred to as not having hope, or feeling that their situation is hopeless, depending on the magnitude of problems associated with poverty and economic disadvantage. The despair and hopelessness associated with poverty are well documented. A large body of research has shown how poverty and disadvantage, when experienced early in life, have consequences that reach into the early childhood years, adolescence, and adulthood (Maholmes & King, 2012). These consequences include negative effects on social, health, and educational outcomes. Studies have also shown large and consistent associations between poverty and negative academic outcomes, including lower reading scores, poorer health, and social behavior problems (Maholmes & King, 2012). Children living in poverty are at greater risk for displaying behavior and emotional problems and difficulty getting along with peers. Long-term poverty is also associated with children's inner feelings of anxiety, unhappiness, and dependence (Bolger, Patterson, Thompson, & Kupersmidt, 1995; McLoyd & Wilson, 1991).

In addition to early experiences of poverty, we have become increasingly aware that children who experience deep and persistent poverty are likely to have economic hardships and associated problems in adulthood (Wagmiller & Adelman, 2009) ranging from a greater risk of low birth weight babies to other health, social, educational, and parenting outcomes (Redd et al., 2011). Conger, Conger, and Matthews (1999) reported that children who grew up in poverty are more likely to have low productivity and low earnings compared to children who did not grow up in poverty, and adolescents are more likely to drop out of school and consequently engage in delinquent or antisocial behavior. These poor educational outcomes are also associated with challenges in adulthood, including unemployment or underemployment and limited access to health care and other important social services and resources (Maholmes & King, 2012). Family poverty is also associated with higher risk for teen childbearing, less-positive peer relations, and lower self-esteem. All these outcomes feed into the vicious cycle of poverty.

The challenges associated with poverty are seemingly intractable. As current economic conditions become less stable, children are at the greatest risk for slipping deeper into poverty. Given this trend, it is not surprising that children would be on a trajectory of poor developmental outcomes as a consequence of living in or being affected by poverty.

However, a less well-understood story is that of the poor children who seem to fare well despite their risks for poor outcomes. The circumstances surrounding their economic situation may not ultimately change, but some children and families are able to manage or overcome many of the consequences of poverty. Regrettably, few if any population-based statistics are available on the children and families living in poverty who have managed to avert these consequences—leaving us with only popular stories and anecdotes about children reared in adverse circumstances who overcame these adversities to become successful adults. In many ways, the lack of any empirical treatment of this phenomenon has fostered the notion of rugged individualism and a bootstrap theology that few can endorse. Yet such perspectives do not lead to an understanding of the environment in which a child grows and develops or how elements of this environment can be brought to bear on a child's outlook on life, creating conditions in which hopefulness will flourish. Nor does this individualistic view make a case for developing policies and programs that could promote hope and increase the likelihood that more children and families will escape the stranglehold of poverty.

The story of three young men who grew up in Chicago's South Side is instructive. The three friends decided that they wanted to become doctors and made a pact to support each other so they could make it out of their difficult circumstances together (Davis et al., 2003). All three are now successful doctors and write prolifically about their struggle to achieve. Most importantly, they have crafted their experiences into a set of "lessons learned" in order to help others achieve similar outcomes. Their story sheds light on the influences, both positive and negative, of their ecological context: first, the powerful influence of a role model who gave them a vision of what they could be in life. Peer support was also an important process in their story, as was support from caring adults. Thus, having someone believe that they could, in fact, achieve these goals was important for inspiring hope and engendering optimism (Davis et al., 2003).

Intrigued by human interest stories and advances in research on resilience, as well as the empirical studies that are now available, I was impelled to explore this phenomenon of hope in more depth, looking at it in the context of poverty. I am convinced that this phenomenon deserves far more attention. If we can understand how hope functions as a mechanism that enables children and families to navigate difficult circumstances and defy the odds stacked against them, perhaps we can learn from these processes—developing strategies to be adopted and designing policies and programs that create opportunities for more children and families to flourish. It is my contention that hope matters a great deal and plays an important role in overcoming adversity. Hope matters for the children and families who discover its motivational efficacy. Hope matters for those presumed to be lost causes but who have untapped potential to succeed. Hope still matters for those of us who study, educate, legislate, and provide services to children and families. We need to find ways to look beyond what seems hopeless and to provide resources and support so that the hopes placed in us by poor children and their families are not futile but are fulfilled.

The purpose of this book is to explore the role of hope in promoting positive outcomes for children and families who live in poverty and experience the problems associated with economic and social disadvantage. This includes persistent lack of adequate income; the inability to acquire the basic goods and services necessary for daily living and survival with dignity; low levels of health and education; lack of access to services, transportation, and other resources; inadequate physical security; lack of voice or political influence; and social exclusion (Bradley & Corwyn, 2002; Department of Health & Human Services, 2012).

To start, let me introduce the individuals whose stories and insights are the centerpiece of this book. These accounts, obtained through semi-structured interview protocols (Harrell & Bradley, 2009), shed light on how hope has enabled low-income families to manage the day-to-day complexities of their lives and to achieve their most fundamental goal: providing a better life for their children.

Meet "Ashante," an African American male in his 30s. I interviewed Ashante on a college campus, where he is pursuing a graduate degree in African American studies. He speaks of the philosophies, theories, and ideologies of people of African descent, both on the continent and in the African Diaspora. He looks forward to having an academic career where he can write and lecture about these ideas and help school the minds of young scholars about the importance of knowing one's cultural heritage. However, Ashante's path to graduate school was not typical. In fact, very little about his experiences leading up to matriculation in graduate school was typical of the average college student. From a very early age, Ashante participated in the culture of gangs and of the streets. While spending time in prison for his exploits, he had an epiphany. I share how this experience changed his life and helped him take steps toward a more hopeful and productive future.

Similarly, "Carlton" had an awakening of sorts. While shuffling from homeless shelter to homeless shelter and struggling to overcome addiction to alcohol, Carlton knew he needed to make a change in his life—if not for his sake, then for his daughter. A middle-aged African American man, Carlton now reflects on his journey and shares the pride of single-parenting and the challenges of recovery.

Everyone needs to have a "Josephine" in their life. An African American mother of five, near retirement age, Josephine shares the wisdom of her hard-fought victories. I met Josephine through a transitional housing program of which she was once a client. She now works at this program, skillfully guiding other parents through the inevitable twists and turns on the road toward well-being. She knows firsthand how perplexing this journey can be, having to come from "uptown" to "downtown" in homelessness shelters, fighting to keep her family together.

Few parents have the intimate knowledge of child development as "Amanda" does. She earned a PhD in developmental science and works in child protective capacities. Amanda's story represents the influential role of family functioning on child outcomes. A European American mother of a toddler, Amanda reveals the challenges of growing up in family dysfunction and how her early life experiences gave her the drive and ambition to create a caring and nurturing home environment for her child.

In addition to my interviews with these parents, I also met with staff in the intervention programs that serve these individuals, and I share their insights and recommendations for programs and policies. "Sarah" is an academic researcher and also directs a trauma program that services American Indian children and families. Her interview provides important insights regarding the roles of family, culture, and spirituality in promoting hope and fostering resilience. "Ramona" represents a program that largely serves immigrant families—primarily mothers and children. Her accounts of family culture, advocacy, and education speak to the important role that having knowledge plays in fostering a sense of empowerment, purpose, and optimism in families. Finally, excerpts of focus group discussions featuring low-income students participating in a national leadership academy shed light on the influential role of parents and teachers in promoting hope in children and youth.

I anticipate that the perspectives from these interviews will personify the scientific literature on hope, optimism, and resilience and help practitioners and policymakers who work with children and families to become more aware of the factors that promote hope in children and, in response, design interventions and policies that allow hope to thrive.

Hope and resilience do not occur in isolation, but they are influenced by the psychological and physical environment in which children and families interact. Bronfenbrenner's (1979) ecological theory frames an important perspective for understanding these psychological resources and how they occur in children and families. His ideas call attention not only to the individual but also to the family, community, and societal factors that work together to influence a child's development and outcomes. Bronfenbrenner's theory suggests that a child is "nested" within interacting systems. The first of these is what he calls a *microsystem* or an immediate influential environment that includes the family: its structure, available resources, and the ways in which the family functions. In addition, the microsystem includes other influential systems, including peer and other social relationships, the community and its resources in terms of services and supports, livability in terms of safety and security or the presence of crime and violence, and, finally, the availability of religious and cultural institutions. School is also included in the microsystem: Its resources, structure, and functioning are important considerations in this theory, as are the relationships and interactions among the school, the family, and the child. Individuals encounter the most social interactions within the microsystem. Here, an individual is not passively observing his or her experiences but is helping to create and construct experiences through interactions within and across elements of this microsystem (Bronfenbrenner, 1979).

The interactions, referred to as a *mesosystem*, include experiences at home related to experiences at school, or experiences at school related to experiences at church, in the community, and so on. In contrast, the *exosystem* does not involve an individual's active role in the construction of experiences. Instead, the experiences tend to be externally driven and beyond personal control. However, these experiences have a direct impact on the microsystem of which the individual is part. An example might be a child's parent being laid off from work or losing a job. This event, of course, could have direct bearing on the parent's ability to provide for a child's basic needs of food, shelter, and clothing, and could lead to maternal depression, increased levels of stress or tension in the home, child abuse and neglect, or even domestic violence.

The societal context is at Bronfenbrenner's *macrosystem* level, which refers to the cultural beliefs, historical narratives, or sociopolitical issues, including policies, that affect how the child and family function. Obviously, cultural beliefs and historical narratives may directly affect a child in terms of child-rearing practices, worldview, or response to challenges. Individuals may not have as much of an influential role in shaping their experiences at the macrosystem level, but they may function as dictated by sociopolitical or cultural norms (Betancourt & Beardslee, 2012).

Finally, Bronfenbrenner's *chronosystem* reflects the cumulative experiences of a person over the course of his or her lifetime. These experiences constitute major transitions (both positive and negative) and environmental events in life. Examples of such transitions might be the loss of a parent, birth of a baby, removal from immediate family to a foster home, imprisonment of a parent, or marriage. The chapters of this book are written to correspond to these ecological system levels. The contexts, processes, and factors that give rise to hope will be reviewed in light of each level. I chose to do this to underscore that just as these ecological systems are interactive and bidirectional, so too are the factors that promote hope and foster resilience. As we will learn from Carlton, Ashante, Amanda, Josephine, and the individuals who work with them, there are many processes and factors that give rise to adaptation and positive outcomes for children and families. Accordingly, policymakers and practitioners must work within and across systems to bring about change.

Throughout the book, I pose provocative questions to enhance understandings of hope and discuss contrasting literatures on important themes. One such question is whether we are "wired *for* hope." Are there pathways and processes in the brain's structure and functions that give rise to hope and optimism? To what extent do experiences of the environment promote changes in the brain that permit or foster positive adaptation to potentially deleterious contexts? Finally, I discuss the brain's capacity for renewal and recovery—essentially giving us the wherewithal to continue learning, adapting, growing, and perhaps hoping, throughout our lives. While the last two decades have seen great strides in understanding brain development and the importance of early stimulation, there is still much to learn. The best available science tells us that an impoverished environment may lead to poor functioning and deficits in certain brain regions (Shonkoff & Phillips, 2000; Kaufman et al., 2000). Burgeoning empirical evidence suggests that the effects of impoverishment can be ameliorated—although more research is needed in this area—but restoration can occur, giving us hope that the long-term and generational grip of poverty can be loosened so more youth will have enhanced capacity to achieve their goals and realize their potential (Blair & Raver, 2012). The potential for continuous learning gives us encouragement as policymakers, educators, parents, and those who care about the children's welfare that our intervention efforts are not in vain. Rather, they should be redoubled to ensure each child a safe passage into adulthood.

The influential role of the family is well documented, and a large body of research shows that family functioning has far-reaching effects on children's developmental trajectories (American Academy of Pediatrics, 2003). In particular, parenting directly shapes how children see and experience the world and how they see their place in the world (Greenberger & Goldberg, 1989; Hughes & Chen, 1997; Maccoby, 1992). Parenting behaviors and practices that are warm, nurturing, and engaging promote secure attachments and help a child to develop self-control, confidence, and the social and emotional skills needed for a variety of life situations (Jackson-Newsome, Buchanan, & McDonald, 2008).

It goes without saying that material assets afford families a range of advantages such as economic security, food security, and housing. Yet even in the absence of material assets, some families possess psychosocial assets such as family support systems, mental health, cultural practices, and a positive worldview that help them manage the day-to-day complexities associated with material poverty. What are some of the salient family psychosocial assets, and how are they cultivated and inculcated in children? How do these promote hope and foster resilience? These questions are explored and, where appropriate, the experiences of Carlton, Josephine, Ashante, and Amanda are shared to address these questions.

Outside the family, the school is arguably one of the most influential organizations in the life of a child. Interactions with teachers, peers, and other personnel indelibly impress upon children certain perspectives on who they are and what they can do in the world. Schools that foster engagement and allow these interactions to occur help facilitate these important impressions and perspectives. However, in addition to the psychosocial aspects of the schooling process, I focus attention on the necessity of ensuring that children and youth have the opportunity to learn. While the debates surrounding this important policy have subsided and attention has focused on other issues, its mandate remains unfulfilled. As disparities in disadvantaged children's learning and behavioral outcomes persist, our attention needs to be turned again to this important goal of eradicating inequities in the educational process. Research consistently points to the important role of quality early educational experiences in stimulating cognitive abilities and regulatory capacities in children—all important processes for learning and engagement (Dawson, Ashman, & Carver, 2000; Greenberg, 2006). Investing in these experiences will increase the chances for economically disadvantaged children to have positive outcomes throughout the schooling process, thus laying the groundwork for success in adult life. The school's role in promoting hope and fostering resilience is highly influential and should be central to our understandings of the processes by which we can protect against the challenges encountered daily by children who live in impoverished communities and homes. Ashante's story is illustrative of the transformative power of educational opportunity coupled with the motivational aspects of hope. Together, hope and opportunity provided the context for Ashante to rebound from adversities associated with a criminal lifestyle.

The ability to engage in positive peer relationships and form meaningful friendships is an important developmental achievement. A youth's mastery of these tasks is associated with positive developmental outcomes (Lerner et al., 2005), prosocial behavior, and positive school adjustment (Gifford-Smith & Brownell, 2003). I will explore the extent to which these interactions and psychosocial processes among peers play a role in promoting hope. I will also broach the important topic of mentoring. The facilitating role of mentoring for promoting positive child developmental outcomes is well documented in the literature. Early research by Russian psychologist Lev Vygotsky referred to the dynamic of this relationship as the "Zone of Proximal Development," in which an expert leads and supports a novice until he or she has obtained the requisite skills to master a task. Vygotsky (1978) sees the Zone of Proximal Development as an area that requires the most sensitive instruction or guidance—allowing a child to develop skills to use on their own. This research has tremendous relevance for thinking about the specific type and timing of mentoring that vulnerable youth may need to achieve their goals. Formal and informal mentors provide the scaffolding necessary to help a youth gain confidence, personal agency, and a sense of self-efficacy (Dubois & Rhodes, 2006). In so doing, mentoring and responsiveness from caring adults can promote hope in youth and inspire them to strive persistently toward their goals.

Neighborhoods are significant in the social identity of children and youth. The specific communities where children grow up; the available resources; the models of success and failure; and the types of businesses, organizations, and places of worship play roles in shaping a child's future orientation and worldview. I explore community and neighborhood assets and how these can promote hope and foster resilience. I also explore the notion of social capital, which researchers refer to as the ability to draw upon one's social networks and groups to acquire the resources and support needed to navigate uncharted territory (e.g., new employment, new neighborhoods, new school contexts, etc.) or to negotiate for resources and support (Coleman, 1988; Runyan et al., 1998; Cattell, 2001). To whatever extent these assets are present, hope has an opportunity to be present and to thrive.

Much like communities and neighborhoods, cultural frames of reference can shape the way a child views him- or herself in the world; most importantly, culture plays a central role in the identification and use of specific coping mechanisms, adaptive processes, and strategies in succumbing to or overcoming adversity (Gutiérrez & Rogoff, 2003). I explore the ways in which cultural values, practices, and norms may protect against aspects of adversity and the role hope plays in this process. In addition, I discuss the important role of culture in promoting hope and fostering resilience, including factors that may influence perceptions of opportunity, worldview, and social capital. I consider ways in which cultural help-seeking behaviors and coping strategies may aid in ameliorating the effects of stress and other issues associated with living in poverty.

Finally, it's important to put in concrete terms how the theories and ideas proposed throughout the book can be used to engender action. The ultimate goal of this volume is to explore where the evidence supporting these ideas and theories may converge and, most importantly, to translate this evidence into discrete action steps that practitioners and policymakers can take to create a hope-promoting agenda. I end this volume with a set of lessons learned, case studies, and principles gleaned from the research and from the interviews with families, which underlie this action agenda.

Of course, the theories offered and ideas discussed are not meant to be exhaustive or prescriptive. They may not, in and of themselves, have an impact on children's outlook on life or their ability to cope in adverse contexts. But taken together, the psychosocial assets, interventions, resources, and policies described may work in tandem and create the conditions that inspire hope and motivation to thrive in the midst of adversity. Moreover, I do not intend to portray "having hope" as a silver bullet for overcoming adversity. Rather, I have observed that some processes seem to allow families to thrive in the midst of difficult circumstances. In some cases these circumstances change and become less constraining, while in others the circumstances are neither easily nor rapidly resolved. Understanding the factors that favor hope over hopelessness may help us work with families to give them the hope, agency, and optimism to self-actualize and achieve their potential.

Resilience and hope do not mean the absence of adversity. In fact, individuals interviewed for this volume describe in vivid terms the pressures and challenges of poverty and economic disadvantage. Yet, somehow, these challenges served to motivate these families to pursue a hopeful pathway. The pathway from having hope and optimism to reaching positive outcomes is often far from linear. In fact, my interviews show that there are multiple pathways to resilient outcomes, with positive and negative experiences interacting at different developmental time points to reach these outcomes. I strongly suspect that hope is present at each of these time points, and it is the presence of hope that allows individuals to persist in their pursuit of better outcomes. Thus, this book is not an exhaustive study, but it provides an initial view through the lens of hope of policies and practices that will help families surmount barriers—both psychological and structural—that might otherwise confine them to the prisons of poverty and economic disadvantage.

Thus the subtitle of this book is *Why Hope Still Matters*. It matters in the extent to which children and families will engage with or even see the value of participating in interventions or will take advantage of available resources. It matters in the effort parents and children put forth to achieve a goal. It matters in terms of whether they feel their goals are attainable. If parents or children feel that putting forth any effort is futile, or that having a dream or aspiration is of no avail, then the policies, practices, and interventions that offer prospects of a positive, fruitful, and more productive future may also fail. The challenges in the lives of children and families living in poverty often lead us to project hopelessness in the way we respond to their needs. Having purposeful optimism is important, and it matters greatly to these families despite the complexities of their lives. For those who touch the lives of these families, a strong and pervasive hope in their ability to self-actualize and fulfill their potential still matters.

2

Thriving in Adversity

Toward a Framework of Hope, Optimism, and Resilience

> *Let my body dwell in poverty, and my hands be as the hands of the toiler; but let my soul be as a temple of remembrance where the treasures of knowledge enter and the inner sanctuary is hope.*
> —George Eliot, *Daniel Deronda* (1887)

One of my favorite sayings is "How you start out is not always how you end up." Underlying this sentiment is the belief that, despite the challenges and complexities of life, one's fate is not necessarily sealed. Starting life with disadvantages doesn't mean that they will define the narrative of one's life, obstacles and setbacks notwithstanding. The deleterious outcomes of poverty and economic disadvantage are well documented (Maholmes & King, 2012). Empirical studies have demonstrated the risks for negative outcomes such as poor physical, mental, and emotional health; school dropout; and other problems that often perpetuate the cycle of poverty (Korenman, Miller, & Sjaastad, 1995; Duncan, Yeung, Brooks-Gunn, & Smith, 1998; Evans, 2004). Popular media highlight the all-too-familiar stories of inner city youths who drop out of school and become involved with the juvenile justice system, or the adolescent mother—both undereducated and underemployed—who is overwhelmed by the stresses of her life. However, for each of these stories there is likely another with a similar beginning but, leavened by hope, a different middle and perhaps a different ending.

Hope is an important psychological resource that has been associated with positive outcomes. It is commonly thought of as an intangible but palpable resource that helps us manage the unknowns in our lives. We rely on hope to yield positive outcomes in difficult circumstances (hoping for the best). We call upon hope for direction and focus in times of uncertainty (hoping for answers). And we refer to hope as a way of explaining the seemingly inexplicable (hope that things will become clearer in time). In addition to these everyday applications, hope has been used as a key strategy in therapeutic relationships with patients having mental health or other rehabilitative needs (Koratamaddi, 2012). Hope is believed to play an important supportive role in the recovery of chronically ill patients, recovery from the pain of bereavement, and psychological healing from difficult life circumstances (Benzein & Berg, 2005; Cutcliffe, 2006; Snyder, Lehman, Kluck, & Monsson, 2006). In fact, as far back as 1905, hope was mentioned in psychiatric literature by Freud, who believed that many benefits of psychoanalysis could be explained by patients' "expectations, colored by hope and faith" (p. 289) in the treatment process (cited in Weis & Speridakos, 2011). Half a century later, Menninger (1959) urged mental health practitioners to study hope, "a basic but elusive ingredient in our daily work" (p. 281) (cited in Weiss & Speridakos, 2011). More recently, cognitive and social psychologists have put forward theories of hope that reflect its influential role in bringing about positive psychosocial, educational, emotional, and health outcomes.

Closely related to hope are two important concepts also associated with positive outcomes: *optimism* and *resilience*. Although each has its own unique characteristics and qualities, I propose that, together with hope, they foster adaptive functioning and well-being. Hope is a psychological resource that motivates and drives future action. It involves a sense of personal agency, planning, and strategic thinking to work toward goals. We can see hope reflected in the old adage: "Where there's a will, there's a way."

While *optimism* involves one's perspective on circumstances and the subsequent behavioral response, *resilience* is thought to involve both the risks and the capacity to adapt despite adversity. Competence and growth are the hallmarks of resilience (Masten et al., 1999; Garmezy, 1993; Garmezy, Masten, & Tellegen, 1984). Taken together, these constructs form a potential explanatory model for understanding the ways in which children and families may fare well despite adversity. In addition, it is my contention that hope, optimism, and resilience potentially give rise to well-being—a general state of satisfaction, health, happiness, and success in life. This is ultimately what we strive for; however, we define and perceive of it. In the sections that follow, I discuss the distinctive elements of each concept and how they are related to each other. I also discuss the notion that the degree to which one has hope or optimism, or is resilient to certain adversities, is shaped by the protective influences of the social and physical environment. The explication of these ideas will serve as the basis for exploring, in subsequent chapters, factors that promote hope and optimism and foster resilience in children and families experiencing adversities associated with economic disadvantage.

Hope: Where There's a Will, There's a Way

Hope as a Cognitive Process

The study of hope has origins in a variety of disciplines and is well established in the literatures of psychotherapy, mental health, and positive psychology. The scholarly work of Snyder and colleagues (1997, 2002) validates hope as a cognitive construct and theorizes about hopeful thinking in children and adults. In much the same manner as Rogers theorized about the human tendency toward self-actualization, Snyder propounded the idea that humans are innately motivated to understand the world in which they live and to manage their environment to ensure predictability and familiarity (Snyder, Feldman, Shorey, & Rand, 2002). Infants come into the world experiencing a variety of sensory stimuli and, over time, they learn to make meaning of these early experiences. Snyder and colleagues (2002) contended that, through the processes of making meaning and anticipating environmental predictability, the fundamental cognitive processes underlying hope are formed. In infants and young children, a positive and nurturing bond with the caregiver is important in the development of hope. This bond gives the child a sense of security and confidence that he or she can overcome obstacles and accomplish his or her goals (Snyder, Feldman, et al., 2002). Such confidence is important as children develop through middle childhood and into adolescence. Peer relationships take center stage at these junctures, and youth are confronted daily with the need to make a host of health-risking or health-promoting decisions. Confidence in the ability to make decisions in their immediate and long-term best interests is a component of hope. Thus having a secure base of attachment with their primary caregiver in early childhood as well as a sense of self-confidence and self-concept are developmental achievements that can lead to hopeful thinking in middle childhood, adolescence, and on into early adulthood.

Snyder and colleagues (2002) defined hope as that which enables people to set clear and *valued* goals, to conceive of the means to achieve those goals, and to have the wherewithal or drive to make those goals happen. They conceptualized hope as a cognitive or "thinking" construct rather than an emotion. Seen this way, hope is not wishful as is commonly thought, but rather an active thinking process that is goal directed and involves planning and belief in personal ability to achieve the goal. These ideas are based on the assumption that specific behaviors or "mental-action sequences" are directed toward achieving specific and *valued* goals, with these behaviors being both purposeful and intentional (Snyder, Rand, & Sigmon, 2002).

To initiate such goal-directed behaviors, two types of thinking must occur: *pathways* and *agency* thinking. *Pathways thinking* refers to a person's *self-perceived* capacity to develop cognitive routes to the desired goal. In other words, individuals must think they are capable of designing feasible strategies for accomplishing their goals (Snyder, Rand, & Sigmon, 2002; Snyder, Feldman, et al., 2002). In pathways thinking, individuals typically develop multiple routes or strategies for achieving their goals to ensure that any obstacles encountered will not prevent their accomplishing the intended goals. Statements of affirmation that characterize pathways thinking include "I will find a way to get this done" (cited in Snyder, Rand, & Sigmon, 2002, p. 258). However, Tong and colleagues (2010) suggested that hope is associated with a belief that goals are somehow attainable regardless of whether the person knows how to achieve them. They argued that hopeful people tend to think that desired goals are attainable even if their personal resources are exhausted. As long as people feel that a specific and concrete goal can somehow be attained, regardless of whether they consider themselves able to generate ways to achieve that goal, they are likely to feel more hopeful (Tong, Fredrickson, Chang, & Lim, 2010).

Hope as a Motivational Process

A central theme of hope is a person's motivation to act—the willpower to engage in continuous goal pursuit. Hope also focuses on a general belief in one's ability to achieve a goal. Conceptualizing a goal (goal thinking) and developing strategies to reach that goal (pathways thinking) are necessary cognitive processes, yet they are insufficient without another—and perhaps most important—component of hope: agency thinking. Agency thinking is the mobilizing aspect of hope, which consists of individuals' thoughts regarding their ability to begin the process of movement along selected pathways and continue toward achieving their goals (Snyder, Feldman, et al., 2002). Statements of motivation characteristic of agency thinking include "I will not give up" (Lopez, Rose, Robinson, Marques, & Pais-Ribeiro, 2009) or "I will not be stopped" (cited in Snyder, Rand, & Sigmon, 2002, p. 258). Such statements are typical of "high-hope" individuals. This agency thinking is related to a similar concept called self-efficacy. This is defined as a belief in one's own capacity to accomplish a particular *task in a specific situation*, as opposed to a global belief in one's overall ability (Bandura, 1977). In describing the differences between self-efficacy and agency thinking, Helland and Winston (2005) suggest that efficacy becomes activated when a person is faced with a significant situation-specific, goal-related outcome that is *valued* by that individual. To pursue this outcome, the person must believe it can be attained.

In an effort to understand the motivational factors common to high achievers, Curry, Snyder, and Cook (1997) examined the role of hope in the academic and sports achievements of college athletes. They observed that athletes had higher hope than did their non-athlete counterparts. Curry and colleagues believed that this is due, in part, to the fact that athletes are generally taught pathways and agency thinking toward goals as important means of coping in a competitive, performance-based environment. Although hope is conceived of as a cognitive rather than an emotional process, the successful achievement of a valued goal can elicit positive emotions that may, in turn, be motivational in setting new and more challenging goals. Athletes who achieve in a highly competitive environment may well be reinforcing cognitive processes that enable success in other domains (Curry, Snyder, & Cook 1997). Generally speaking, youths who are involved in competitive, high-performance activities may have a strong sense of personal agency and learn to apply these motivational mechanisms in daily stressful encounters. This may be an important consideration for economically disadvantaged youth who experience stressful encounters as a fact of daily life. Participation in sports and other types of high-performance activities is important, but perhaps even more critical is having coaching to help develop and reinforce agency thinking in these youth. This could potentially help poor children learn to set challenging goals and to devise multiple strategies for achieving those goals. As a result, the process of successfully accomplishing goals may generalize to other important areas and engender a sense of confidence and agency in coping productively in real-life stressful and high-demand contexts.

Motivational aspects of hope have also been studied in the context of academic achievement and career development. Kenny et al. (2010) theorized about "work hope," suggesting its importance in understanding the motivational state of economically disenfranchised groups, who may find it challenging to sustain hope in a context offering limited economic resources and multiple obstacles to school and work success. Work hope encompasses the goal and pathways components of Snyder's hope theory. Assessment items such as "When I look into the future, I have a clear picture of what my work life will be like" (goal); "I have a plan for getting or maintaining a good job or career" (pathways); and "I am confident that things will work out for me in the future" (agency) were used to measure work hope in study participants (p. 207). In addition, Kenny and his colleagues, wanting to explain the relationship between career experience and achievement motivation, argued that school programs offering work-based learning and career experiences may foster a sense of hope by helping youth to identify work goals, expand their understanding of how to reach those goals, and foster confidence in the likelihood of achieving those goals. What is important about this study is the researchers' assertion that achievement-related beliefs can be internalized through a supportive context. These expectations for educational success, along with motivational supports and the anticipation that school will pay off in the future, all provide students with important psychological resources and reinforce cognitive processes instrumental in helping them persist and achieve their educational goals. The researchers tested these ideas with an ethnically diverse sample of high school students enrolled in a work-based learning program. This program included an academically rigorous schedule and placed students in work sites for one day each week throughout the four years of high school. The findings from their study revealed strong relationships between work hope, achievement-related beliefs, and learning environments characterized by support and autonomy. Work hope appeared to be a meaningful construct in understanding the school motivation of low-income youth of color, whose hopes for the future are challenged by numerous economic and social barriers. The researchers concluded that participation in a work-based learning program may have enhanced the importance of work hope as a predictor of adaptive achievement-related beliefs.

Finally, hope theory has also been applied to the study of leaders and leadership development. Leadership is an important aspect of well-being, especially during adolescence. It is important that youth have confidence in their ability to make appropriate decisions despite tremendous pressure to do otherwise. Helland and Winston (2005) theorized that the three components of hope—goals, pathways, and agency—are present in organizations, as leaders and others pursue valued personal and organizational outcomes. While Hellend and Winston (2005) were referring to professional organizations and business leaders, their hypothesis could equally apply to schools, as they are also organizations. Students serving in leadership capacities in their classrooms, clubs, or other school-wide organizations are presumably motivated to pursue goals for themselves and for their school. Hellend and Winston contended that hope frequently resides within leadership, and effective leadership could "awaken" hopeful thinking. In this vein, it seems important for schools serving low-income youth to provide as many opportunities as possible to cultivate leadership abilities and to provide forums for these abilities to be constructively utilized. Citing positive psychology literature, the researchers referred to hope as an activating force that enables people, even when faced with the most overwhelming obstacles, to envision a promising future and to set and pursue goals.

Hope as a Protective Mechanism

Hope is also regarded as a protective mechanism that influences an individual's ability to overcome disappointments, pursue goals, and avoid perceiving the future as fruitless (Snyder, 1994; Guthrie, 2011; Harley, 2011). As discussed throughout this volume, the protective aspects of hope are critically important for families experiencing the challenges of economic disadvantage. In a qualitative study of hope in low-income, inner-city, African American youth Harley (2011) identified five themes regarding the perceptions of hope: (1) caring connections, (2) education, (3) spirituality, (4) "the basics," and (5) a "gonna make it mentality" (p. 128). Regarding *caring connections*, the youth in Harley's study discussed such prosocial behaviors as listening to parents, obeying rules, doing chores, thinking positive, being respectful, and completing homework. Youths in the study overwhelmingly rated the support received from family members and significant others as "hopeful" and envisioned themselves becoming what significant adults in their lives had already become. Thus adults and family members were models of success that the youth could potentially strive to emulate. In addition, youth identified *spirituality* as a source of hope and described how family members used prayer and church attendance as means of maintaining hopefulness.

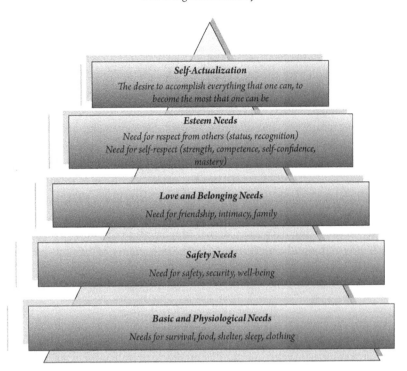

Figure 2.1 MASLOW'S HIERARCHY OF NEEDS.

Adolescents also connected hope with having basic physical needs met, including food, clothing, shoes, shelter, toiletries, and transportation. Harley's finding of a relationship between hope and *"the basics"* harkens back to Maslow's classic Hierarchy of Needs theory (Maslow, 1943) in which self-actualization could be achieved only after a basic set of physiological and psychological needs was met (see Figure 2.1). Clearly, for youth experiencing the challenges of economic adversity, it is not surprising that their hopeful goals would focus on these fundamental needs.

Finally, Harley's *"gonna make it mentality"* theme refers to the positive affirmations associated with agency thinking of high-hope individuals. The adolescents were hopeful about their futures and expected positive outcomes in attaining their goals. Respondents were aware of potential barriers that could impede their progress toward achieving personal goals but held positive beliefs that, with perseverance, such barriers could be overcome. This finding suggests that perceived obstacles do not necessarily decrease the levels of hope in minority adolescents.

As noted earlier, the origins of hope lie in the caregiving relationship established between parent and child (Snyder, Feldman, et al., 2002). While a good deal of this literature focuses on the relationship between mother and child, studies are beginning to address the protective role of fathers in the lives of children. Along these lines, Davis-Maye (2004) wanted to explicate the relationship between perception of paternal support and African American girls' hopes for future success. She examined the significance of the paternal figure among African American girls ranging in age from 9 to 19. With this wide developmental band, findings from this study carry implications not only for the early caregiver relationship but for the role of hope in promoting positive outcomes in later developmental stages. For the purpose of this study, Davis-Maye defined hope as reflecting a person's belief in his or her ability to achieve certain goals, thus affecting academic achievement, healthy emotional development, and successful transition to adulthood. She proposed that hope is a protective mechanism that influences adolescents' knowledge about and ability to perform self-care in the face of stressful events. Of the girls in the study who reported high levels of paternal support, slightly more than two-thirds reported having moderate levels of hope, and nearly one-third reported having high levels of hope. The relationship between paternal support and hope was strongest for the younger girls in the study, suggesting again the importance of early attachment relationships between parent and child.

Hope as a Coping Mechanism

Coping abilities and the specific strategies used to manage stressful life circumstances are central to psychological adjustment and overall well-being. The pathways and agency thinking outlined in hope theory enable one to acquire the tools and resources necessary to cope in stressful conditions. As children grow and develop, so too does their coping ability. Roesch and colleagues (2010) studied hope and the propensity to cope in a sample of African American adolescents, seeking to challenge the assumption that minority youth would report lower levels of hope and consequently have fewer coping abilities. They argued that adolescents who score high on the pathways thinking component of hope may display greater use of coping strategies because they are better able to see multiple ways to reduce the impact of a particular stressor. The authors hypothesized that youth rated as having high *dispositional* hope would use more direct problem solving, planning, positive thinking, and overall coping than those rated as having low hope. Roesch and colleagues found that both pathways thinking and agency thinking were significantly associated with specific daily coping strategies: pathways with direct problem solving, planning, positive thinking, religious coping, and distracting actions; and agency with support for actions. These effects were evident after controlling for gender, age, and perceived stressfulness of the event. Roesch's work is important for understanding hope and its relationship to coping in low-income minority youth. In addition to using standard research measures to understand coping and hope, Roesch and his colleagues asked participants to use an open-ended format to write the most stressful or bothersome event that had occurred to them in the past day. This allowed the researchers to examine a broader range of perceived stressors confronting the study participants, as well as the range of coping strategies employed to ameliorate the effects of those stressors. This process provides a broader understanding of the ways (often not codified into standard assessments) in which low-income minority youth respond to adverse situations, and could lead to developing more sensitive measures of coping abilities and hopeful thinking in minority youth.

Similarly, Ong and colleagues (2006) examined the question of how variations in hope modify the everyday experience of stress and emotion in later adulthood. He found a noteworthy interaction between hope and daily stress, indicating that high-hope individuals, in general, react less to stressful situations than do low-hope individuals. Also noteworthy was a finding that the stress-damping impact of daily hope on negative emotion was most pronounced among high-hope individuals.

Finally, conceptualizations of hope by Snyder and other colleagues have been validated and used as a predictor variable in a variety of studies, and the framework of hope has been used to devise therapeutic, occupational, and educational interventions. While samples of economically disadvantaged minorities were not always the primary targets of Snyder's empirical research, his theoretical framework clearly applies to this population—as shown by the work of Harley, Kenny, Davis-Maye, and others discussed in this overview. Findings from these studies indicate the importance of hope as a framework through which to understand how children and families living in economic disadvantage manage the complexities of their lives. Miller and Powers' (1988) conception of hope sums up the findings from these studies: *an anticipation of a future that is good and is based on mutuality, a sense of personal competence, coping ability, psychological well-being, purpose and meaning in life, and a sense of the possible.*

Optimism: The "Can Do" Spirit

Most people use the terms *hope* and *optimism* interchangeably, but theorists point out that although optimism is related to hope, it is conceptually distinct (Helland & Winston, 2005). Optimism involves the *perceived* ability to move toward goals with desired outcomes and to avoid undesirable outcomes (Carver & Scheier, 1999; Helland & Winston, 2005). However, researchers point out that the anticipated and actual outcomes of the goal pursuit, especially negative outcomes, are often attributed to external (chance, luck) rather than internal (personal agency, efficacy) forces (Helland &Winston, 2005). So, hope theory focuses on setting goals to attain a positive future outcome, whereas optimism focuses on whether the goal attainment is attributed to external rather than internal resources.

Scheier and Carver (1987) use the term "dispositional optimism," which they define as the generalized expectations that tend to generate effective goal-directed behavior; briefly, it is a tendency to expect positive outcomes. These positive expectations may result from individuals' belief that they are in control of good outcomes and a belief that good things will happen (Gillham & Reivich, 2004). According to Carver et al. (2010), this expectation of positive events is a relatively stable tendency.

A body of research suggests that optimism predicts many positive outcomes, such as physical and psychological health and well-being (Nes & Segerstrom, 2006; Segerstrom, 2007). Optimists have been shown to have greater success in school, work, and other important contexts. Notably, they report less depression and anxiety, enjoy greater marital satisfaction, and tend to live longer (Scheier & Carver, 1992; Gillham & Reivich, 2004). These outcomes may be due in part to optimists' approach to coping and managing stressful situations. According to Segerstrom (2007), optimists have an "active" approach to problem solving, which helps them negotiate challenging and stress-inducing situations, whereas less optimistic individuals may adopt avoidance strategies in stressful situations (Murberg, 2012). The work of these researchers suggests that optimists are persistent—particularly when tasks become difficult or when they encounter obstacles—and greater persistence increases the likelihood that a solution will be found. Optimists may take better care of themselves and are more likely than pessimists to participate in preventive health care, seek out information about potential health risks, and change their behavior to decrease risk levels (Gillham & Reiveich, 2004). Optimism also leads to changes in behaviors that may drive changes in mood, productivity, performance, and health. For example, Murberg (2012) examined dispositional optimism as a protective factor for somatic health problems and examined the links between negative life events and somatic symptoms (physical ailments). In a study of Norwegian high school students, Murberg found that adolescents who scored high on the optimism scale had significantly lower reports of somatic symptoms. She also found that, among students who were exposed to stressful life circumstances, an optimistic outlook may have been beneficial in buffering the negative effects of stressful life events on somatic symptomatology. Murberg concluded that the protective effects of optimism on somatic symptoms provide support for promoting an optimistic view among adolescents. Recognizing the buffering effects of optimism on adolescents should encourage professionals to make greater use of this internal psychological resource to alleviate the adverse impact of stressful events on physical health. Along these lines, Segerstrom (2005) examined relationships between immunologically mediated diseases (such as cancer or HIV) and dispositional optimism, and proposed what she referred to as an "engagement hypothesis" to explain why optimism may not always produce positive outcomes. She hypothesized that, under difficult circumstances, more optimistic people remain engaged with difficult circumstances, whereas more pessimistic people disengage, avoid, or give up. Giving up can be physiologically protective, because stressor exposure is minimized in the short term by giving up rather than remaining engaged. Segerstrom concludes that in many cases, both dispositional optimism and specific expectations appear to buffer the immune system from the effects of psychological stressors. However, a short-term physiological cost must sometimes be paid for the optimistic strategy of engaging difficult stressors rather than disengaging and withdrawing. However, this may be ameliorated in the long term by problem solving and resolving the adverse situation (Segerstrom, 2005).

Optimism and Self-Efficacy

Optimism is related to general self-efficacy in the sense that self-efficacy involves an individual's belief in their own ability to perform a specific task (Bandura, 1977), whereas optimism involves expectations of good outcomes (Scheier & Carver, 1987) and beliefs about one's ability to control or influence those out-comes (Urbig & Monsen, 2012). Findings from research conducted by Urbig and Monsen (2012) linked dispositional optimism to individual behaviors that involved engaging in and succeeding at challenging goals. They contended that if individuals believe they are in control and are optimistic due to higher self-efficacy, then more effort or active coping might help increase their perceived chances of success. The researchers also argued that while actively coping (planning and problem-solving) and passively coping (waiting for a lucky chance) individuals are persistent because they are optimistic, their coping behaviors differ due to the structure of beliefs associated with their optimism. In other words, an individu-al's optimism can cause or be linked to very different beliefs about self-efficacy. This has implications for understanding how people persist in the face of adverse events. Optimism may drive them to persist, but their different underlying beliefs about sources of efficacy and control may determine whether their coping is active or passive.

Optimism and Adjustment

Dispositional optimism is also a predictor of adjustment in children (Kochanska et al., 2007). This may be due to maternal warmth and authoritative and competence-promoting parenting practices (Jackson, Pratt, et al., 2005; Taylor, 2010; Taylor et al., 2012). We know that the nature of the parent-child relationship is highly influential in the way a child views the world and perceives his or her place in the world (Jackson-Newsome, Buchanan, & McDonald, 2008). The psychologi-cal and emotional health and well-being of the parent may affect his or her parent-ing style, which may, in turn, affect a child's outcomes (McLoyd & Wilson, 1991; Shaw, Levitt, Wong, & Kaczorowski, 2006). Thus children are likely to internalize the optimism or pessimism conveyed by parents and other significant individuals in their lives (Gillham & Reiveich, 2004).

Kochanska and colleagues (2007) wanted to learn whether parental per-sonality traits could buffer the negative impact of adversity on the childrearing environment. Notably, they found that parents in high-risk environments who reported an unhappy childhood, and who had a more pessimistic outlook on life, tended to use more coercive and punitive parenting practices. By comparison, parents in these high-risk environments who could recall a relatively happy childhood and positive school experiences were likely to use more positive parenting strategies. The high-risk environment did have a detrimental effect on parents who reported little sense of optimism, distrusted others, and felt socially alienated. These parents showed less warmth, affection, and positive affect when interacting with their toddlers. Adversity, however, had no such detrimental effect on parents who were optimistic, trusting, and well integrated with their social world.

Similarly, a study conducted by Taylor and colleagues (2010) found that maternal optimism among African American mothers was associated with greater resilience to the negative effects of economic stress. The mother's optimistic response to adversity may lead to positive interactions with her children who, in turn, may internalize those optimistic problem-solving approaches.

In other research with Mexican American mothers, Taylor and colleagues (2012) found that economic pressures did not predict depression, distress, or anxiety for mothers who demonstrated high levels of optimism. This result supported the idea that optimism is an important psychological resource that buffers against many adverse consequences of stressful life circumstances. It's important to note that optimism may be functional for different reasons or have different meanings in different contexts. For example, Jackson, Pratt, et al. (2005) noted that in individualistic contexts, which particularly encourage and reward autonomy, self-reliance, and belief in one's unique potential, optimism may generate positive outcomes; however, in more collectivist cultures, confidence in one's support network may play a larger role in fostering the same outcomes. Thus more research needs to be done with disadvantaged populations to learn how optimism functions in high-risk and other diverse cultural contexts.

Optimism and Social Support

Finally, with regard to the social implications of optimistic thinking, Segerstrom (2007) investigated whether an association between dispositional optimism and growth of social and status resources is a function of an individual's persistence and performance. Noting that optimists persistently pursue their goals and use effective strategies to do so, Segerstrom suggested that they were likely to accumulate resources over time. These resources include status resources such as seniority, leadership, money, and possessions, and social resources such as friendships, social networks, and significant relationships with family and romantic partners. Optimists are more successful than pessimists in pursuing status and social resources, partly because they are likely to persist in school and complete their education, which may give entrées into social status situations and social resources that might otherwise be unavailable. Optimists also actively pursue relationships and are perceived as more popular than their pessimistic counterparts. Accumulation of these resources is important, especially for disadvantaged families, in that they are frequently associated with better mental and physical health as well as longevity. Segerstrom (2007) conducted a follow-up study of law school graduates after a 10-year period to determine their accumulation of resources, whether greater resource growth would contribute to increases in optimism, and whether these increases would have positive implications for mental and physical health. She found that dispositional optimism results in long-term resource growth and that resource growth increases optimistic beliefs. Optimism predicted increases in income but not social network size; however, she found that social network growth was predictive of increased optimism.

While optimists have been shown to achieve positive outcomes, people whose optimistic outlook is unrealistic may have interpersonal difficulties if they do not take responsibility for problems or minimize the meaning and importance of the negative outcome or conflict. Without a realistic appraisal of their circumstances, they may not be prepared to cope when adversity occurs (Gillham & Reivich, 2004).

As we will discuss in the next section on resilience, some degree of adversity or challenge must be present in individuals' lives to help them learn coping strategies and appropriate problem solving behaviors for adapting to these challenges.

Fostering Resilience in Children, Youth, and Families

Resilience is a term commonly used to describe people who have the ability to "bounce back" from difficult situations. This phenomenon is referred to in everyday conversations about people who appear to have the ability to overcome obstacles that many would have difficulty managing. In many ways, we think of these individuals as having rare, special abilities or an internal force of will that enables them to surmount obstacles. While resilience does indeed entail an ability to adapt, other factors must also be considered. It's important to consider the nature of adversity, the degree of exposure to adversity, and the context that facilitates adaptation. As briefly discussed in Chapter 1, Bronfenbrenner's ecological theory (1979) provides important insights into contextual factors and how they interact to affect an individual's ability to adapt to life's circumstances. These insights are particularly valuable for understanding how children reared in economic disadvantage fare in the face of the associated kinds of adversity. His ideas call attention not only to the individual but also to the family, community, and societal factors that work together to influence a child's development and outcomes. In so doing, Bronfenbrenner's theory of development frames a broader ecological perspective for understanding resilience and how it occurs in children and families. Children do not develop in isolation but are part of many interacting and influential systems that shape their development and play a role in the ways they adapt to adversity.

Theory of Resilience

The study of resilience has a long history, emanating from the fields of developmental science, psychiatry, and education (Masten, 2012). Much of what we learned from early research on resilience was derived from clinical observations. The concept of resilience was first introduced in the literature as a stable personal characteristic. Pines (1975), noting that some children appeared to function well despite exposure to adversity, referred to those children as "invulnerable." This conceptualization suggested that some quality inherent in the child protected them against the challenging circumstances and subtly implied that some children have capacities enabling them to be resilient while others do not.

Early resilience researchers studying the mental health outcomes of poor children observed that not all children reared in poverty succumbed to negative outcomes. Over a 40-year period, Werner (1993) studied children born on the island of Kauai and examined the long-term effects of growing up in high-risk environments. She found that about one-third of the children in her study had grown up to be productive adults. An important observation was that some of the children who had learning or behavioral problems at early stages of development did not exhibit these problems as adults and were, in fact, leading low-risk children on measures of behavior and achievement. This paradigm-shifting observation led Werner to conclude that resilience is not a static quality but can be observed at various points along the developmental continuum. Similarly, during the initial planning stages of the Project Competence study, Garmezy and colleagues described the resilience phenomenon in terms of "stress resistance," which they defined as manifestations of competence in children despite exposure to stressful life events (Garmezy, Masten, & Tellegen, 1984; Masten & Tellegen, 2012). In this view, in order to study resilience, competence had to be factored into the equation along with exposure to stressors and the attributes of the child or family. This approach requires examining positive adaptation and adversity in tandem in order to infer resilience in any individual or group of people. Accordingly, resilience was to be understood as *patterns* of positive adaptation in the context of risk or adversity, thus underscoring its dynamic nature. As with Werner's findings, the Project Competence investigators also recognized that resilience developed and changed over time—an individual might show resilience at one point in life and not in another, or in one domain or context but not in other domains.

Contemporary research conceptualizes resilience in terms of developmental and dynamic processes. Rather than being viewed as a static internal trait, resilience is now seen as a series of ongoing reciprocal transactions between the individual and the environment (Luthar & Zelazo, 2003; Luthar, 2006; Vanderbilt-Adriance & Shaw, 2008). Thus, to be resilient, Luthar and colleagues (2006) argued in much the same manner as Garmezy, two critical conditions must exist: (a) exposure to significant threat or severe adversity, and (b) the achievement of positive adaptation despite major assaults on the developmental process (Cicchetti, 2010; Vanderbilt-Adriance & Shaw, 2008).

Risks and Adversity

Risk factors are negative occurrences or adverse phenomena in the environment, or within the child, that place the child at risk of having poor outcomes (Garmezy & Rutter, 1983). These factors are present at the individual, family, and community levels. Individual risks for poor outcomes may include temperament, chronic illness, or mental disorders (Caspi et al., 1995). Family risks may include harsh parenting styles, maternal depression, job loss, food insecurity, poverty, and economic disadvantage (Repetti, Taylor, & Seeman, 2002). Community risks may include poor neighborhood quality and cohesion, or lack of resources (Leventhal & Brooks-Gunn, 2000). The nature and intensity of risk and adversity are important in resilience research, and the resilience to these risks involves more than avoiding negative or poor outcomes (Vanderbilit-Adriance & Shaw, 2008). To the contrary, resilience results from *successful engagement* with risks rather than evasion of risks (Kaliel, 2003). This is reminiscent of individuals that measured high on various hope and optimism factors, who tend to engage longer and more persistently in a risk context in an effort to solve the problem and manage the impact of that risk.

It should be noted here that, unfortunately, children exposed to risks for poor outcomes are unlikely to experience only a single risk or to have sequential exposure to single risks. In adverse contexts such as poverty, children are exposed to multiple risks—some of which occur randomly while others may be chronic, extending throughout the course of development. For example, a child growing up in economic disadvantage may experience harsh parenting, a chaotic home environment, an unsafe neighborhood, or an under-resourced school. Sanders and colleagues' (2008) study of "health resilience" demonstrated how poverty and other structural inequalities link to additional risks such as poor dietary practices, which may increase the risk of poor health outcomes. As the number of risk factors increases, so does the probability of negative outcomes (Rutter, 2000). The cumulative impact of these risks interacting simultaneously, and over time, may be more than a child can overcome without supportive processes that "clear the way" for a child to successfully navigate the difficult terrain of life (Sameroff & Rosenblum, 2007). Toward that end, researchers and clinicians are beginning to explore the idea that cumulative assets or strengths built over time may ameliorate and protect against the cumulative effects of multiple and interacting risks. Certain assets or protective factors may be more influential at critical junctures in the maturation process, thus supporting the developmental and dynamic nature of resilience.

Protective Factors and Adaptation

Factors within the child or environment that reduce, mitigate, or minimize the risks discussed above are referred to as *protective factors*. These are defined as characteristics within the child, family, or community that reduce the negative effects of adversity on the child and allow the child to adapt in adverse contexts (Masten & Reed, 2002; Seccombe, 2002; Kalil, 2003). Protective factors include such personal characteristics as a child's positive temperament and self-concept, self-efficacy, problem-solving skills, and good health. Family characteristics include warmth and affection, maternal optimism, family structure, emotional support, and employment status. Community characteristics may encompass safety and security, social resources, opportunities for civic engagement, and religious participation (Seccombe, 2002). Such protective factors may be "leveraged" to ameliorate the effects of risks and bring about positive child outcomes. For example, a healthy birth might protect against harsh parenting; supportive peer relationships might be protective against a violent neighborhood; or an internal locus of control might protect against peer rejection.

Protective factors are thought to encompass those personal or environmental resources that function as compensatory or buffering agents that interact with risk to either directly reduce the risk or change the predictive relationship between risk factors and outcomes (Kalil, 2003; Masten, 2001; Scales, 1999; Luthar, 2006). Protective factors include capacities, processes, and resources such as effective parents and supportive relationships, cognitive problem-solving and self-control skills, motivation to achieve, and personality characteristics associated with maintaining well-controlled, stable functioning in emotional, social, and motivational domains (Werner, 1990; Masten et al., 1999; McCabe & Clark, 1999; Masten, 2001). In her longitudinal study of Hawaiian youth, Werner characterized adaptation and resilience as a "balancing act" between the dual presence of risk and protection, which suggests that successful adaptation results from the influence of protective factors (cited in Kalil, 2003, p. 12).

As discussed earlier, researchers are careful to point out that adjustment and adaptation are specific to context and situation (Sapienza & Masten, 2011; Masten, 2001). Thus a child may be resilient to certain risks in one context but still susceptible to poor outcomes in another domain or context. It is important to identify an individual's assets, strengths, and competencies, as well as environmental assets, in order to understand how they work together to protect against risks in a particular context—and then determine ways in which to build on those strengths to reduce vulnerabilities in other contexts.

Building Competence and Promoting Resilience

As previously noted, competence is a hallmark of resilience. Positive outcomes observed in adolescence and adulthood may have their origins in the development of important competencies and skills during childhood. Masten, in reviewing the prolific body of work on competence, resilience, and adaptation that she and colleagues contributed to the field (Masten, 2012; Masten & Tellegen, 2012), recalls that many of the adaptive children they studied generally became adaptive adults. For the most part, exposure to adversity did not play a major role or hinder the emergence of basic adaptive capacities and resources. But when high adversity in childhood and adolescence was accompanied by little indication of protection, and evidence of limited adaptive capacity was compounded with cumulative risk factors, adaptive problems were often observed in childhood as well as adulthood (Masten, 2012; Masten & Tellegen, 2012). For this reason, researchers and practitioners alike underscore the importance of reducing children's risk and enhancing protective factors while at the same time building their developmental assets or strengths (Scales, 1999; Scales et al., 2006). This makes intuitive sense, and research supports the idea that the more assets and competencies young people have, the fewer risky behaviors they engage in and the more they experience positive developmental outcomes (Scales, 1999). And notably, this seems to be the case for the more highly vulnerable youth—they especially seem to benefit from the protective impact of a broad range of developmental assets. Toward this end, Scales and colleagues identified 40 developmental factors that range from support, empowerment, boundaries, and expectations to relationships, positive identity, commitment to learning, and positive values. The broader scope of assets opens opportunities for developing interventions and prevention programs, as well as other resources to help youth engage in positive behaviors, reducing the risk of poor outcomes.

In a similar vein, Howard (1996) argued for the importance of identifying and targeting social and behavioral competencies that may underlie or promote positive adaptation in high-risk environments. In a review of resilience research on African American children exposed to violence, Howard referred to a "triad of protective factors" linked to adaptation and positive outcomes (p. 255):

- Modification of stressors by personal resources such as temperament, social engagement, and cognitive skills
- Cohesive families that are warm and nurturing and have caregiving styles that reflect confidence, provide guidance, and encourage self-esteem
- External support such as teachers, neighbors, or institutional structures that provide support and counsel

Similarly Lee, Cheung, and Kwong (2012) reviewed the relationship between resilience and positive youth development and outlined five core competencies involved in the process of adaptation (p. 3):

- Cognitive competence—good cognitive abilities
- Emotional competence—self-regulation of emotion and impulses
- Moral competence—positive self-perceptions
- Behavioral competence—talents valued by self and society
- Social competence—general appeal or attractiveness to others

Consistent with the notion that resilience is relative, not absolute, and varies over time, circumstances, and maturation, Howard (1996) pointed out that the opening of opportunities at major life transitions (e.g., emerging adolescence, transition to adulthood) provides a second chance for youth exposed to earlier adversity. During key transition periods, individuals with certain dispositional qualities (e.g., optimism) and resources may seek out and construct environments (pathways and agency thinking) that provide rewards and reinforcement. Notably, Howard concludes that both having and actively drawing upon these qualities help reset youth's behavioral trajectory to move away from negative adaptation toward competence and positive adaptation. This underscores the notion that resilience and adaptation are processes that involve personal and active engagement. As in hope theory, the actions of goal setting, planning, thinking, and problem solving must accompany the presence of dispositional qualities for children to successfully chart a path toward success.

This understanding is important for working with populations deemed particularly at risk for poor outcomes. As assets and strengths within these groups become better understood, the opportunities to promote adaptation and foster resilience can be greatly enhanced. With this goal in mind, Teti et al. (2012) examined resilience in African American males to understand the nature of the socio-structural challenges they experience and to identify strengths that may elicit resilience in the face of these challenges. Study participants indicated five major categories as strengths:

- Perseverance
- Commitment to learning and growing from hardship
- Reflecting and refocusing to address difficulties
- Creating their own supportive environment
- Drawing support from religion/spirituality

The study participants discussed their commitment to "keep goin' despite adversity," trying harder, and refusing to quit. Given the participants' reliance on supportive communities wherever they could find or create them, and on religion or spirituality, the authors suggest that an ecosocial model that acknowl-edges the importance of social and community-level protective factors might be the best way of understanding and fostering resilience among low-income urban Black men.

Sanders et al. (2008) examined protective factors from a health promotion per-spective and underscored the importance of different types of support as a critical factor in achieving better health outcomes for poor African American families. The study examined emotional support (empathy, love, caring, and trust), instrumental support (tangible aid such as sharing of tasks or actions, loaning of money), and informational support (teaching of skills, advice, and providing information about problem solving) and found that access to these types of support was associated with fewer depressive symptoms. The authors assert that the extent to which indi-viduals feel a sense of mastery and efficacy may determine if they will access these supportive processes.

Finally, in a study of resilience in poor children, Buckner, Mezzacoppa, and Beardslee (2003) found self-regulation to be a strong predictor of resilience, even when taking into account factors such as parental monitoring, self-esteem, or intelligence that typically explain such outcomes. Youth who scored high on measures of self-regulation also showed positive executive functioning and emotional regulation. Executive functioning skills are important because they enable planning, coping behaviors, diligence, organization, and problem-solving behaviors. Youth with these skills are able to manage their emotions and behav-ior, which may lead to positive reinforcement from their surroundings—and eventually to positive behavior and adaptation across multiple domains of development.

Family Resilience

As delineated in Bronfenbrenner's ecological model, children function within a broad social ecology. While they possess individual competencies and adaptive capacities, they are also affected by the capacities in the family—their most influ-ential context. As mentioned earlier (and to be discussed in Chapter 4), relation-ships between and among individual family members have enduring effects on a child's adjustment. Families that experience economic disadvantage are consid-ered to be at risk for poor educational, social, psychological, and health outcomes (McLoyd, 1998). Most studies have focused on the psychopathology and nega-tive life trajectories of these families. Increasingly, however, scholars are begin-ning to devise theoretical models that focus on the strengths of these families and how these strengths can translate into positive outcomes, potentially breaking the cycle of negative outcomes. One such model, the family resilience framework (Walsh, 2006), focuses attention on family strengths under stress rather than on family pathology. This approach assumes that no single model fits all families or their situations; therefore, functioning is assessed in the context of each family's values, structure, resources, and life challenges. Processes that optimize functioning and the well-being of family members are observed to vary over time, as challenges unfold and families evolve across the life cycle. This family-resilience-based approach arises from a strong conviction that families have the potential to recover and grow from adversity. Walsh contended that resilience-oriented services enhance family empowerment, bringing forth shared hope, developing new and renewed competencies, and building mutual support and collaborative efforts among family members. Walsh identified belief systems as one of the central components of this model. The ways in which families find meaning in adversity, and normalize adversity and distress, are outgrowths of their respective belief systems. Family beliefs also influence how they explain or interpret their experiences, as well as the extent to which they believe they have a positive outlook or hope, an optimistic view, or confidence in their ability to overcome the odds. A notable belief is that, together, families can "master the impossible"—but at the same time accept those things that cannot be changed. Such beliefs indicate an ability to transcend life's circumstances and to focus on larger values and purposes, future goals, and dreams (Walsh, 2006).

By strengthening family resilience, researchers, practitioners, and policymakers are able to build family resources for effectively addressing the adverse experiences associated with economic disadvantage.

Every Child Has the Capacity for Resilience

I end this chapter by challenging the notion that only children with specific innate abilities or unique personal qualities can be resistant to stress and resilient to certain adversities. To the contrary—all children have the capacity to adapt and to be resilient! Masten (2001) eloquently called this capacity "ordinary magic" and declared that it is the great surprise of resilience research. She contended that resilience does not spring from rare and special attributes, but from the everyday magic of ordinary, human resources in the minds, brains, and bodies of children; in their families and relationships; and in their communities. This understanding has profound implications for those whose goal is to promote hope, competence, and human capital in individuals and society (Masten, 2001, 2010).

All children, especially those at greatest risk for poor outcomes, need the support of protective processes described earlier in this chapter. Clearly, the role of the family is critically important and has powerful protective and ameliorative effects on children's ability to adapt to adversity—both in the short term and in later life. In addition, the personal and cognitive processes of hope and optimism promote competence and resilience and must be fostered in children. By doing so, opportunities can be created throughout development for children in difficult circumstances to have the best possible chance of achieving their goals and finding success in life. Toward that end, the chapters that follow build on these theories of hope and resilience and discuss important concepts relevant to programs and policies that could help achieve these goals.

3

Wired for Hope?

Examining Lifelong Capacities for Learning, Growth, and Recovery from Adversity

I am fundamentally an optimist. Whether that comes from nature or nurture, I cannot say. Part of being optimistic is keeping one's head pointed toward the sun, one's feet moving forward. There were many dark moments when my faith in humanity was sorely tested, but I would not and could not give myself up to despair. That way lays defeat and death.
—Nelson Mandela, *Long Walk to Freedom: The Autobiography of Nelson Mandela* (1995)

In this chapter I revisit Carl Rogers' notion of self-actualization—the idea that we have a natural drive toward achieving our highest potential. In thinking about Rogers, I began to wonder whether there are biological underpinnings for this kind of drive. So, I ask the question *"Are we wired for hope?"* Is there something inherent in human nature that pushes us to reach beyond our circumstances, no matter how adverse, to achieve our goals? If so, what does this mean for children who begin their lives in very difficult circumstances? There is a common presumption that children who experience significant adversity early in life are likely to continue along that difficult pathway throughout life and and very little can alter their trajectories. Research does indeed underscore the long-term and deleterious impact that early adverse experiences associated with poverty can have on children's overall development, including brain development (Maholmes & King, 2012). However, recent advances in the neurosciences have opened a window into understanding how the brain works and have shed light on important processes that may make it possible to foster a more optimal course of development for these children. For example, research suggests that an enriched environment (the variety of activities and resources allowing for physical activity, learning, speaking, and social interaction) stimulates areas of the brain that promote language acquisition, cognitive development, and emotion regulation (Hart & Risley, 1995; Knudsen, Heckman, Cameron, & Shonkoff,

2006). All these are important capacities that help children accomplish developmental tasks and reach important milestones. Conversely, the absence of this early stimulation may result in underdevelopment of critical cognitive capacities, leading to challenges in mastering grade-level academic competencies such as literacy and numeracy (Hart & Risley, 1995). Practitioners and policymakers observe that children who have difficulty reading by the third grade are likely to have other academic problems and are less likely to do well in school (Slavin & Madden, 1989). This observation has been especially associated with poor minority children, who disproportionately achieve at lower levels than their counterparts (Ladson-Billings, 2006). African American boys—a particularly vulnerable group of children—who do not read by the third grade are deemed especially at risk for school failure, behavioral problems, and eventual engagement with the juvenile justice system, the so-called cradle-to-prison pipeline (Children's Defense Fund, 2009). This phenomenon leads to other negative outcomes, ultimately deepening the effects of impoverishment. Thus, an important notion explored in this chapter is whether this pathway from impoverishment to deleterious outcomes is immutable. Do people have the capacity, despite early adversity, to rebound from these experiences? What opportunities are there to develop and implement efficacious interventions throughout development that might help reduce and even eliminate this "pipeline to prison" phenomenon and/or other nonoptimal situations? It is my intention in this chapter to highlight in broad strokes the findings and insights from brain research that might help inform efforts to improve outcomes for disadvantaged children. This discussion is not intended to assume causal relationships, paint a deterministic picture of development, or make statements unsubstantiated by solid evidence. Rather, its goal is to explore whether opportunities exist for promoting development and optimal functioning, so that children reared in adverse conditions may have the best possible chance of rebounding from early adversity and resetting their course toward a positive developmental outcome.

Challenging Our Assumptions: Understanding Brain Development

It is important *not* to assume that a child starting life in adverse circumstances is incapable of healthy functioning later in childhood or adolescence. Research on the developing brain suggests that opportunities for change and growth extend into adulthood (Hawley, 2000; Stiles, 2000; Child Welfare Information Gateway, 2009). The social and economic costs of loss of human potential and resources for remediation are far greater than the costs of preventing these problems, so this research provides exciting new clues to therapies and interventions that might be most helpful for children who, through no fault of their own, have had difficult life experiences (Heckman, 2006, 2008).

Paradigm-shifting volumes such as *From Neurons to Neighborhoods* (Shonkoff & Phillips, 2000) have offered tremendous insight into the impact of early adversity on normative brain development, calling attention to the consequences of deprivation and stress. Through this work, we have also learned about the brain's adaptive capacities and its potential to recover from early adversity and to continue learning, growing, and developing over the course of a life. Such scientific advances are especially promising for children whose lives begin in contexts that militate against optimal growth and development.

Nearly all children, whether born to adversity or advantage, start their lives with the basic capacities needed for success in life. Scientists say that a newborn has more than 100 billion neurons—many more than are needed to accomplish the developmental tasks of infancy, childhood, adolescence, and adulthood (Child Welfare Information Gateway, 2009). These neurons are created during fetal development and migrate to form parts of the brain that govern the bodily functions necessary for life (Johnson, 1997; Nelson, 2000; Perry, 2002). Neurons migrate to the areas governing basic functions such as breathing and heart rate, and to higher regions of the brain that govern how we feel (limbic system) and how we think (cerebral cortex). In newborns and infants, the brainstem and spinal cord are better developed than the higher brain regions. These higher regions, which include the limbic system and cerebral cortex, will develop throughout key developmental periods and are modified through experiencing the environment (Nelson, 2000; Perry, 2002; Child Welfare Information Gateway, 2009).

Brain development is essentially a complex interactive process that entails creating, strengthening, and discarding connections among neurons (see Figure 3.1). These connections, called synapses, organize the brain into pathways that connect the parts of the brain that govern everything we do, from breathing and sleeping to thinking and feeling (Child Welfare Information Gateway, 2009).

Synaptic development occurs at an astounding rate during a child's early years in response to early experiences. At its peak, the cerebral cortex of a healthy toddler may create 2 million synapses per second, and by the time children are 3 years of age, their brains have approximately 1,000 trillion synapses, indicating tremendous potential for learning and development (Child Welfare Information Gateway, 2009). Some of these synapses are strengthened through experience and remain intact, but many are gradually discarded. The process of synapse elimination, called *pruning*, is a normal part of development and signals the specialization or strengthening of the synaptic connections that remain (Nelson, 2000; Child Welfare Information Gateway, 2009). By adolescence, about half of the synapses have been discarded or pruned. However, brain development continues throughout the life span, enabling continued learning and adaptation to new circumstances. During these processes,

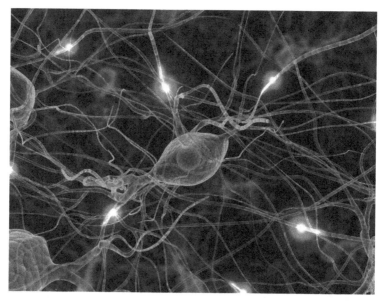

Figure 3.1 NETWORK OF ACTIVE NEURONS.

new synaptic connections are formed or existing connections are strengthened, suggesting deeper learning and specialization (Nelson, 2000; Tsujimoto, 2008; Child Welfare Information Gateway, 2009).

Myelination, the production of the myelin sheath, is another important process that occurs in the developing brain. This process ensures the rapid transmission of neural signals and allows impulses to be efficiently transmitted along the nerve cells (Child Welfare Gateway, 2009). The myelin sheath insulates various neural processes and is needed to help the nervous system function properly. If myelin is damaged (as in demyelinating diseases such as multiple sclerosis), the impulse transmission slows down (Till et al., 2011). As we will discuss later, a child's experiences affect both the rate and the extent of myelination, as well as other important processes. Greater understandings of such critical aspects of childhood brain development may help shed light on young children's capacities for adaptation, resilience, and response to adversity.

It is well documented that stressful early life experiences significantly affect brain structure and function (Kaufman, Plotsky, Nemeroff, & Charney, 2000; Middlebrook & Audage, 2008). In early childhood, especially, stress has been found to either promote growth or damage the developing brain architecture (Fox & Rutter, 2010; Shonkoff et al., 2012). In any given situation, the effect is dependent on the intensity and duration of the stressful experience, the individual differences in children's physiological responsiveness to stress, and the extent to which a supportive adult is available to provide individualized support and help the child deal with adversity (Kaufman, Plotsky, Nemeroff, & Charney, 2000; Dawson, Ashman,

& Carver, 2000; National Scientific Council on the Developing Child, 2005; Middlebrooks & Audage, 2008; Shonkoff et al., 2012). Positive, tolerable, and toxic stress are three kinds of stress that affect the developing brain (National Scientific Council on the Developing Child, 2005; Shonkoff et al., 2012). *Positive stress* is associated with moderate, short-lived physiological responses. This type of stress may be brought on by such normative developmental tasks as meeting new people or experiencing the first day at school. When these experiences occur in the context of stable and supportive relationships, the levels of cortisol and other stress hormones return to a normal range and assist the child in developing a sense of mastery and self-control. Similarly, *tolerable stress* is associated with physiological responses that could disrupt brain architecture, but it is relieved by supportive relationships that facilitate adaptive coping, thereby restoring heart rate and stress hormones to their baseline levels. However, *toxic stress*, the most deleterious type of stress, is associated with strong and prolonged activation of the body's stress management systems in the absence of the buffering protection of adult support (National Scientific Council on the Developing Child, 2005; Shonkoff et al., 2012). Factors associated with toxic stress include extreme poverty with continuous family chaos, recurrent physical or emotional abuse, chronic neglect, severe and enduring maternal depression, persistent parental substance abuse, or repeated exposure to violence in the community or within the family (Perry, 2001; Zeanah et al., 2003; Fox & Rutter, 2010). The essential feature of toxic stress is the absence of any consistent, supportive relationships to help the child cope and thereby return the physiological stress responses to baseline levels (National Scientific Council on the Developing Child, 2005). The timing and duration of these early stressful life events, whether positive, tolerable, or toxic, have implications for optimal brain development and functioning and may affect subsequent development of important neural capacities. For example, researchers have examined the long-term effects of early deprivation by studying how children in orphanages fare over time, after having experienced extreme neglect and lack of social stimulation (Zeanah et al., 2003; Beckett et al., 2006). Beckett and colleagues (2006) found that there are long-lasting effects even after these children are adopted into supportive and nurturing families. Children who experienced such deprivation for more than six months after birth had lower IQ scores at age 11, despite having been removed from the deprived environment for seven years or longer (Beckett et al., 2006; Armenian Medical Network, 2006). Interestingly, the researchers observed that after being adopted into these homes, the children who had been more significantly affected in the early environment made progress over time, catching up a little with those who had not been so badly affected by the early deprivation (Beckett et al., 2006; Armenian Medical Network, 2006). Although the researchers observed intellectual impairment in some children as they followed them to age 11, they also noted that the window of opportunity for intellectual gains was indeed wider than originally expected, suggesting perhaps that targeted interventions could ameliorate some observed impairments at later stages of development (Beckett et al., 2006). Similarly, Zeanah and his colleagues (2003) studied the neurobiological consequences of early and prolonged deprivation on children reared in institutions, with the goal of examining the degree of recovery that foster care could potentially provide. They compared children who had never been institutionalized, abandoned children reared in institutions, and abandoned children placed in institutions but then moved to foster care. Young children living in institutions were randomly assigned to continued institutional care or to placement in foster care, and their cognitive development was tracked until the child was 4½ years of age. The cognitive outcomes of children who remained in the institution were markedly below that of the children who had never been institutionalized, and also below that of the children taken out of the institution and placed into foster care. Notably, the researchers observed improved cognitive outcomes for the youngest children in their study who were placed in foster care, suggesting that a nurturing family could have ameliorative effects even on young, abandoned children (Nelson et al., 2007).

Sensitive Periods

Remarkably, by 3 years of age, a baby's brain is nearly 90 percent of its adult size! This phenomenal growth largely depends on receiving stimulation, which spurs activity in particular regions of the brain and provides the foundation for learning (Child Welfare Information Gateway, 2009). Researchers generally agree that there are key opportunities in the developmental process, referred to as *sensitive periods*, when certain parts of the brain are optimally susceptible to particular stimuli or experiences (Thompson & Nelson, 2001; Perry, 2002; Knudson, 2004). However, synapses and neuronal pathways that are not sufficiently and repeatedly activated may be discarded, and, unfortunately, the potential capabilities they promised may be diminished (Perry, 2002; Stiles, 2000; Child Welfare Information Gateway, 2009). For example, infants are genetically predisposed to form strong bonds of attachment to their caregivers; however, the attachment process can be disrupted if those caregivers are neglectful or unresponsive or if they create an abusive or otherwise threatening environment (Aisnworth, Blehar, Walters, & Wall, 1978; Child Welfare Information Gateway, 2009). As a consequence, the child's ability to form healthy relationships throughout development may be impaired.

Impoverishment and adversity during the sensitive period can also have severe and long-lasting detrimental effects on later brain capabilities (National Scientific Council on the Developing Child, 2007a). Although a sensitive period enables a neural circuit to optimize its architecture for the individual's needs and environment, this period of extreme receptivity also makes the brain region more vulnerable to the damaging effects of adversity (National Scientific Council on the Developing

Child, 2007a). Experiments in which animals were subjected to significant stress have demonstrated that, when adverse conditions last through the end of a circuit's sensitive period, the changes in the circuit's architecture become stable and tend to persist in the adult brain (National Scientific Council on the Developing Child, 2007a). While the brain has some capacity to mitigate the adverse effects of the altered circuit's architecture, the affected neural circuits do not process information as well as those exposed to appropriate experiences during the sensitive period (National Scientific Council on the Developing Child, 2007a). Degraded information transmitted by an altered neural circuit can prevent high-level circuits from receiving the information needed to optimally shape their architectures— even when a rich environment has been restored later in life (Thompson & Nelson, 2001). Much more needs to be learned about these sensitive periods and how long the windows of opportunity remain open for stimulating and activating important neural pathways. Clearly, early interventions that target caregiving practices and provide resources for parent education and training can help optimize development during these important periods.

Second Chances: Plasticity and Resilience

Having discussed the basics of growth and development of the brain, and possible ways in which difficulties might arise, I will now explore opportunities for continued brain development, learning, and growth. Advances in research shed light on the brain's ability to adapt to adversity and also on the idea that growth and change occur throughout life. This realization opens new avenues for thinking about possible strategies for building important skills at different stages of development, as well as for designing interventions and developing programs and policies that promote resilient outcomes in disadvantaged children.

Brain Plasticity: Growth and Change. There is now a general consensus in the field of neuroscience that neurons, even in the adult human brain, have the capacity to regenerate. However, for many years, at least until the 1990s, researchers doubted that this kind of growth and neurogenesis was possible (Kohman & Rhodes, 2013). More recently, with systematic study and advances in tools and technologies to more closely examine these processes in the brain, researchers have been able to study the brain's capacity for regeneration, reorganization, and recovery, and are discovering exciting ways in which these important processes can occur even in the aging adult brain (Stiles, 2000; Pulvers et al., 2007; Kohman & Rhodes, 2013). Researchers use the term *plasticity* to describe the processes of growth and change that enable the brain to adapt, compensate, and reorganize in response to repeated stimulation and environmental inputs (Stiles, 2000; Nelson, 2000). Stiles (2000) characterizes this dynamic process as a progressive adaptation to contingencies of input and the

demands of the learning environment and argues that the basic processes of plasticity are pervasive in childhood and continue through adulthood.

The extent of a brain's plasticity varies with the state of development and the
particular brain regions involved (Perry, 2006, cited in Child Welfare Information
Gateway, 2009). For instance, regions of the brain that control functions such as
breathing and heart rate are thought to be less adaptable than the regions that process thoughts and feelings. Thus, plasticity in the former regions may decrease as a
child gets older, although some degree of plasticity does remain (Stiles, 2000; Fox,
Levitt, & Nelson, 2010). As we now understand it, plasticity enables us to keep
learning throughout life and could potentially foster resilience or adaptation in the
context of certain adverse events (Fox, Levitt, & Nelson, 2010).

The ongoing adaptations of the developing brain happen because of genetics
and experience (Child Welfare Information Gateway, 2009; Blair & Raver, 2012).
Our brains prepare us for certain experiences by laying down the basic neuronal
pathways needed to respond to those experiences. When babies hear people speaking, for example, the neural pathways involved in speech and language receive the
necessary stimulation to organize and function (Perry, 2006, cited in Child Welfare
Information Gateway, 2009). The more babies are exposed to people speaking,
the stronger the neuronal pathways and synaptic connections become. However,
if appropriate exposure does not occur, the pathways developed in anticipation of a
developmental event may be discarded (Child Welfare Information Gateway, 2009).

As discussed previously, the various processes of creating, strengthening, and
discarding pathways enable a child's brain to adapt to his or her unique environments (Perry, 2002; Blair & Raver, 2012). This ability to adapt to the environment
is a part of normal development, and children growing up in various contexts learn
how to function in those environments. But because the brain can adapt, it will
adapt to a negative environment just as readily as to a positive one. In their examination of the effects of poverty on child development, Blair and Raver (2012) warn
that adaptation to low-resource environments has both short- and long-term costs
and benefits. A child's hypervigilance in a stressful context may be protective in the
short run in terms of physical safety, but may yield longer-term costs with respect
to psychological health and the ability to form trusting relationships in other, less
stressful contexts (Blair & Raver, 2012). Though much more difficult to accomplish at later stages, development can be shaped by experience and re-optimized,
according to Blair and Raver, opening up avenues for repair and recovery through
interventions.

For the brain to take full advantage of this plasticity, experiences must be tailored
to activating the relevant neural circuits and engaging the individual's attention for
the task (National Scientific Council on the Developing Child, 2007a). Based on
examples of adult stroke patients, cognitive rehabilitation methods are thought
to be most effective because they work directly with cognitive mechanisms of the
brain such as memory, speech, attention, and motor patterns (Koratamaddi, 2012).

Cognitive rehabilitation is designed to help the brain form new neural pathways, working without the affected region to promote positive adaptation and resilience (Koratamaddi, 2012).

Similarly, Rabipour and Raz (2012) discuss the burgeoning enterprise of brain training and intervention programs and practices hypothesized to improve cognition and behavior. Brain training is thought to improve general cognitive ability and behavioral outcomes as a result of repeated activity or focused meditation. They reviewed studies that support the claim that brain training has the potential to produce changes measured at the behavioral as well as the neuroanatomical and functional levels. Accordingly, they observed that the greatest changes in neuroplasticity leading to improved cognitive function occur with repeated practice of a skill over a specified period of time—through cognitive training programs involving musical training, physical exercise, or video gaming, for example. Training regimens based on these types of activities are thought to tap into many neural systems. For example, training through video games may tap into memory, spatial, and visuomotor functions, thus strengthening adaptive abilities across a number of domains (Green & Bavelier, 2008).

Resilience and Self-Regulation. According to researchers who study child development, resilience refers to a dynamic process that encompasses positive adaptation within the context of significant adversity. Luthar and colleagues (2000) argue that two critical conditions must exist for this kind of adaptation to occur. The first condition is exposure to significant threat or severe adversity; the second is the achievement of positive adaptation despite major assaults on the developmental process. By this definition, resilience is understood as a dynamic developmental process rather than a fixed construct or trait that only some people are fortunate enough to have (Luthar, 2006; Cicchetti, 2010; Masten, 2001). The presence of more factors in children's lives that are protective and buffer individuals against risks associated with adversity increases the likelihood that they will adapt in a positive manner.

Self-regulation is an important factor linked to resilient outcomes (Masten, 2001; Buckner, Mezzacappa, & Beardslee, 2009). Broadly speaking, it allows an individual to manage thoughts, feelings, and behaviors, and helps foster goal-directedness in different contexts across time (Buckner, Mezzacappa, & Beardslee, 2003). Self-regulation is especially important in poor children in that it is thought to promote proactive coping as well as problem-focused coping (Buckner, Mezzacappa, & Beardslee, 2003). Such regulatory capacities emerge from what are often referred to as executive functions—the psychological processes involved in the conscious control of thought (Anderson, 2002; DeLuca & Leventer, 2008). Examples of these processes include inhibition; future-time orientation; consequential thinking; and the planning, initiation, and regulation of goal-directed behavior—all of which are essential for school readiness and academic success (Greenberg, 2006). Early stresses in the lives of children living in poverty affect how they develop the executive functions essential for success in preschool and later school experiences (Blair et al., 2011; ScienceDaily, 2011). Executive functions are thought to be processed in the prefrontal cortex of the brain, although there is emerging evidence that other regions of the brain are also involved (Blakemore & Choudhury, 2006). These abilities mature at different rates—some peak in late childhood or adolescence while others continue to progress into early adulthood. Development of executive functioning corresponds to the neurophysiological development of the growing brain; as the processing capacity of the frontal lobes and other interconnected regions increases, the core executive functions emerge (Anderson, 2002; De Luca & Leventer, 2008). As these functions become established, they continue to mature throughout development, with more complex functions developing in late adolescence and early adulthood (Anderson, 2002; De Luca & Leventer, 2008). The ability to manage regulatory capacities is essential to adaptation in various contexts. For example, *effortful control*, an important subset of executive functions, is important for children's adjustment and also for its protective effects, which contribute to children's resilience when they are faced with risk or adversity (Lengua, 2012). Effortful control is likely to help temper emotional response and behavioral reactions to stress and interpersonal challenges and to facilitate more adaptive responses. These responses might, in turn, bring about more supportive responses from others, giving rise to positive feedback and support. High degrees of effortful control have been related to children's resilience, flexibility, and persistence (Lengua, 2012).

Notably, caregiving appears to be involved in the development of a range of children's self-regulatory abilities (Hofer, 1995; Kopp, 1982; Bernier, Carlson, & Whipple, 2010). These abilities can, similarly, be observed not only in psychophysiological domains of development but also in behavioral and cognitive domains (Gunnar & Donzella, 2002). In her work on the context for understanding self-regulation, Carlson (2003) discussed three dimensions of parenting that are thought to promote executive function in children: maternal sensitivity, scaffolding, and mind-mindedness. *Sensitivity*, which consists of appropriate and consistent responses to infants' signals, allows parents to have successful experiences of having an impact on the child's social environment. *Scaffolding* involves the parent offering or modeling age-appropriate problem-solving strategies for the child to emulate. Finally, *mind-mindedness*, or the parent's tendency to use mental terms while talking to the child, is thought to offer children verbal tools with which to progress from being externally regulated to becoming self-regulated (Bernier, Carlson, & Whipple, 2010). Together, these three dimensions are thought to be involved in the development of children's executive functioning, each in a distinctive and influential way. Bernier, Carlson, and Whipple (2010) theorize that the early development of executive function is an aspect of children's cognitive development that appears likely to be susceptible to strong caregiving influences. They go on to assert that inasmuch as the prefrontal cortex is an area of the brain that develops more slowly than other regions, there is a large window of neural development during which caregiving can have a significant impact on the developing brain structures.

It remains to be seen whether additional research will illuminate even further how early caregiving practices impact the brain structures involved in executive functions, and how the effects of these practices can be ameliorated or sustained throughout development. We now know that healthy development of executive function skills can be supported through specialized practice and training, and that neuroplasticity validates the possibility of successfully promoting the development of these skills (Nelson, 1999a, 1999b; Bodrova & Leong, 2007). One such interventional approach shown to be effective in supporting the self-control and goal-orientation aspects of executive functions is "Tools of the Mind," an evidence-based early-childhood intervention focused on teaching self-regulation as well as other important skills such as literacy and math (Bodrova & Leong, 2007). The program uses a core curriculum of 40 activities that promote executive functioning, including self-regulatory private speech, dramatic play, and aids to facilitate memory and attention (Diamond, Barnett, Thomas, & Munro, 2007). The strategies currently used in this program have been shown to significantly improve the self-regulatory skills of children from low-income families (Diamond, Barnett, Thomas, & Munroe, 2007; Bodrova & Leong, 2007).

Thus, interventions that target important executive functioning skills have strong promise and potential to enhance competencies in disadvantaged children. Such interventions may tap into neuroplastic processes in the brain, potentially leading to changes in brain structure and function that may indeed give a child a "second chance" at developing important cognitive and behavioral skills essential for school success. More research is needed to fully understand whether these types of interventions are effective at later stages of development and whether caregiving practices throughout the school-age years can be brought to bear on important neural processes and give rise to resilience in children.

Discoveries of Hope and Optimism

As discussed earlier, the brain's capacity for renewal and continuous growth and learning provides exciting opportunities to examine how children can recover from less-than-optimal early developmental experiences. Advances in the neurosciences may yield discoveries about neural pathways and connections that can mitigate the effects of exposure to stressful experiences and foster positive outcomes. One such advance is the discovery of brain regions that promote an optimistic outlook on life. Sharot and colleagues (2007) studied what is called "optimism bias"—a human tendency to expect positive events in the future even when no evidence supports such expectations. While investigating how the brain generates this pervasive optimism

bias, she discovered that specific regions of the brain—the amygdala and the ros-
tral anterior cingulate cortex (rACC)—showed greater activation when study participants were asked to imagine positive, rather than negative, future events. The
same regions are involved when depression and pessimism are observed (Sharot,
Riccardi, Raio, & Phelps, 2007).

According to these researchers, expecting positive events and generating compelling mental images of such events may serve an adaptive function, by motivating
present behavior toward a future goal (similar to the processes involved in hope
theory's agency thinking). Her study highlights how the brain generates a tendency
to engage in the projection of positive future events to create positive images of
the future (Sharot et al., 2007). Sharot's (2011) work also demonstrates the brain's
capacity to adopt a less negative perspective on stressful life events and to positively
reassess negative outcomes as a function of past and future experiences. Notably,
the rACC has strong reciprocal connections with the amygdala and other brain
regions that convey emotional and motivational information. Sharot posits that the
rACC may work hand in hand with emotional centers of the brain to downplay negative emotional responses. This mechanism may be adaptive, promoting an internal
drive to achieve high-stakes goals (Sharot, 2011). Sharot and her team further note
that the rACC has been implicated in tasks involving self-reflection, such as making positive self-referential judgments, reflecting on hopes and dreams, indicating
preferences, and judging the trustworthiness of others (Sharot et al., 2007). The
findings from Sharot's work suggest that when people learn, their neurons encode
desirable information that can enhance optimism and, at the same time, omit undesirable information.

Similarly, research by Fox (2012) examines cognitive biases toward a pessimistic or an optimistic outlook on life. While an individual's personality type
may predispose one to see the proverbial glass as half empty or half full, Fox pro-
poses that the neural pathways underlying optimism and pessimism are highly
malleable and able to change. Referring to these pathways as the "sunny brain"
and "rainy brain," she contends that even small changes in avoiding negative,
pessimistic thinking can strengthen sunny-brain circuitry and promote a more
balanced and healthy reaction to adverse events. Such changes may potentially
prevent depression and anxiety disorders. Fox theorizes that optimal mental
health involves stronger "sunny-brain circuits." These circuits can be strengthened and reinforced through cognitive behavioral therapy, cognitive-bias retraining exercises, and other strategies tested in her lab. The new therapeutic focus
on positive thinking and optimistic approaches to problem solving strengthens
the targeted neural systems, enhancing the opportunities for positive outcomes
(Fox, 2012).

Finally, an exciting discovery by UCLA scientists has highlighted a biological link to optimism. Saphire-Bernstein and colleagues (2011) studied the
genetic bases of optimism, self-esteem, and mastery and found the oxytocin

receptor gene (*OXTR*) to be implicated in these psychological characteristics and mental-health outcomes. This reportedly was the first study to report a gene associated with these important psychological resources. Oxytocin is a hormone produced mainly in the hypothalamus, from which it is released into the blood via the pituitary gland or sent to other parts of the brain and spinal cord (DeAngelis, 2008). When oxytocin binds to oxytocin receptors, it influences behavior and physiology. Oxytocin acts as a neurotransmitter in the brain and plays a role in maternal behavior, social relationships, and bonding (DeAngelis, 2008). Saphire-Bernstein and colleagues noted a growing literature supporting the role of *OXTR* in the structure and function of specific brain structures—the amygdala, hypothalamus, and dorsolateral anterior cingulate cortex (dACC)—related to psychological resources such as optimism, self-esteem, and mastery. These researchers found that specific variants of the *OXTR* gene are highly associated with depressive symptoms, which may be largely mediated by how the function of *OXTR* influences these psychological resources.

The important message conveyed through the researchers' work is that genes are not deterministic. They emphasize that even people whose gene variants predispose them to depression are able to learn coping skills. Furthermore, people who rate themselves as having lower levels of psychological resources might still benefit from training themselves to be more optimistic, have higher self-esteem, and have a greater sense of mastery. While many questions remain to be answered, this line of inquiry has enormous promise for shedding light on approaches to overcoming adversity. To what extent can an optimistic outlook help economically disadvantaged children and families cope with difficult circumstances? And what are the mechanisms involved? Once again, the fundamental roles of parenting and maternal warmth and nurturing are implicated in the functioning of these basic psychological resources, thus underscoring the powerful interactions of environment and biology.

A Hopeful Conclusion

The research reviewed in this chapter supports the notion that, to a large extent, we may indeed be wired *for* hope. However, much more research is needed to fully understand how the buffering psychological resources of hope, optimism, and personal agency are linked to brain structure and function. Rogers' notion of self-actualization focused on internal drive states and natural tendencies to strive toward a desired goal. For children who begin life experiencing the challenges associated with economic disadvantage, their internal drive and natural tendencies may be overshadowed by the day-to-day exigencies of life. However, if we indeed have neurobiological mechanisms for hope, for achieving our goals, and for overcoming adversity, then it is possible that education, training, and targeted interventions may enable poor children to reach their potential, even if their early life experiences were far from optimal.

As discussed earlier, sensitive periods are believed to exist at the optimal times for development and learning. While evidence suggests that both children and adults may be able to make up for missed experiences later in life, the process is likely to be more difficult. This is especially true if a young child was deprived of certain stimulation, resulting in pruning of the synapses and loss of the neuronal pathways relevant to that stimulation. Plasticity of the brain often allows children to recover from missing certain experiences, but children will learn and master each step more easily as they progress through each developmental stage if their brains have built an efficient network of pathways. The implications for later interventions in development are clear—the task will be harder, more expensive in terms of societal and individual effort, and potentially less durable (National Scientific Council on the Developing Child, 2007a; Knudsen, Heckman, Cameron, & Shonkoff, 2006). This understanding suggests the need for parents, schools, and service providers to invest in early intervention programming, especially when family risk factors are recognized.

A central theme running through the research reviewed above is the powerful ameliorating effects of a warm and nurturing relationship, especially during the sensitive periods of development. Even in the context of extreme stress, the buffering role of caregivers or supportive adults helps promote coping with and adaptation to adversity.

A social neuroscientist, Shelly Taylor, spoke of her surprise to see how clearly social relationships forge our underlying biology, even at the level of gene expression:

> Chief among these social forces are the ways in which people take care of one another and tend to one another's needs. An early warm and nurturant relationship, such as mothers often enjoy with their children, is as vital to development as calcium is to bones. The benefits that tending provides to children, especially those with genetic risks, are substantial. From life in the womb to the surprisingly resilient brain of old age, the social environment molds and shapes the expression of our genetic heritage until the genetic contribution is sometimes barely evident. A mother's tending can completely eliminate the potential effects of a gene; a risk for a disease can fail to materialize with nurturing, and a genetic propensity may lead to one outcome for one person and the opposite for another, based on the tending they received. (Wolpert, 2011)

Interventions aimed at developing and strengthening parenting competencies may serve to provide the basic neuropsychological, emotional, and social skills a child needs to adapt positively to adverse circumstances. We know the importance of parents' explanatory styles and how responses to adversity have an impact on the coping strategies children learn to employ (Peterson & Steen, 2002; Taylor et al., 2010). Interventions devised to help parents tap into "sunny-brain" neural circuits may not only help ameliorate stressors associated with economic disadvantage but may also be protective for the child. Chapter 4 undertakes a more elaborate discussion of the important role of parents.

I started this chapter by alluding to the challenges of African American males and the so-called pipeline-to-prison phenomenon. The research discussed in this chapter has promising implications for providing targeted interventions for these children throughout their educational experience. In undertaking such interventions, we may provide these youth with multiple opportunities at multiple time points to develop and master important skills that may inspire hope and build confidence in their academic abilities. Investments in these children must be provided early and continued to ensure that the remedial effects are sustained (Heckman, 2007). As pointed out by Blair and Raver (2012), viewing development as a dynamic and complex process rather than from a deterministic, deficit-compensation point of view opens up opportunities for new and exciting approaches to ensuring that children have the best possible opportunity for success.

4

Parenting and Family Matters

Contrasting Parenting and Family Processes—Examining
Family Strengths and Assets

> Listen to the mustn'ts, child. Listen to the don'ts. Listen to the shouldn'ts,
> the impossibles, the won'ts. Listen to the never haves, then listen close to
> me...Anything can happen, child. Anything can be.
> —Shel Silverstein, *Where the Sidewalk Ends* (1974)

I begin this chapter by reintroducing Carlton and Amanda. Carlton is a single father who at the time of this writing was raising his 11-year-old daughter. He struggled with recovery from alcoholism, which led to his being homeless and moving from location to location to find support. Carlton did not grow up experiencing the challenges of economic disadvantage. He was raised in a two-parent family in which his father was in the Army and his mother was a homemaker. Carlton reflects: *"I didn't want for anything and had everything I needed."* However, in the process of growing up, Carlton was introduced to alcohol and became an addict. His journey toward recovery was variable, with many issues and challenges along the way. However, his strong desire to ensure his daughter's well-being and safety was a motivating factor for seeking rehabilitative services, counseling, and transitional housing support. This desire put him on a stronger, more determined course toward recovery and ultimately placed him in a healthy position to care and provide for his daughter. Carlton's childrearing practices and ideologies came largely from his own upbringing. Guided by the stern presence of his military father and the flexibility and nurturing of his stay-at-home mom, Carlton created a template by which he engages with his parents and his daughter: *"It's an open friendship, relationship. A father and daughter thing. I can just look at her sometimes [demonstrating how he looks at her] and she know—don't do that. My father did it with me, my mother did it."*

In contrast, Amanda's story speaks of motivation and resolve to create a different life for herself, not despite her family upbringing, but because of it.

Amanda experienced adversity during her childhood because her parents were going through a divorce. The tension in the household that led up to the divorce reportedly affected the parent-child relationships as well as the relationships among the siblings. The strain of these broken relationships, financial difficulties, and other associated problems influenced the parenting styles and behaviors in the home, and these in turn affected family relationships and exacerbated family problems. According to Amanda, however, these parenting styles and behaviors promoted adaptive behavioral responses, fueling Amanda's drive to have a better life and giving her willpower to withstand the compulsion to be drawn into family chaos. For Amanda, maintaining positive family relationships meant moving across the country to attend college. Through her academic experiences, and subsequent knowledge about child development, Amanda was able to put her family's functioning into perspective and to use that knowledge to rear her own children.

In many ways, Carlton's story demonstrates the importance of identifying and focusing on family strengths and "assets" as a means of helping parents cope with the challenges of adversity. Despite their difficulties, many poor families like Carlton's possess important strengths or assets—including strong relationships, positive parenting styles, cohesiveness, and extended family—that may protect against the effects of poverty, allowing the families to achieve success, however they define it. Even in families where it may appear that the risks are more prevalent than the protective factors, closer examinations of family processes such as the establishment of core values, whether or not these are clearly articulated, are important assets as well. Family strengths research models highlight qualities of strong families, which include characteristics such as appreciation and affection, spending time together, and commitment to one another (Walsh, 2006). Structure, routine, and orderliness, the processes operating in Amanda's home, help foster stability, predictability, and security—important factors associated with children's emotional well-being and self-regulatory capacities.

Identifying and understanding strengths and assets, as opposed to focusing on deficits, within poor families are important steps toward promoting the cognitive and motivational aspects of hope that pave the way for adaptation to adversity (Snyder, Feldman, Shorey, & Rand, 2002; Lopez, Rose, Robinson, Marques, & Pais-Ribeiro, 2009). The strengths-based approach may inform programs and practices to help families build the competencies needed to adapt to adversity. Important questions for policymakers and practitioners to consider are whether and to what extent these assets can be leveraged across the various ecological system levels to cultivate additional strengths and assets, enabling families to have access to resources that may help sustain these strengths over time. I explore these ideas throughout this chapter, and discuss ways that families draw upon these strengths to manage the complexities of their daily lives. Carlton's and Amanda's perspectives on parenting are shared to highlight lessons learned from their triumphs and challenges.

The Strength of the Parent-Child Relationship

Few relationships are more profound or have more enduring effects than the relationship between parent and child (American Academy of Pediatrics, 2003; Brooks, 2013). Even before a child is born, parents lay the groundwork and create an environment for establishing an attachment bond and promoting their child's optimal growth and development. The prenatal care a mother obtains to maintain her own health and emotional status plays a role in how her child comes into the world (Gortmaker, 1979; Olds et al., 1986). In addition, the mother's capacity to respond to the child's needs and provide a nurturing and supportive postnatal environment are essential to promoting the child's well-being (Martins & Gaffan, 2000; Shaw, Levitt, Wong, & Kaczorowski, 2006).

A secure attachment bond between the parent and child is essential to a child's emotional well-being (Bowlby, 1969; Ainsworth, Blehar, Waters, & Walls, 1978). Establishing this attachment bond during infancy is important because the process of attachment plays an essential role in initiating pathways that enable children to develop such crucial skills as social relations, self-confidence, and emotion regulation (Ainsworth et al., 1978; Sroufe, 2005). These skills are important as children mature and begin to interact in social contexts outside the home. A child who is securely attached to his or her parents has been shown to have a strong self-concept and a positive outlook, which afford the opportunity to take appropriate risks, develop positive peer relationships, engage in prosocial behavior, enjoy fruitful relationships with others, and have a positive sense of themselves in the world (Bowlby, 1969, 1988; Sroufe, 2005). In contrast, a child who is insecurely attached may have difficulty developing social competencies and regulating his or her emotions (Bowlby, 1969, 1988; Sroufe, 2005).

While research has typically focused on the mother's role in establishing this bond, the father's role is also very important during this tender stage of development (McCabe & Clark, 1999; American Academy of Pediatrics, 2003). We are beginning to examine more closely the ways in which attachment bonds are established between father and child and the hope-promoting role that fathers play as their children grow and develop (McCabe & Clark, 1999; Bretherton, 2010; Cabrera & Tamis-LeMonda, 2013). As discussed in Chapter 2, researchers found a link between paternal support and hope in young girls in the study, suggesting the importance of early attachment relationships between father and child.

We also know that the quality of the parents' relationship with each other is critically important, as it affects the behavior of both parents in their childrearing practices (American Academy of Pediatrics, 2003). Whether or not both parents reside in the home, strong parental relationships allow the mother and the father to be more responsive, affectionate, and confident in rearing their children and helping them achieve important milestones from infancy through adolescence and into adulthood (Amato, 1994; Harris, Furstenberg, & Marmer, 1998).

So, it is also important for families to build on and maintain close relationships even as the child approaches and goes through adolescence. Indeed, a good deal of research is devoted to understanding the links between parenting, family processes, and early child development. However, we need a better understanding of the buffering role that parents may play, even at later stages of development. Adolescence is a tumultuous and risky time for teenagers and is certainly challenging for parents, regardless of socioeconomic status. The teenage years hold the greatest risk for engaging in unsafe activities including early sexual debut, substance use, delinquency, and other behaviors that might reduce adolescents' chances of breaking the generational cycle of poverty (Hardaway & Mcloyd, 2009; Spera, 2005). Strong, positive relationships between adolescents and their parents may help the adolescent navigate the difficult transitions from the preteen years through adolescence and into emerging adulthood (Steinberg, 2001). This is important because, as discussed earlier, research tells us that early experiences of poverty and disadvantage can have far-reaching consequences in nearly every domain of development (Maholmes & King, 2012). Studies have shown large and consistent associations between childhood poverty experiences and negative academic outcomes including lower reading scores, poorer health, and social behavior problems in adolescence and later adulthood (American Academy of Pediatrics, 2003; Maholmes & King, 2012). In addition, children living in poverty are at greater risk for displaying behavioral and emotional problems and difficulty getting along with peers. Moreover, experiences with long-term and persistent poverty are also associated with feelings of anxiety, unhappiness, and depression (Bolger, Patterson, Thompson, & Kupersmidt, 1995; McLoyd & Wilson, 1991). The consequences of such experiences may place youth on a path toward experiencing poverty as young adults and potentially rearing their own children in such emotionally difficult contexts. Thus, the strength of the parents' relationship with the adolescent may play a particularly protective, stabilizing role, especially in environments high in violence or with risks of gang initiation or juvenile delinquency (Hardaway, Mcloyd, & Wood, 2012). The protective function of strong, stable relationships needs to be better understood and supported as a means to buffer against both the psychological and behavioral consequences of poverty.

Evidence-based interventions are available to help parents build stronger relationships with their children and learn interaction and communication strategies that help maintain this relationship throughout the various stages of development. Home visiting models in which one-on-one support is offered in the home by qualified practitioners call attention to the importance of intervening early with families who may be at risk for poor, unhealthy parenting practices (Olds, Henderson, Tatelbaum, & Chamberlin, 1988; Olds & Kitzman, 1990). One such home visiting intervention, called the Nurse Family Partnership (NFP), starts early to help provide the wherewithal to foster these important relationships (Olds, 2006). It offers a program of home visitation by a prenatal and infancy nurse, in an effort to improve the health, well-being, and self-sufficiency of low-income, first-time parents and their children. The NFP program activities are designed to link families with needed services to promote good decision making about personal development, and assist parents in making healthy choices during pregnancy and in providing proper care to their children. The program also helps women build supportive networks and relationships with families and friends that, as discussed later in this chapter, have been shown to foster resilience. Notably, the NFP has been successful in improving parental care of children, including fewer incidences associated with maltreatment, as well as better infant emotional and language development, fewer subsequent pregnancies, greater workforce participation, and reduced dependence on public assistance and food stamps.

Another intervention program, Parent-Child Interaction Therapy (PCIT) places emphasis on improving the quality of the parent-child relationship and changing the patterns of parent-child interaction (Funderburk & Eyberg, 2010). While the PCIT is a treatment program for young children with conduct disorders, the principles of the program certainly have relevance to parents in need of support in managing their children's behavior, especially in instances where the stresses of economic disadvantage or other risks may obscure and place a strain on otherwise obvious opportunities for building these relationships (Borrego, Anhalt, Terao, Vargas, & Urquiza, 2006; Bigfoot & Funderburk, 2011; Fernandez, Butler, & Eyberg, 2011). In PCIT, parents learn specific skills to establish or strengthen a nurturing and secure relationship with their child while encouraging prosocial behavior and discouraging negative behavior. This treatment focuses on two different parent-child interactions: child-directed interactions (CDI) and parent-directed interactions (PDI). During the CDI phase, parents learn nondirective play skills, similar to those used in play therapy, and engage their child in a play situation with the goal of strengthening the parent-child relationship. During the PDI phase, parents learn to direct the child's behavior with clear, age-appropriate instructions and consistent consequences, with the aim of increasing child compliance. (For more thorough discussions, see Child Welfare Information Gateway, 2013, and http://www.pcit.org/.)

The Strength of Flexible Parenting Styles

The parents' approach to childrearing may be instrumental in establishing a strong attachment bond and connection. In the research literature, parenting styles encompass the parenting behaviors and practices as well as the particular perspectives about childrearing (Darling & Steinberg, 1993; Gray & Steinberg, 1999). These styles may be based on parents' belief systems, cultural practices, perceptions of neighborhood safety, or worldview (Chao, 1994; Pinderhughes, Nix, Foster, & Jones, 2001; Morris, Silk, Steinberg, Myers, & Robinson, 2007; Roche, Ensminger, & Cherlin, 2007). For example, parents who believe that children should be seen and not heard might have a more restrictive style than parents who believe that children should have the opportunities to explore, to learn, and to experience the world for themselves. As we learned from Carlton, parenting styles may also be based on prior experiences. Parents who enjoyed a warm, inclusive family environment as children may provide a similar environment for their own children. Conversely, if a parent grew up in a context in which their parents "ruled with a strong hand," they may be less supportive of expressions of emotions or less likely to consider how children might be involved in family decisions (Morris et al., 2007). Researchers have shown that parenting styles that show warmth and responsiveness and are nurturing are critically important to the positive development of a child's psychological, behavioral, and emotional development (Simon & Conger, 2007; Jackson-Newsome, Buchanan, & McDonald, 2008). Baumrind (1966, 1967, 1971), who is credited with the conceptualization of parenting styles, suggested that children do better educationally, socially, and behaviorally when their parents are responsive to their needs, monitor their behavior, and engage with them in ways that promote independent decision making, critical thinking, and age-appropriate judgment. Baumrind conceptualized this combination of monitoring, responsiveness, and encouragement of independence as an *authoritative* style of parenting. *Authoritative* parents establish a warm and nurturing relationship with their children but, as the name implies, set firm limits for their children's behavior. These parents give their children a range of options and choices within those boundaries, and they allow their children to participate in family decisions. *Authoritarian* parenting, a second style, is characterized as demanding and controlling. Parents using this style are typically less flexible and are often deemed to lack responsiveness and warmth. These families are generally governed by rules and may exact harsh punishment if rules are not followed. In contrast, *permissive* or *indulgent* parents are sometimes thought of as overly nurturing and nonpunitive. They tend to provide few standards for behavior and are extremely tolerant of misbehavior. This may lead to disorganized and chaotic homes, which may be stressful for children and parents alike. Research suggests that chaos and disorganization in the home is a signal that other adaptive processes may not be operative (Repetti, Taylor, & Seeman, 2002).

Structure, consistent routine, and orderliness are important in helping to develop important competencies and self-regulatory capacities associated with positive academic, social, and emotional outcomes in children (Evans, Gonnella, Marcynyszyn, Gentile, & Salpekar, 2005). The importance of orderliness in the home is discussed in my interview with Gladys, a support worker at the transitional housing program that Carlton attends:

> *We have one family right now we're working on whose housekeeping was really deficient. We do weekly inspections. We go into the home and we have an inspection chart and they have to pass that. They get put on probation if they consistently have an apartment that's in disarray. In this case, it's a symptom of the family and some of the chaos within the family, some of the disorganization, and some dysfunction in the family. She has done very well over the last couple of months. She struggles because it's hard for her to keep this up, but it makes a huge difference in the atmosphere of the home and for the children and having a place to sit, having a place to sleep, and having a place to do their homework. It does have an overall positive effect. She is doing counseling as well, and that helps in the process of healing the situation and working on some of those issues that keeping her home in disarray is a symptom of.*

Thus, responsiveness and attention to such mechanisms of family functioning as orderliness and structure are important markers of well-being for both the parent and the child. These qualities are typically observed in families in which the authoritative parenting style predominates. Interestingly, researchers (Simons & Conger, 2007) put forward the notion that while having both parents use authoritative styles is ideal; having one parent with this style can buffer a child from the negative effects of less optimal styles used by the other parent. This, they argue, is a "compensation effect" whereby the benefits of authoritative parenting outweigh the problems associated with indulgent or authoritarian parenting. Simons and Conger point out, however, that despite the buffering power of authoritative parenting, it cannot assuage the effects of an uninvolved mother.

Nonetheless, the research generally converges around the idea that the authoritative parenting style and associated behaviors have been found to be most beneficial to children—fostering resilience, giving them tools to build important competencies, and promoting autonomy and good decision making (Gray & Steinberg, 1999; Simon & Conger, 2007). Children growing up in authoritative households are generally thought to have several positive outcomes, including academic achievement, positive school behavior, and completion of high school (Beyer, 1995; Gray & Steinberg, 1999), thereby increasing their chances of pursuing postsecondary education or securing future employment. In contrast, children of authoritarian and permissive parents tend to have relatively poor academic outcomes, as well as other social and behavioral problems (Fletcher et al., 2008).

It is important to point out that parenting styles and behaviors are not unidimensional. Rather, they are integrative (Darling & Steinberg, 1993) and have been shown to have interactive effects on children's behavior and well-being (Maccoby & Martin, 1983). Indeed, a family's broader ecological context may dictate more flexible use or combinations of various parenting styles and behaviors to manage the day-to-day complexities of family life (Darling & Steinberg, 1993; Fletcher et al., 2008). The ability to discern the need for flexibility is an asset that could help foster family functioning in a given circumstance. This is important because parents living in environments where their children face daily risks of physical harm may need to be more adaptive and nimble in their approach to parenting and therefore may use a variety of approaches as their situation requires. Insights from my interviews with the families suggest that a parent who leans toward an authoritative style may, in circumstances deemed harmful or dangerous for their children, become more directive and restrictive (Carlton). A permissive parent may at times find it necessary to be authoritative during times of transition or change (Amanda); likewise, an authoritarian-rule governed parent (Josephine) may find it necessary to embrace other styles, although, without support, these changes may be temporary. During our interview, Carlton discusses his ability to be flexible in his approach to parenting:

> **Interviewer:** *How would you describe your parenting style? Are you permissive? Do you have rules?*
> **Carlton:** *I'm in between. I have rules. I don't let her do what she wanna do. First thing is homework. She can watch TV, she can play her games, but she can't play 'em all night. Homework has to come first. I try to let her figure out things on her own. She'll go in there and look in the refrigerator and she'll say dad what's to eat? And I'll say what do you want? And we agree. I teach her about compromise.*
> **Interviewer:** *Do you ever find it necessary to bend the rules?*
> **Carlton:** *Yeah, a lot of times. It depends on the situation. Sometimes I have to work late. Sometimes she goes to aftercare. Sometimes I have meetings at Hope and a Home. So I'm pretty flexible on how late she goes to bed. Not real late, but just a little later. I understand that everybody needs a little bit of "me time" or a little wind down time. So I give her that little wind down time after the meetings . . . I take her with me sometimes.*

Thus, in these contexts, the situational use of parenting styles may be an important coping strategy that enables parents to maintain a sense of order and structure in their household, and at the same time facilitate in their children the development of cognitive skills and personal agency as theorized by Roesch and colleagues (2010) in Chapter 2. Parents who are able to be more flexible in their parenting style—whether of necessity, through trial and error, or as a result of their own rearing—may reflect a keen attunement to a child's emotional, psychological safety needs. However, as Fletcher et al. (2008) point out, parents' decisions to modify rules, expectations, and consequences for misbehavior should result from give-and-take discussion. If parental demands and expectations change without discussion or in response to negative responses from children, these shifts may result in more problematic development for the child. This may be particularly the case for children in households where discussion is often lacking regarding parental rules and priorities.

For children in poverty, more directive parenting style may be protective in high-risk contexts (McCabe & Clark, 1999). *Directive* differs from harsh parenting styles, in that parents may provide more explanation of their decisions and focused monitoring, whereas harsh parenting is typically devoid of explanation and is punitive in nature—a style that children may perceive as less caring and nurturing (Ceballo & McLoyd, 2002). McLoyd (1998) studied parenting styles of poor African American families and found that strict and highly directive parenting (i.e., well-defined house rules, clear sanctions for breaking rules, close supervision) combined with high levels of warmth help poor, inner-city children resist environmental forces outside their home that would normally contribute to poor child outcomes. Further, some directive parenting behaviors distinguish poor, inner-city children who exhibit high academic achievement from their low-achieving counterparts exposed to similar stressors (Baldwin, Baldwin, & Cole, 1990; Clark, 1993; Jarrett, 1995).

As Carlton revealed in his interview, most parents have dreams and aspirations for a better life for their child and, as a result, engage with the children in ways that they believe will help bring these dreams to fruition, whether or not the parents have achieved their own personal goals in education, employment, or even in personal relationships. Toward this end, parents may need support in using styles and practices that are most effective for their children and in their particular family context. Interventions that tap into these important processes can help parents learn to become more flexible and adaptive in their parenting of their children. In so doing, the interventions also help parents model for their children important strategies for problem solving, critical thinking, and decision-making—all of which are elements of the agency thinking described in hope theory.

Such intervention strategies as the Triple P–Positive Parenting Program and the Strengthening Families Program (SFP) help promote effective parenting practices. The Triple P is a multilevel system or suite of parenting and family support strategies for families with children from birth to age 12, with extensions to families with teenagers aged 13 to 16. The program has been developed to be used with families from many cultural groups and is designed to prevent social, emotional, behavioral, and developmental problems in children by enhancing their parents' knowledge, skills, and confidence (Sanders, Markie-Dadds, & Turner, 2003). Outcomes of program implementation connect changes in problematic parenting practices with fewer child behavioral problems at home and at school. Also, parents were observed to have greater confidence in their parenting ability and have more positive attitudes toward their children.

Similarly, the SFP is a family skills training program designed to increase resilience and reduce risk factors for behavioral, emotional, academic, and social problems in children (Molgaard, Spoth, & Redmond, 2000; Kumpfer, Alvarado, Tait, & Whiteside, 2007). The program comprises skills sessions that help parents to increase desired behaviors in children by using attention and rewards, clear communication, effective discipline, substance use education, problem solving, and limit setting. Life skills for children are part of the program. These are designed to help children learn effective communication, understand their feelings, improve social and problem-solving skills, resist peer pressure, understand the consequences of substance use, and comply with parental rules. Notably, the SFP includes family life skills sessions in which families engage in structured family activities, practice therapeutic child play, conduct family meetings, learn communication skills, practice effective discipline, reinforce each other's positive behaviors, and plan family activities together.

The Strength of Shared Values

Parents pass along to their children attitudes and behavioral characteristics that are essential to rising above the risks associated with economic disadvantage and poverty. According to one researcher (Mayer, 1997), such values as diligence, honesty, good work ethic, thriftiness, and reliability reflecting "good parenting" improve children's life chances, independent of their effect on parents' income. Carlton describes how he tries to teach his daughter these important values:

> I try to teach her values like mostly of being honest. I try to teach her honesty and being open minded...I try to give her different ways of looking at things. I try to teach her about money and how to save money. I have a jug in my room. Every day I put change in. Then when it gets filled up I take her and we'll go down to the store and we'll dump it over—she'll push it in. Sometimes [there's] 200 dollars and I try to tell her that this is from saving pennies, and nickels and quarters. When you save your money, you'll have money. And that's how I pay my bills sometimes. I leave my money in the bank and I go in there and cash [the jars of change] in and I start all over again. I [also] try to teach her how to be

a young lady. Young ladies don't have their room junky and ladies don't do this and that. Her room is a mess right now, but I teach her responsibility: "Now, you're the one that messed it up, now go in there and clean it up."

Carlton has clear values about honesty and thriftiness that he wants his daughter to embrace, and his approach to parenting reflects those values. As discussed in the previous section, parenting styles and behaviors help to inculcate these values and perspectives and give rise to *socialization practices.* Here I refer to socialization practices as the ways in which parents transmit values to their children regarding their view of the world (Greenberger & Goldberg, 1989; Hughes & Chen, 1997; Maccoby, 1992). It involves parents' perceptions regarding their "place" in society in relation to others, their explanations of life events, and the value they place on education, work, and civic responsibility and other important qualities. For example, parents who instill messages of social equality help their children learn that despite economic limitations, they have the same right as others to high-quality education and other important processes that will contribute to the child's success in life. Parental monitoring behavior, making homework and school a priority, and allowing children to be inquisitive are all socialization practices that give children the tools needed to engage not only with others in their families, school, and local community but also with people in broader, less familiar social contexts (Hart & Risley, 1995; Maccoby, 1992).

Moreover, the lenses through which a parent views the world—glass half empty or glass half full—are influential in shaping how children interpret the events in their lives, how they respond to difficult challenges. Recall in Chapter 2 the discussion on optimism as a tendency to expect positive outcomes (Carver et al., 2010) and that this expectation often leads to goal-directed behavior (Scheier & Carver, 1987, 1992). Bamford and Lagatutta (2012), in their work on children's knowledge about positive and negative thinking, hypothesized that individual differences in child and parental optimism and hope would predict children's reasoning about the emotional benefits of thinking optimistically in negative situations. They found that the higher a parent rated themselves on measures of optimism and hope, the more beneficial their children rated the emotional effects (feeling happy or sad) of thinking positively. The researchers suggest that parents can provide direct modeling or teaching that may help their child interpret appropriately and cope with negative situations.

Similarly, Jones and colleagues (2002) studied the role of maternal optimism in relation to positive parenting and child psychosocial adjustment. They asked whether maternal optimism would have significant interpersonal effects, whether mothers reporting a more positive outlook would use positive parenting behaviors, and whether children of optimistic mothers would show positive psychosocial adjustment. The researchers did indeed find positive associations between mothers' optimism and their children's adjustment and suggested that programs could be targeted toward helping parents understand how they can foster optimism in children through positive parenting strategies.

As discussed earlier, relationships within the family make a profound difference in children's outcomes and experiences. Expressing *affection and warmth* solidifies the bond between parent and child, thereby giving the child a sense of belonging, confidence, and assuredness in the family relations (Jackson-Newsome et al., 2008). We learn from Amanda the importance of affection and warmth on a child and the long-term influences of parenting behaviors on a child's perspectives and practices when he or she becomes a parent:

> *I don't parent the same way my parents did. I try to do the opposite of what my parents did. I remember my mother physically pushing me off her lap and saying "no time for this." There was no affection.... It felt like we were part of some type of factory. I'm sure it was unresolved family experiences for her. I've come to have compassion for her. I think she was holding on by a thread. The rigidity for her was a way of coping and holding on....*

Beyond the obvious immediate benefits for the child, the expression of affection and warmth among family members may result in lower levels of stress and tension within the family context and may help foster a greater sense of efficacy and competence in parenting (Seccombe, 2002; Jackson-Newsome et al., 2008).

Finally, a family environment in which there is mutual respect and openness to communicate important family values, concerns, and points of view is a fruitful and protective context within which to socialize impressionable children and adolescents. McLoyd and her colleagues (2011) found that most parents they studied, irrespective of income groups, reported their relationship with their child as very close and feel they can share important matters very well. Data from the National Survey of Children's Health (2007) support this and show that a majority of parents surveyed across family types and federal poverty income levels feel that they can share important ideas with their children (sees Figures 4.1 and 4.2).

The Strength of Family Cohesion and Extra-Familial Support

One challenge of poverty is that it leads to social exclusion and isolation, often due to the lack of financial means among poor people to become engaged in the broader social milieu. Rural areas are also socially isolated, making it difficult for

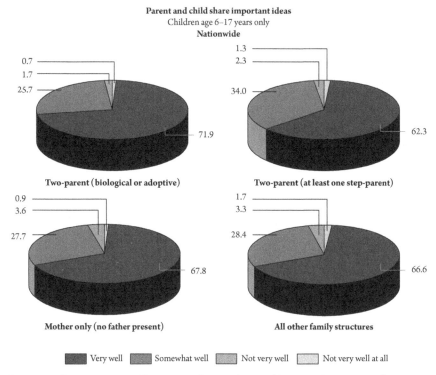

Parent and child share important ideas
Children age 6–17 years only
Nationwide

Two-parent (biological or adoptive): 0.7, 1.7, 25.7, 71.9

Two-parent (at least one step-parent): 1.3, 2.3, 34.0, 62.3

Mother only (no father present): 0.9, 3.6, 27.7, 67.8

All other family structures: 1.7, 3.3, 28.4, 66.6

Legend: Very well | Somewhat well | Not very well | Not very well at all

Figure 4.1 PARENTS AND CHILDREN SHARE IDEAS (FAMILY STRUCTURE). National Survey of Children's Health. NSCH 2007. Data query from the Child and Adolescent Health Measurement Initiative, Data Resource Center for Child and Adolescent Health website. Retrieved 10/12/2012 from www.childhealthdata.org.

poor rural families to gain access to resources or to travel to obtain important services. However, research has shown that some poor families who have important *social networks* can reduce isolation and facilitate access to important resources that might not otherwise be available (Jarrett, 1999; Cattell, 2001). These networks include friendships, associations, and other relationships outside the family context that provide information, as well as other material, social, financial, or emotional resources to the family. Such social networks expand a person's asset base, as the relationships can be used to engage with others, share resources, increase employment opportunities, improve quality of life, or even help develop entrepreneurial initiatives that could ultimately support the financial goals of the family (McLoyd, 1998; Gilchrest & Kyprianou, 2011). Children also benefit from parents' social networks because they enhance the psychological well-being of the parents and provide additional resources for child care, youth social engagement, and development of peer friendships and other important sources of support (Ceballo & McLoyd, 2002).

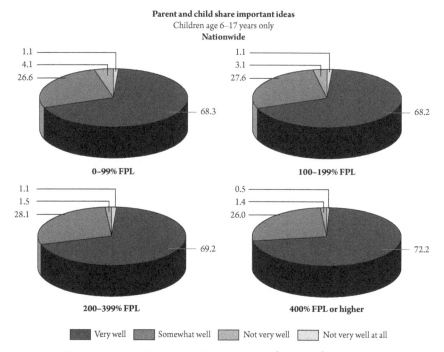

Figure 4.2 Parents and Children Share Ideas (Income). National Survey of
Children's Health. NSCH 2007. Data query from the Child and Adolescent Health Measurement
Initiative, Data Resource Center for Child and Adolescent Health website. Retrieved 10/12/2012 from
www.childhealthdata.org.

The *extended family* is a type of social network inside the family context. It
is often deemed a critical asset for disadvantaged families in that, collectively,
members fill gaps in terms of needed resources and support. They also enhance
parenting capacities, promote family cohesion, and help inculcate the values,
and socialization needed to foster optimal child development. The extended
family includes members beyond the immediate nuclear family, who often
reside with or are in close proximity to the family. These may include biological relatives such as grandparents, aunts, uncles, in-laws, and cousins (Taylor,
2010). Distant relatives or close family friends considered "adopted" family members may also be part of this extended family network. Each member
of the family has an important function to play in supporting the family and
addressing immediate needs and challenges the family may experience. These
functions may be determined by particular cultural perspectives on the nature
of the roles and responsibilities family members must take on (see Chapter 8).
Notably, the extended family can serve to provide the mother the emotional
support she needs to help manage the challenges and stressors of daily life.

Mothers who have emotional support they need (i.e., relationships that provide security, intimacy, and reassurance) are less likely to be distressed and more likely to demonstrate competence, to be better adjusted, and to use appropriate discipline strategies with their children (Taylor & Roberts, 1995; American Academy of Pediatrics, 2003; Taylor, 2010). Similarly, children achieve better social and behavioral outcomes when their mothers have emotional support with their parenting tasks (Chrisler & Moore, 2012). For example, research by Taylor (2010) focuses on the importance of "kinship social support" as a positive agent in adolescent adjustment and as an important protective factor for adolescents moderating the negative effects of poor parenting and ineffective communication between adolescent and parent. Reciprocally, parenting abilities are enhanced when children are well adjusted (Sanders, Markie-Dadds, & Turner, 2003). Brody and his collegues (1999) explored these ideas by studying the positive contributions that children can make to a parent's psychological well-being. They hypothesized that, among rural single mothers, the daily experiences of rearing a child who is competent at self-regulation may help these mothers develop more confidence in their own parenting skills. As well, according to Brody, a competent older sibling may also contribute to developing competencies in his or her younger sibling by providing social support, caring, tutoring, and modeling prosocial behaviors that foster positive outcomes in the younger child. Brody hypothesized that these interactions may elicit "basking" processes, or vicarious well-being, in which parents' and siblings' psychological well-being is enhanced through each other's accomplishments and competencies.

The presence of a *social father* is also observed in many extended families and can be considered an important family asset for a number of reasons. A *social father* is someone who is not the biological or adoptive parent but who acts as a surrogate father or a male father figure (Kalil, 2003). Often, these social fathers are cohabiting partners of the mothers; however, in some families they may be a grandfather, uncle, minister, or close family friend. The social father role is an asset in many low-income families, particularly because many homes are headed by single mothers, the biological father is absent, or co-parenting is not feasible (Coley, 1998). As with biological fathers who are present, social fathers may contribute both directly and indirectly to children's cognitive and emotional adjustment (Coley, 1998; Coley, 2001). In addition to their direct contributions to children's well-being through personal interactions, social fathers may have a positive influence on maternal mental health by providing support and assistance, thereby helping to improve maternal parenting behavior and the quality of the home environment provided for children. These improvements, in turn, may be associated with positive child outcomes (Kalil, 2003). Findings from studies conducted by Berger and colleagues (2008) of fathers' parenting practices with young children suggest that social fathers engage in practices that are of equal quality to, if not better than, those of some biological fathers. The studies reported that, overall, social fathers who are cohabiting partners engage in higher levels of cooperation in parenting than do some biological fathers.

Thus, having the resources of an extended family to draw upon is extremely helpful for facilitating positive outcomes. Extended families are able to share family resources, perpetuate family values and practices, and provide continuity and support to children. Extended family can also act as a safety net when human, material, and other resources may be limited (Seccombe, 2002). If parents alone are unable to create an environment where these protective factors can be tangibly experienced, then siblings, grandparents, or other members of the extended family may step in to provide those important experiences.

Few things signify family cohesion and togetherness more than having meals together. In many cultures, *family meals* are not just about consuming the food but also about sharing values, furthering oral traditions, and spending time with immediate and extended family. In a research brief outlining the strengths of poor families, Valladares and Moore (2009) noted significant differences between poor families and more financially stable families in the number of meals the whole family eats together. In their analysis of the National Survey of Children's Health data, they found that 63 percent of parents in poor families said they eat together as a family "six or more days in the past week"—which was significantly more than the 53 percent of parents in moderate-income families and the 47 percent in higher-income families who also reported. On the face of it, this seems counterintuitive, given economic disadvantage is associated with a host of family life stressors that might get in the way of processes such as family dinners. However, in the hustle and bustle of modern life, families across the income spectrum are challenged to find time when they can come together as a family for meals or other activities promoting family cohesion—albeit for different reasons. That low-income parents report having meals together with some degree of frequency is an important base on which to strengthen other hope-promoting aspects of family functioning. This result is particularly important because research shows a consistent positive association between frequency of family meals and developmental assets (family support, peer influence, boundaries, and expectations) and a negative association with high-risk behaviors (Rockett, 2007). Valladares and Moore (2009) observed that eating together as a family is particularly effective for adolescents in that it helps diminish the likelihood that these youth would engage in risk behaviors. Thus, family meals may be one of the mechanisms that foster other strengths discussed previously, such as socialization practices or building strong relationship bonds. Other processes such as routines and orderliness may also need to be operative in order for the mealtime to occur with frequency and regularity. These meals together provide a forum for discussion and may help parents guide their children through the many difficult situations and make other developmentally relevant decisions, as Carlton points out:

> *Sometimes we talk and I always ask how was her day. And she ask how is mine. She'll tell me ideas she has and what she wants to do. She wants to have a sleepover. We talk about all kind of things. We compromise about most things.*

Family dinners have the potential to yield psychosocial benefits important to help solidify resilience to external stressors, help parents monitor children's activities, and strengthen relationships within the family, and they have health benefits as well. Aside from the obvious benefit of daily nutrition, family meals can give rise to other assets and health-promoting strengths such as use of humor, which may help alleviate the impact of external stressors and thus increase the possibility of averting poor outcomes in children and youth. For example, the benefits of humor for promoting health have been known for some time (Martin, 2008). Humor appears to have a stress-reducing quality, as well as the ability to strengthen the immune system against illness (Celso, Ebener, & Burkhead, 2003; Martin & Lefcourt, 2004). According to Spaulding (2008), the benefits of laughter range from reducing inflammation to increasing problem-solving ability. Research supports the idea that those who laugh and have a good sense of humor may suffer from fewer health problems than those who don't (Martin & Lefcourt, 2004) and that humor and positive affect act as important buffers against the stresses of adversity and difficult circumstances (McGhee, 2010). Less systematic research has been done on the role of humor or laughter in parenting practices and fostering resilience in low-income families. Interventions are needed to help foster an environment where laughter can abide and positive parenting practices can be cultivated. Even when parents must be directive, through these assets they can still communicate caring and warmth and foster an environment where children and youth know that they are valued and loved. A student participant in the Comer leadership academy alludes to this in her discussion of parenting:

> *To me, I think one of the things that stood out in my family is humor. My parents are constantly, always, always making my brother and sister and me laugh. It's unbelievable because most of the time we have so much tension in the house because there's school work to do. They're very serious about education and getting us to do the work. They don't even let us out half the time. But they're our entertainment, let me tell you that! They are our entertainment. They keep us busy at home with the school work but we always have family time and we always have dinner together. That's one thing we always have to have. My dad*

will not let us eat unless we're all sitting at the table together. And it's so much
fun because, to me, I've always grown up with the humor that they have and it's
just always been great having laughter [to] lighten things up in your life, to me
that's something really important.

Taken together, the strengths and assets discussed in this chapter reflect important starting points for helping economically disadvantaged families function more optimally. Many of these families have multiple strengths, just as they may have multiple risks. The strengths and risks may be operative and interacting at all levels of the ecological system discussed in earlier chapters. It is important for policymakers and practitioners working with families to find ways to cultivate those strengths and leverage them to help ameliorate the risks. In so doing, parents develop the important tools to manage the complexities of their lives, giving them the wherewithal to nurture and support their children's development.

More on Parenting Interventions

In one of my interviews, a family member indicated that she didn't realize that some of her basic parenting behaviors were indeed protective, although she was intensely focused on survival, keeping the family intact, and protecting her children from any risk of harm. Conversely, other families may not know that their basic parenting behaviors exacerbate the risk of poor outcomes. The latter is especially true for young adolescent parents, who may lack models of effective or positive parenting that could guide their own childrearing practices. Even more seasoned parents experiencing the stresses of daily life may be unaware of how their behaviors can help or hinder a child's ability to develop at optimal levels and achieve his or her potential in life. The selected interventions discussed earlier may help foster self-awareness, knowledge of child and adolescent development, and the acquisition of more effective parenting skills. There are many other programs available to promote hope and foster resilience in families. Home visiting intervention models, when implemented effectively, may lead to positive outcomes in delivering preventive interventions to parents, especially those with young children. The most positive and enduring benefits for children and families appear to occur when home visiting strategies are well integrated with other evidence-based practices (Chrisler & Moore, 2012). Education and training intervention models use curricula and a variety of educational and training tools to improve parenting skills. The goal of these types of interventions is to improve outcomes through information, awareness, and coaching. Education and training models, coupled with opportunities for practice and feedback, have been shown to increase the likelihood of behavior change. Finally, therapeutic and treatment interventions combine didactic and interactive processes to address the mechanisms underlying a child's problematic behavior. The interventions often focus on modifying cognitive and behavioral processes to produce positive outcomes. Many of these types of interventions are well documented in the literature, while others may be less well known but nonetheless effective.

Practitioners and policymakers are often faced with the challenge of trying to discern which programs work best, for whom and under which conditions, and where it may be best to invest precious resources. A discussion of the specific details of programs' effects is beyond the scope of this book; however, many evidence-based models have been systematically reviewed by the Substance Abuse and Mental Health Services Administration (SAMHSA) National Registry of Evidence-based Programs and Practices (NREPP). More details about the effectiveness of intervention programs can be found at http://www.nrepp.samhsa.gov/.

Concluding Words of Hope

I highlight in this chapter the importance of identifying and building upon the strengths and psychological assets that families possess to underscore the notion that families do have resources that can help tamp down the risks associated with economic disadvantage. These strengths need to be cultivated and enhanced so that parents can be intentional in their childrearing practices and strategic in the way they utilize their assets. In recognizing effective parenting practices, family structure, and processes as strengths, families can learn through appropriate interventions how to maximize these resources to help them manage the complexities of their lives and ultimately achieve a level of success for themselves and for their children. This is the underlying premise of hope theory—that the active processes of goal, pathways, and agency thinking working together provide the basis for creating change and navigating life circumstances. As Snyder and colleagues (2002) point out, it is through the processes of making meaning and anticipating environmental predictability that the fundamental cognitive processes underlying hope are formed. A positive and nurturing bond between the parent and child help foster these important cognitive processes. The reciprocal benefit of this bond gives both parent and child a sense of well-being and confidence that obstacles can be overcome and goals accomplished (Snyder et al., 2002). Carlton's story reflects his extraordinary motivation fueled by this bond. His primary motivation for recovery, finding and maintaining a stable home, and steady employment was his daughter's well-being. His ability to be flexible in his parenting style and to create a warm and caring environment for his daughter provides an example for her to follow as she watches how he maneuvers through the complex contours of single fatherhood.

This is important because the stressors related to economic conditions, work-life balance, housing, and food insecurity require extraordinary flexibility and adaptability in order to manage, much less overcome those challenges. Interventions that help parents learn how to strike these important balances are critically important. By learning the skills to manage their child's behavior in engaging and responsive ways, as opposed to exacting harsh punishment, parents can promote their child's development, help cultivate family assets, and maintain their own emotional and physical health. This, in turn, can strengthen parents' ability to solve problems when difficult issues arise. Like Carlton, parents who acquire these skills can model for their children how to solve problems in difficult circumstances and, at the same time, maintain strong and productive relationships.

It is worth pointing out that material resources do make a difference in how a parent provides a supportive, responsive environment. Families living at or below the poverty line may be less likely to have an enriched, highly stimulating home environment with a variety of educational materials or other aids to support their children's cognitive development. The Hart and Risley study of the 1990s pointed to disparities in educational preparation and the fundamental skills these children need in order to keep pace with children from families in better economic circumstances. Without early interventions in parenting, these disparities persist well into later childhood and throughout the school-age years. Increased economic resources would go a long way toward helping families to establish such an environment. Support is needed to help parents create a tangibly enriched environment with books, educational materials, and resources and, most importantly, to learn how to create this environment for their child using the psychosocial resources they already have—love, nurturing, warmth, and responsiveness. Programs that partner with schools, community agencies, and churches can help provide tangible resources and strengthen parents' psychosocial resources so that they realize their influential role in their children's ability to successfully reach developmental milestones and achieve their potential in life. Policies that give rise to funding and investments in these resources in schools and communities and that allow these partnerships to be sustained over time are well worth the investment and will have long-term and far-reaching benefits to the children, the families, and the community as a whole.

Finally, Carlton's story makes us aware that parents, even those who are experiencing the challenges of adversity, want their children to have the opportunities that they didn't have. They have dreams and aspirations for their children and are taking the steps necessary to bring those dreams to fruition. Hope still matters for these families because they envision a path their children could take that would lead them toward those dreams. The examples these parents set and the sacrifices they make to provide for their families' basic needs, to educate their children, and to create a home environment where the child feels safe and cared for will inspire optimism and a sense of purpose in their children now and in the years ahead.

I end this chapter with words of wisdom from Carlton:

> *I would tell most people to just give themselves a chance—give their children a chance. Be open-minded. Be optimistic. There's different ways of doing things and different ways of looking at things...Just believe in yourself, because you're all you got. I just believe that everybody has a chance to do something in this world—in their life. It's not all about you. Not all the time. It's about helping somebody else. Not just yourself.*

5

Do You Believe in Me?

Promoting Hope through Quality Education and Opportunities to Learn

> *Hold fast to dreams for if dreams die Life is a broken-winged bird that*
> *cannot fly.*
>
> —Langston Hughes, *Dreams* (1994)

Education is so important in children's lives, not only for instilling knowledge and teaching concepts and ideas, but also as a means to inspire dreams, unlock talent, and give a child a vision of what he or she can be in this world. This is especially important for economically disadvantaged children whose circumstances may obscure their dreams and visions of a bright future. Research shows that these children have greater risks for poor educational outcomes and, as a consequence, may repeat the cycle of poverty and economic disadvantage as they mature and have families of their own (Anderson-Moore et al., 2009). However, mere access to education alone may not be sufficient to counteract the compelling risks associated with economic disadvantage. For these children, the promise and ideals of education for a better quality of life must be buoyed by important protective factors that allow hope to flourish and that increase their likelihood of overcoming adversity. I'll discuss these processes first by recalling the story of Ben Carson, who initially considered himself a poor student because he always performed academically at lower levels than his classmates. This poor performance, coupled with behavior problems in the school and community, led Carson's mother to intervene and become more directive in her parenting style. She limited the amount of time he spent watching television and playing outside. Most importantly, she required Ben to do his homework every day, to read at least two library books a week, and to give her a written report even though her own education was inadequate for evaluating what he had written. One outcome of her intervention was that Ben was able to identify rock samples his teacher brought to class because he recognized them from a library book he had read (Academy of Achievement, 2012). This experience was transformative for Carson. In the course of complying with his mother's direction, Carson had become a learner! His newly developed sense of academic self-efficacy enabled him to excel and graduate from high school with honors. In addition, these successful academic experiences helped inspire Carson to dream of a future as a physician—a goal that seems unattainable for many inner-city children. His future orientation and goal directedness led Carson to a successful career as neurosurgeon. Carson's story reveals an important factor that is vital in helping children to experience the benefits of the educational process and to use those experiences to rise above their adverse circumstances. The first of these are efficacy beliefs—an important correlate of hope. As discussed in Chapter 2, efficacy is a general belief in one's ability to achieve a goal. In close relation to efficacy, agency thinking, the mobilizing aspect of hope, consists of individuals' thoughts regarding their ability to begin and continue movement along selected pathways toward achieving their goals (Snyder, Feldman, Shorey, & Rand, 2002). These thoughts and beliefs (sense of efficacy) in one's ability to perform specific tasks influence the actions taken to achieve the goals. As Helland and Winston (2005) pointed out, efficacy becomes activated when a person is faced with a significant situation-specific, goal-related outcome that is *valued* by that individual.

Throughout this chapter, I focus on efficacy beliefs as a facilitator of actions and behaviors that drive the nature and quality of children's educational experiences. I discuss how efficacy beliefs are manifested in four processes, which are protective and may help buffer the effects of disadvantage and remove barriers to educational attainment and achievement, thus paving the way for adaptation and resilience. These processes are parental intervention and engagement, transformative relationships, opportunity to learn, and culture of achievement through policy. The first of the processes emphasizes the role of parents—not just parental involvement as widely discussed in the literature (Epstein, 2001), but what I call parental intervention and engagement—an active, directive process that is goal directed and lays important foundations for improved academic outcomes. In this view, the parents' role is not limited to traditionally organized and planned invitations for involvement by school staff. Rather, it is a decisive intervention on the part of the parent—irrespective of the school's structured activities—to ensure his or her child's pursuit of academic goals, as observed in the Carson example. Highlighted in this discussion are parental efficacy beliefs and how these beliefs foster behaviors and socialization practices that give rise to positive outcomes for children. Transformative relationships, a second process, play a pivotal role in promoting hope and fostering resilience in children. Naturally, teacher-student relationships are important in the educational enterprise. Most of us can think of a positive relationship with at least one teacher. Those relationships are important, but the most critically important relationships in schools are those that *transform* the way children see themselves as learners and those that help them recognize their own potential to be successful in future academic or other endeavors. The self-awareness and the academic efficacy beliefs fostered through these relationships help children see their own potential to accomplish specific educational tasks and, more important, to overcome the educational challenges associated with economic disadvantage. Furthermore, the extent to which teachers and school staff believe that they can influence outcomes for children is a motivating factor. The third process designates "opportunities to learn" as a gateway to a child's sense of future orientation and optimism about the future, and paves the way for the development of the competencies necessary to realize the academic goals inspired through the preceding factors. This factor characterizes how system-level processes reflect the value of the children it serves and how this value translates into programs, policies, and practices that promote optimal educational outcomes. The last is culture of achievement, as perpetuated through broad-based policies and resultant programs and interventions. This process speaks to how society values its most vulnerable citizens and sheds light on the power of political efficacy to change deeply held beliefs and practices in such a way as to change the trajectory of outcomes for these children and their families. Taken together, these processes reflect a belief that outcomes for disadvantaged children can be influenced, and these beliefs give rise to actions, policies, and programs that help facilitate a child's safe passage through the school-age years.

Parental Intervention and Engagement

Parent involvement in the educational process is touted in the research literature as an important correlate of children's educational outcomes (Epstein, 2001; Comer, 1980; Comer et al., 1996). Studies show that children whose parents are involved in their education have better educational and psychological outcomes (Hickman, Greenwood, & Miller, 1995; Hoover-Dempsey & Sandler, 1997; Hoover-Dempsey et al., 2005). Indeed, parents who continue to be involved, even as their child approaches adolescence, can have a major impact on social outcomes and such adolescent risk behaviors as substance use and early sexual debut (Eccles & Harold, 1993; Hill et al., 2004). For many economically disadvantage parents, participation in school-directed involvement activities may not always be feasible. Often, parents are asked to attend meetings, volunteer during the school day, or participate afterschool programs. These types of involvements may place parents at risk of jeopardizing employment—as many parents have multiple jobs or work nonstandard schedules. Moreover, transportation and other resources necessary for involvement may be lacking and therefore serve as an additional barrier for involvement (Eccles & Harold, 1993; Lamb-Parker et al., 2001).

However, as demonstrated by Mrs. Carson, these barriers do not preclude parents from having an impact in their children's education. Parents can and do influence their children's educational outcomes through beliefs and practices. What I refer to as parents' *intervention* and *engagement* is representative of their values, their attitudes about the importance of education in changing life circumstances, and their beliefs about their ability to effect change in their child's best interest. These values and beliefs reflect Taylor and colleagues' (2004) notion of academic socialization practices. These encompass the variety of parental beliefs and behaviors that influence children's school-related development. Drawing from Brofenbrenner's ecology theory, they offer a model that places academic socialization in socioeconomic and cultural contexts by characterizing "what parents do" and "who parents are" in these contexts and by identifying how academic socialization practices shape children's attitudes and efficacy beliefs across various stages of development. In many ways, Ben Carson's story is illustrative of "what parents do" and underscores the importance of active parental engagement in children's education. This engagement extends beyond the typical parent involvement in the schools (often initiated or directed by school personnel) and, instead, involves parents directly intervening to change their child's attitudes and behaviors. Despite the fact that Carson's mother had a limited educational background, she intervened to stop undesirable behavior, created conditions for learning in the home environment, and, through her directive parenting style, ensured that Carson went to school prepared to learn.

What parents do reflects *how* they socialize their children. Academic socialization practices in the early home environment are critical for stimulating children's cognitive and self-regulatory capacities, preparing them for the formal schooling process and engendering academic self-efficacy—a child's confidence in his or her own ability to perform various academic tasks and a belief that challenging academic concepts can be mastered (Shunk & Pajares, 2002). Parents, regardless of socioeconomic status, want their children to be successful and have a strong desire to set their children on a solid course for having positive outcomes in school and beyond. Such engagement at this stage of development involves providing an emotionally supportive and cognitively stimulating environment, laying an important foundation upon which to build in later stages of development. As discussed in Chapter 3, these environments help facilitate brain development—allowing children to meet important developmental milestones and laying the foundation for building cognitive and regulatory capacities at later stages of development (Shonkoff & Philips, 2000). This early engagement and intervention is essential for economically disadvantaged families in that these children are at highest risk for poor educational outcomes. Parents' sense of efficacy regarding their ability to nurture and support a child's development during this tender period sets the stage for the ways in which parents will socialize their children as they achieve these milestones and approach school age.

Parent engagement and intervention are equally important during the school-age years, as children formally enter the school system and are faced with potential social and cultural discontinuities. What parents do during this juncture transmits to children their values and perspectives about the importance of education, their beliefs in their child's ability to master academic content, and their strategies for managing social and cultural discontinuities. Intervention and engagement can take on a variety of forms as a function of these values, perspectives, and beliefs. In the excerpt below, Carlton describes his persistent efforts to enroll his child in a school that will give her the attention and support she needs:

> *Interviewer: So you picked the school?*
> *Carlton: I had been trying to get her in the school for three years. The first year that had her grade wrong. Second year, the lottery was too filled. This year, I called the guy every day. I think he just gave me a spot (laughter). One day we were at number 55 in the lottery. The next day I got a call and he said I have a spot for your daughter! I was real persistent about getting her in that school. It paid off.*
> *Interviewer: What is it about this school that made you want to be so persistent?*
> *Carlton: It's a public charter school, the setting is smaller. The teacher can pay more attention to the student and it also goes up to the 12th grade.*
> *Interviewer: Why is that important?*
> *Carlton: Consistency. She never had that before I had custody of her. Her mother moved from place to place to place. So she's missing her foundation of education. And what she's lacking, they'll take care of that. I believe that…*
> *Interviewer: Do they encourage parent involvement?*
> *Carlton: First thing the new school did was work on her IEP. They weren't consistent with that at the former school. The old school started the process at the end of the year. So that following year they should have picked up on that and they didn't, so I had to push it a little bit. I go to all the PTA meetings. I go to all the conferences, I go to everything—whatever she has. She was on the soccer team, I go to all the games. I do everything possible a parent should do with a child.*

What is important in this excerpt is Carlton's recognition that his daughter was not being fully served in her former school. This recognition led to persistent actions on his part to ensure that his child's needs were being properly addressed. Parents may not know the right questions to ask or be knowledgeable of processes that should occur, but they do recognize discontinuities and are often aware that inequities exist. Carlton's interventional efforts and physical presence in school convey an important message to his daughter about the importance of a quality education and also that her father, despite the fact that he is in recovery, has the wherewithal to intervene and remove barriers on her behalf.

Unfortunately, many economically disadvantaged parents may not have the wherewithal to intervene or provide support as strategically and persistently as

Carlton did. In contrast to Carlton's intervention, Ashante's experience tells a different story:

> *Even when I was in undergrad, my uncle would say I want to throw your books in the garbage. You don't need all these books. If I see them laying around, I'm gonna throw them in the garbage. I was seeing that lack of value of education.*

Ashante's account of his family's value of education underscores their influential role in either promoting or thwarting a child's enthusiasm for learning and academic achievement. Programs designed to bolster parent engagement should first reinforce the value of education and then help parents learn how to better advocate for their children and to have a better sense of the kinds of educational and supportive experiences that should be provided to their child.

A study by Hill (2004) of the influence of parent involvement in middle school children showed low-income parents being involved in ways that were directly associated with youth's higher aspirations, but not to their school behavior problems or achievement. This may be due to the fact that parents from backgrounds of lower socioeconomic status (SES) may not feel comfortable with or capable of assisting their children in ways that bring about achievement outcomes (Comer, 1980; Elder & Caspi, 1988; Conger, Ge, Elder, Lorenz, & Simons, 1994). Dr. Hill (2004) asserted, however, that the relationship between parent academic involvement and youth aspirations does attest to the benefits of parents being actively engaged in the academic lives of these youths, influencing further education, career choices, and, ultimately, financial matters. Therefore, while the involvement of some low-SES parents may or may not yield changes in achievement outcomes, that these parents communicate their expectations for their adolescents' future success and upward mobility may be efficacious enough to foster the *motivation* to achieve.

Toldson's *Breaking Barriers* report (2008) underscores this point and highlights the important role parent engagement plays in African American males' academic progress. His study found that parents who helped their children with school-related problems and who were comfortable talking with teachers, who encouraged their children to do well in school, and who maintained high expectations all had higher-performing children. Toldson found that the strongest indicators of academic success for African American males were parents who often told children they were proud of them and parents who let students know when they did a good job.

Thus, academic socialization includes parents communicating their expectations for achievement and value of education, fostering educational and occupational aspirations in their adolescents, discussing learning strategies with children, and making preparations and plans for the future—even linking material discussed in school with their childrens' interests and goals (Hill & Tyson, 2009).

Academic socialization may also involve building on existing strengths to bring to fruition identified goals. We discussed in Chapter 4 the importance of having meals together as a family strength. It is during these mealtimes when families can foster higher aspirations, instill confidence in the child's ability to be academically successful, and discuss goals and future plans. Whether or not the parent has the capability to directly help with academic tasks, they may do so indirectly by engaging their children in these mealtime discussions, providing a consistent place and time for children to do homework, monitoring the completion of academic tasks, and applying a guiding hand to adolescents' burgeoning autonomy and independence (Rockett, 2007; Hill & Tyson, 2009). In his book titled *Maggie's American Dream*, renowned child psychiatrist Dr. James Comer discusses how mealtimes during his childhood were characterized by active discussion and verbal banter and debate. Pointed questions were posed to the children about their academic progress, assignments, and other important information that helped maintain the parents' awareness of progress and also where potential intervention may be needed.

These socialization practices are also connected to parenting styles and behaviors. As previously discussed, authoritative parenting styles are thought to foster strong parent-child attachment bonds and to strengthen important regulatory capacities in children by creating a nurturing and caring home environment while also setting boundaries and allowing children to have an appropriate voice in family matters. There is a general consensus among researchers that children growing up in authoritative households are thought to have several positive outcomes, including academic achievement, positive school behavior, and completion of high school (Beyer, 1995; Gray & Steinberg, 1999). Research by Steinberg and colleagues (1992) corroborates these ideas. They examined the ways in which authoritative parenting, parental involvement in schooling, and parental encouragement to succeed influence school achievement of adolescents. They found that authoritative parenting (high acceptance, supervision, and granting psychological autonomy) led to better school performance and stronger school engagement in adolescents. They conclude that parental involvement that occurs in the context of an authoritative home environment is much more likely to promote school success among these youths.

More directive styles characteristic of economically disadvantaged families also reflect important academic socialization practices (McLoyd, 1998). For example, Carlton describes his style as flexible, encompassing both directive and authoritative elements. In this excerpt, he shares his discussion with his daughter and reveals how he helps her adjust during the transition to the new school:

> **Carlton:** *I just transferred her to a local school and she didn't like it at all the first day. She was going to another school for three years. That first day was: "I don't understand, why do I have to go to this school?" And I said it's not about*

> your friends it's about your education. It's about getting better. These people
> here will pay more attention to your education than they did in the other
> school.
>
> **Interviewer:** Does your daughter realize how important the decisions are that
> you have made for her? Or does she think he's just making me go to this
> school?
>
> **Carlton:** She doesn't see the importance of it. She sees me making a change.
> I told her there's nothing wrong with change. As long as it's for the better. She's
> more cooperative. She's getting used to the school. She's met some friends. I try
> to tell her you still have your friends, but you're just not going to the same
> school...it's going to be ok. [She'll say] "No, it's not." [I'll say] "It's gonna be
> all right."
>
> A week later she start getting adjusted...we went to back-to-school night. She
> seems to be adapting and listening to what the motto of the school is. She has a
> thing of adapting. Like me. I can adapt to any situation.

In this example, through compassion, insistence, and reassurance, Carlton shep-
herds his daughter through the challenge of moving to a new school that happens
to be in a different community, requiring significant daily travel, and that is much
more diverse than his daughter's previous experience, adding an additional layer of
complexity to the transition.

Parents like Carlton and Mrs. Carson found opportunities for intervention and
identified areas where they could exact their influence to make a difference in
their child's life. Their examples not only describe "what they do" but also tell a
story of "who they are." As Taylor and colleagues' (2004) academic socialization
model suggests, "who parents are" reflects *why* parents socialize their children in
particular ways. They argue that the transmission of values and attitudes about
school may be a function of deeply held beliefs, cultural practices, or even their
apprehensions about their own capacities to enhance their child's cognitive abilities. These beliefs and apprehensions may in turn affect their child's school success
or failure. As Hill (2004) pointed out, economically disadvantaged parents may
not have had a positive experience with the schooling process, and those experiences may influence their attitudes and perspectives about involvement in their
child's educational process. This is not to suggest that all negative experiences
translate into lack of value. On the contrary, they may be a driver of engagement
and a motivation for parents to be sure that their children have the experiences
that they didn't have.

Parents may not be able to accomplish these important processes on their own
but may be empowered though their social networks to be engaged with their child's
education. Sheldon (2002) suggests that social networks are a strong predictor of
whether or not a parent will have active engagement in a child's education. This
may be due to the fact that other parents in their neighborhoods or churches are

actively involved, and there might be an implicit expectation that the parent would be involved in some meaningful way. In addition, the breadth and scope of a parent's social network provides parents with more resources from which to draw (Sheldon, 2002). Thus, the social pressure of these networks may encourage or even instigate involvement. The collective engagement and interaction may also offer children other models to observe and may create micro-ecologies of school-age children to study together and engage in school activities together under a broad base of parent supervision (Sheldon, 2002). Moreover, I discussed previously that extended family and kinship ties, a type of social network, are also valuable resources (Taylor, 2010). Extended family may provide additional perspectives and role models for parents to emulate and for children to observe and learn from. As with other parenting socialization practices, the extended family may alleviate aspects of parental stress and give parents the wherewithal to meaningfully engage in their child's educational process.

As stated earlier, parents may not be feel particularly efficacious in how to advocate on behalf of their children or may not understand how they can take advantage of existing resources to help promote academic outcomes for their children. Programs are needed to help build on parents' strengths and assets and to help foster in them a greater sense of parenting efficacy in academically socializing their children across the developmental spectrum. The Parents' as Teachers (PAT) program is an example of an early childhood intervention that can help parents learn how to promote optimal development and advocate for their children during the early stages of development. The program enrolls families during pregnancy, and they can remain in the program until their child enters kindergarten. Parent educators work with parents to strengthen protective factors and ensure that young children are healthy, safe, and ready to learn. Notably, a component of the program, *family well-being*, emphasizes family strengths, capabilities, skills, and building protective factors. More information about this program can be found at http://www.parentsasteachers.org/.

Programs such as this are desperately needed to help parents support and advocate for their children beyond the early childhood stages. Most programs targeting school-age children focus on school participation and traditional involvement activities. While these types of programs are important, other programs that help parents use their strengths and assets to advocate for their children may prove useful. The Parent Leadership Training Institute (PLTI), sponsored by the Connecticut Commission on Children, is such an intervention. It goes beyond mere involvement to teach parents to become advocates for their children; it uses principles of democracy to help parents develop important skills. The program offers 10 weeks of classes, and among its priorities is a goal to expand the capacity of parents so that they can become change agents for their children and families. More information can be found at http://www.cga.ct.gov/coc/plti.htm.

Transformative Relationships

Just as the parent-child relationship and bond lay a foundation for emotional security and well-being, the relationships in school, especially with the teacher, can also be affirming. Students spend a significant part of their lives in schools, and as consequence they look to the teachers and other adults to be responsive to their needs and interests. Most of us can recall having a thoughtful, caring teacher who made us feel welcome in the school and at ease in the classroom with our peers. But how do these relationships go beyond being nurturing and supportive to transformative? How does the teacher-student relationship help children see who they can be as learners and envision a brighter future for themselves?

The research suggests that the quality of the relationship between the teacher and student can have an important and long-term impact on a child's social and academic outcomes, laying the groundwork for the ways in which children will perceive of and experience school in later grades (Hamre & Pianta, 2001; Hughes & Kwok, 2006). In addition, a respectful, trustworthy, and encouraging teacher-student relationship has a significant influence on the success of an impressionable child for whom this teacher may be a major source of motivation, stimulation, and support (Baker, 1999; Birch & Ladd, 1997). Children may view the teacher as an important attachment figure and may look to him or her for emotional support and security. While researchers warn that too much dependence could potentially have negative effects, there is a general consensus among scholars that this kind of positive, supportive, and affirming relationship helps promote positive outcomes (Crosnoe et al., 2004). As discussed by Hughes and Kwok (2006), a supportive relationship with a teacher is critically important for children in their early experiences in schools. As children experience transitions, meet their peers, and separate from home—perhaps for the first time—a supportive relationship can help buffer the effects of stress and disconnection from familiar people and surroundings. It may also help to allay apprehensions about new social and cultural expectations. Thus, a strong teacher-child relationship may be protective and serve as a coping mechanism to help children respond to these new sets of expectations and experiences (Klem & Connell, 2004; Hughes & Kwok, 2006). This relationship sets the tone for the broader classroom environment, fostering fruitful interactions among the students in the classroom and an environment in which students can be engaged to learn (Comer, 1980; Ames, 1992).

Another important transformative factor is self-efficacy—both for the teacher and for the student. Teachers' efficacy beliefs are referred to as a teacher's judgment of their own capabilities to bring about desired outcomes of student engagement and learning—indeed a conviction that they can do so even among those students who may be difficult or unmotivated (Bandura, 1977; Coladarci, 1992; Tschannen-Moran & Hoy, 2001). Not only does teacher efficacy relate to teachers' classroom behavior, but it also affects the effort they invest in teaching, the goals they set, and their level of aspiration. Teachers with a strong sense of efficacy tend to exhibit greater levels of planning and organization, openness to new ideas, and willingness to experiment with new methods to better meet the needs of their students. Notably, these beliefs influence teachers' persistence and resilience when there are setbacks or when things do not go smoothly in classroom practice (Tschannen-Moran & Hoy, 2001).

For the student, a positive teacher-student relationship helps strengthen a child's self-concept and foster a sense of academic self-efficacy (Baker, 1999; Schunk & Pajares, 2002). Academic self-efficacy relates to the student's beliefs in his or her capacity and competence to perform academic tasks (Schunk, 1991; Schunk & Pajares, 2002). It is motivational and is related to positive psychosocial and achievement outcomes (Bandura, Barbaranelli, Caprara, & Pastorelli, 1996). Children who have a high degree of self-efficacy related to academic tasks are more likely to perform well and exhibit fewer behavioral and social problems in class. Zimmerman (2000) referred to self-efficacy as an essential motive to learn, indicating that students' self-beliefs about academic capabilities figure prominently in their motivation to achieve. Accordingly, self-efficacy beliefs have been shown to influence key indices of academic motivation, such as the level of effort students apply to their work, persistence with difficult tasks, and emotional reactions to challenging academic content (Zimmerman, 2000).

To shed light on these processes, I reintroduce in this section students participating in a leadership academy sponsored by the Comer School Development Program. These elementary through high school students attended schools in low-income communities in various urban and rural communities. Each school participated in an intervention program designed to promote positive relationships among teachers, students, and other school staff. The students were chosen by their peers and school leaders to participate in this academy. In this excerpt from a focus group discussion, the students expressed their views on the transformative impact of the teacher-student relationships:

> **Interviewer:** *Do you have good relationships with your teachers? If so, why is it important?*
>
> **Student A:** *Well, I think my third-grade teacher and I had a great relationship. I can talk to her about a lot of things. So that's basically what I think. You should form a relationship with the student and then because—she knew my family, so I couldn't act up in her class or anything and so I learned from her a lot. I learned a lot from her and so it made it a lot easier for me to learn in her class.*
>
> **Student B:** *Me and my second-grade teacher bonded very good and, like she said, that I couldn't act up in the class…And I did learn a lot and I just thank my second-grade teacher for all she did for me.*

Student C: *I had a teacher that I could always confide in because he was so down to earth. There need to be teachers that you can just talk to, not only guidance counselors but teachers in your own classroom that you could just run to and talk to whenever you need anything. And he made it so easy for me to solve my problems and he was just really helpful.*

Student D: *If you have a female teacher, if that person has a female teacher, the female teacher could act like a mother. If he doesn't have a mother to look up to, to be supportive, if his mother passed away or something, she could be like a second mother. If it's a male he could do the same thing.*

Student E: *The teacher could try to interact with the kids more. Like some teachers just go and they just want to get their job done and they want to get home. But we have some teachers who can connect with the kids more and find out about them and try to help them and just let the children know that they care about what they're thinking, what they're doing.*

Student F: *...to let them know that they care. I mean, they need someone to care, so just let them know that you care, if it's just writing a little "good job" on their test or something, it don't matter, because you actually took the time to write good job to them, and so that makes them feel special, like they care.*

Student G: *I found a note in my room. It was a note that my sister's teacher wrote to her. She said "you're one in a billion" or something like that. You should just write notes to students. It will make them feel special. And just say something positive and encouraging, like I know transformative be the best you can be, I know you'll go far in life, I believe in you, I care about you. Just anything like that. It will make them feel special and will let them know that they are somebody and they can do whatever they want in life.*

Several important considerations emerge from this discussion. First, students appreciated open communication—the ability to have access to the teacher and to be able to talk authentically without fear of reprisal about the issues that concern students. This kind of responsiveness to students may be considered a reflection of teacher caring and commitment to student success. And this in turn may foster greater effort on the part of the student. Muller (2001) studied caring in teacher-student relationships and found that the academic behavior of the students in her study was influenced by the extent to which students' perceived that teachers cared and were committed to their success.

Finally, some of the students revealed that the teachers had relationships with, or at least knew, their parents. This suggests that not only is the parent connection to the school important, but in instances where the teachers and parents live in the same community or make use of the same community resources children take notice and seem to benefit from these connections. While parent-teacher relationships are often variable—especially relationships with parents of low-income minority children—efforts to build stronger connections with parents can signal to the student that the two people who are arguably the most important and influential in their lives are working together on their behalf to promote their well-being.

For students like African American males who are at risk for poor outcomes, all of the factors discussed in this section can make an important difference in their school experiences and academic outcomes. Toldson (2008, 2011) reported that high-achieving Black male students tend to have a more positive perception of school, enjoy more congenial relationships with their teachers, and perceive school as a safe environment. Thus, the more Black males report liking school and the less they report being bored by school, the better their educational outcomes. Black males also need to believe that what they are learning is important for their future and that the schoolwork is meaningful. Open and frank communication between the teacher and student can help foster this belief.

Toldson further asserted that high-achieving Black male students reported that their teachers were interested in them "as a person," treated them fairly, encouraged them to express their views, and gave extra help when needed. Also, teachers who were effective routinely let their students know when they did a good job. Black male students who were successful, according to Toldson, perceived their teachers as respectful people who treated them like they mattered and as nurturing people who focused the students' strengths, instead of making them "feel bad" about their weaknesses.

Unfortunately, as Hughes and Kwok (2007) noted, minority and children of low socioeconomic status (SES) are less likely than White or higher SES children to experience such supportive relationships. This has important implications for professional development to help teachers learn to build strong and positive relationships with children and parents from low-income backgrounds. Workforce and diversity issues in school communities that serve predominantly low-income minority families must also be taken into consideration to help promote positive and transformative relationships.

In summary, transformative teacher-student relationships can inspire a sense of academic self-efficacy in students deemed at risk for poor outcomes. It is not enough, however, for a single teacher to be responsive and to have affirming relationships with students. In order for children to achieve optimally, the entire school community must work together to ensure consistency and continuity of values and ideals, codes of conduct, and high expectations. The collaborative infrastructure and supporting resources must be in place so that the high expectations are allowed to come to fruition. A student leader aptly discerns the importance of this collaboration:

> *So having good communication, knowing that people are there for you, having sort of like a second family is very important. Because that's what those people are there for, the teachers and the counselors and any adult in the building,*

*really, that's what they're there for, to help you out not only in what you're learn-
ing but your life and your life choices.*

These collective relationships are often referred to as the "school climate"—in
other words, the interactions among all involved create an environment conducive
to achieving positive outcomes for children and for the adults who work with them
(Comer, 1980; Comer et al., 1996; Haynes, 1996; Wang, 2009). A school's climate
is so central to a child's ability to perform well in school that interventions like the
Comer School Development Program use this theory of change as one of their first
points of engagement with a school (Comer et al., 1996). The Comer program
asserts that schools must address the issue of climate in order to provide a supportive context in which learning can take place. It uses what they refer to as a nine-
element model to promote collaboration with faculty, staff, and parents. This model
has shown how interventionists can help build these relationships in ways that will
have a transformative influence on how children see themselves now and in the
future. It does so by focusing the adults' attention on the physical, cognitive, social,
emotional, language, and ethical development needs of the student as a means to
solve learning and behavioral problems. This steers the emphasis away from blaming children for their circumstances and focusing on deficits toward a strengths-
based approach to promote positive student outcomes (Comer, 1980). Thus, the
collective efforts of all involved help to inspire optimism on the part of students that
the adults in the school will keep them from slipping through the cracks.

This is important because, as reported by Hopson and Lee (2011), there are significant associations between family poverty, social supports, students' behavior,
grades, and perceptions of school climate. They found poverty to be associated with
poor grades and behavior, while students' positive perceptions of school climate
were associated with positive grades and behavior. Notably, students' perceptions
of school climate were found to moderate the association between poverty and
behavior—thus, students from poor families who perceive a positive school climate
exhibited behaviors similar to their peers from higher-income families (Hopson &
Lee, 2011).

Schools serving children from low-income backgrounds must find ways to cre-
atively and collaboratively educate children, despite the considerable challenges
they bring to school. When a school's climate is engaging and fosters a sense of
belonging (McMahon, Parnes, Keys, & Viola, 2008), and resources and support
mechanisms are in place to address their needs (Comer, 1980), children can experience school as a place where they can visualize a brighter future and articulate
those dreams and aspirations. The guiding hand of school staff and faculty can put
children in position to realize those dreams.

Overall, individual teacher-student relationships and collaborative schoolwide
interactions provide psychosocial supports that help children achieve their educational goals. These transformative relationships have protective effects, enhance

academic self-efficacy, and promote a sense of purpose and self-worth—not only for the children and families who benefit from these collective efforts but also for the teachers, service providers, and administrators who serve them.

Opportunities to Learn

For many children, the question is not whether there is a desire to learn but whether there are opportunities to learn. Data from the NSCH 2007 show a majority of children across all income levels and family structures care about doing well in school and are engaged in school (see Figures 5.1 and 5.2). Therefore, the fact that children care about their school performance is an important asset that can translate into academic persistence and ultimately better school outcomes.

To the extent that children living in poverty have access to a quality education and the opportunity to learn, doors will open to them that may help break the cycle of poverty. Quality education opens doors of opportunity not only for a child's future but also for their prospective families, interrupting the intergenerational transmission of poor education outcomes, underemployment, and associated disadvantages. It is widely accepted that the educational level of the parents, especially the mother,

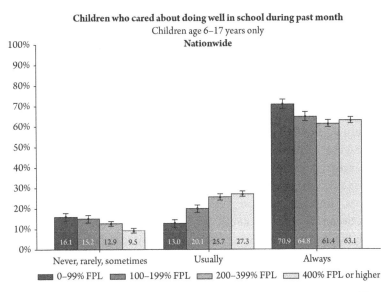

Figure 5.1 CHILDREN WHO CARED ABOUT DOING WELL IN SCHOOL BY FEDERAL POVERTY LEVEL (FPL). National Survey of Children's Health. NSCH 2007. Data query from the Child and Adolescent Health Measurement Initiative, Data Resource Center for Child and Adolescent Health website. Retrieved 10/12/2012 from www.childhealthdata.org.

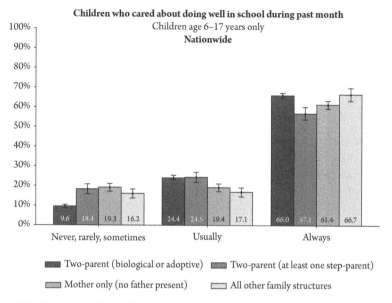

Figure 5.2 CHILDREN WHO CARED ABOUT DOING WELL IN SCHOOL BY
FAMILY TYPE. National Survey of Children's Health. NSCH 2007. Data query from the Child and
Adolescent Health Measurement Initiative, Data Resource Center for Child and Adolescent Health
website. Retrieved 10/12/2012 from www.childhealthdata.org.

is a strong predictor of a child's outcomes (Davis-Kean, 2005). As we discussed in
Chapter 3, a highly stimulating early home environment enriched with conversa-
tional language provides opportunities for children to explore, ask questions, and
develop confidence and readiness for school; and a parent's own educational background and experiences help develop the abilities to provide this rich and stimulating environment (Hart & Risley, 1995). Thus, as children grow into adulthood and
become parents, their educational experiences enable them to provide an enriched
and stimulating environment for their own children to grow and develop. The quality of a child's educational experiences has far-reaching consequences. The earlier
children encounter high-quality instructional and social learning programming, the
better positioned they will be to take advantage of and benefit from future quality
experiences. However, *A Nation at Risk*, the pivotal 1983 report commissioned by
then-U.S. Secretary of Education Terrel H. Bell called attention to the perceived
decline in the quality of the American education system, declaring that "the educational foundations of our society are presently being eroded by a rising tide of
mediocrity that threatens our very future as a Nation and a people" (The National
Commission on Excellence in Education, 1983). So while education is thought to
be the great equalizer, for many children the playing field is not level. Children living
in impoverished neighborhoods are often consigned to under-resourced and underperforming schools, at best assuring mediocrity. In his book *Savage Inequalities*

(1991), Jonathan Kozol chronicled the lives of children living in inner-city communities across the country and attending city schools. He described in graphic detail the inequalities in terms of per-capita spending for students; the overcrowded, unsanitary, and often understaffed school environments; and how these schools lacked the basic tools of good educational practice and programs.

The condition of schools sends a message to children about the value placed on their education and development. Thus, efforts to address the fiscal inequalities of schooling are as important to promoting hope and fostering resilience in children as are the qualitative, relational experiences of schooling. Opportunity to learn also implies the absence of barriers that prevent learning (Stevens & Grymes, 1993). This includes making sure students are exposed to challenging curricula, learning materials and resources, and adequate learning facilities, as well as student-centered policies that create conditions for students to achieve at optimal levels.

The National Council of Teachers of English (NCTE) wrote:

> The opportunity to learn is the inherent right of every child in America. Educators, parents, and other members of a child's many communities share a common interest in the educational success of each child and in the role of education in our democratic society. Full, positive participation in democracy is contingent upon every child's access to quality education. Such access to high-quality education should not be dependent upon the specific community in which a child lives. By focusing and building upon the strengths of learners, Opportunity-to-learn standards can help ensure equitable access to high-quality education for all students in America. (NCTE, 1996)

Although the rhetoric and reforms around the formal opportunity-to-learn standards have subsided since the 1990s, this statement still rings true today. In fact, the NCTE reaffirmed their statement in 2012. Regrettably, however, a recent report indicated that schools do not challenge enough students and reported that from one-fifth to one-half of students in grades 4 through 12 say that schoolwork is "too easy" (Murphy, 2012). The report also stated that many students do very little writing as part of their schoolwork. Studies show that students become less engaged with school as they progress from elementary to middle to high school, and by high school as many as 40 to 60 percent of students have become chronically disengaged from school (Klem & Connell, 2004).

All too often, this lack of a challenging curriculum reflects a school community's beliefs about children's ability to perform well in school. Dweck's (2006) research focuses on challenging the mindset and beliefs of teachers and students about their ability to perform well in school. She theorized about, and tested, two sets of beliefs about intelligence that may be held by school staffs and students. A *fixed mindset* reflects the belief that intelligence is a static trait, so that students either have or do not have the ability to achieve to high standards. Alternatively, a *growth mindset* reflects the belief that intelligence can be developed by various means, including effort and instruction. Dweck argues that a growth mindset can be fostered or taught, and can decrease or even close achievement gaps. Drawing upon Steele's notion of stereotype threat (Steele, 1997), Dweck theorizes that when Black and Latino students adopt a growth mindset, their grades and achievement test scores are more similar to those of their non-stereotyped peers.

While one of the most important undertakings of our society is to provide educational experiences so that children have opportunities to learn, taking advantage of these opportunities can be a challenge, especially for families living in poor communities where schools are often under-resourced, the range of services is limited, and the resources and services that are available are all too often delivered in a disjointed and siloed manner. Schools in districts with limited resources may have to make difficult decisions about how to distribute those resources in ways that target the specific challenges of low-income students. Operating on their own, schools and districts may lack the human or fiscal capital to target interventions and address the needs of poor children, and efforts to address these challenges must often be pursued outside the physical school setting.

School-community collaboration is a strategy that brings the school's resources together with the resources of various community agencies, institutions, and organizations to pursue a shared vision (National Education Association, 2011). Also referred to as family-school-community partnerships, all parties involved take responsibility and, to some degree, are accountable for the learning and experiential opportunities as well as social support provided to children (Epstein, 2001; Van Roekel, 2008). Collectively, the collaborators form what Kerensky (1975) referred to as an *educative community*, where everyone in the community is accountable for the quality of education. This sense of accountability is especially important for families whose children attend school in low-income, under-resourced districts. Such collaborative efforts can help improve the children's learning opportunities and enhance their intrapersonal assets, thereby promoting overall well-being and serving the intended purpose of schooling—to give students tools and mechanisms that will sustain their hopes for and expectations of the best possible outcomes in school and in life.

Dryfoos (1994) makes the connection between these partnerships and youth development, indicating that young people thrive when they are surrounded by supportive adults and effective parents. Drawing upon attachment research, Dryfoos (1994; Dryfoos & Maguire, 2002) points out that one strength of these models is that they facilitate important transformative relationships between students and caring adults. In addition, these partnerships allow schools to extend their reach beyond the confines of the school building and draw on the resources of a willing partner for assistance in accomplishing their goals, especially when their own resources are limited or unavailable. Some outcomes of these collaborations have shown improved performance in reading and math, as well as improved social and behavioral outcomes (Schargel & Smink, 2001). A variety of collaborative or part-nership models have shown positive results along several developmental domains, and the results have been especially pronounced for children in low-income school communities (National Education Association, 2011). An example of this is the community schools model, which attempts to address the needs of the whole child by having a comprehensive focus on academics as well as on health and social ser-vices, youth, and community development. These services can be school-based or school-linked, and the school serves as the hub of a community, so that it benefits the parents and community members as well as the students. These collabora-tions may also offer primary, dental, and mental health care; activities to increase literacy; career counseling; expanded-learning opportunities; early childhood education; and nutrition education, including Women, Infants, and Children (WIC) classes, among many other services (Dryfoos & Maguire, 2002; Coalition for Community Schools, 2012). To increase the opportunity for family participa-tion, these community schools generally remain open long after school hours and operate during weekend hours as well (Dryfoos, 1994, Dryfoos & Maguire, 2002; Blank et al., 2003). Availability of these services is important because families liv-ing in under-resourced or isolated areas may have difficulty accessing services such as preventive health care, mental health support, employment training, and other resources that could improve their ability to provide for their child and ensure that the child has resources needed for optimal learning. What is most important is that the combination of these resources increases the opportunity to learn and leads to improved student academic outcomes. Together, these benefits have far-reaching effects—improving children's educational attainment and ultimately strengthening the competencies needed for future employment.

Promoting a Culture of Achievement through Policies

The interpersonal aspects of a school's context are not the only factors that influence the outcomes for children. The policy climate in which a school functions can also promote a culture of achievement that frames the boundaries of communication within a school and sets the tone for how schools provide educational services to children and families. By "policy climate" I refer to the regulatory and operational policies set by local school governance councils, as well as by the local and state boards of education. The term also refers broadly to the structure of the school (i.e., condition of school facilities, class sizes, grade-level configurations) and the funding priorities of the local school district and the state. Taken together, the prioritiza-tion of these elements in a school translates into a belief system and set of values about what is important in children's education. This sends a message to students, whether stated or implied, about their value and is, in effect, a vision statement for a child's future. Schools have the important role of building human capital to ensure the future economic, intellectual, and social viability of our nation. To the extent that education programs, practices, policies, and funding coalesce around a common vision for the children they educate, a school system may have a significant capacity for promoting hope in its most vulnerable children.

One example of such a vision is the Montgomery County Public School (MCPS) system in Maryland, which made a strategic effort to address the needs of its most vulnerable students. The overarching goal was to ensure that students would be college-ready when they left the system. A pivotal study commissioned by the district pointed out that low-income minority students were performing at least one standard deviation below the mean on standardized assessments. The district recognized the necessity to examine the processes being used to meet the needs of its students and, in examining the processes for achieving their goals, identified equity as a major issue. Ironically, school officials discovered that their efforts to treat students equally actually led to unequal performance:

> We had thought that equality—being equal to all children—was the way to go. In fact, we found that it was the most unequal thing that we could do. So we started to think about this whole concept of differentiation…(Montgomery County Public Schools, 2009)

They found that poverty in the county was well defined geographically. Mobility rates were high within that defined area, with nearly 80 percent of the students receiving free and reduced-cost lunches; about 75 percent of the students were minority children. Further analysis revealed that the system had not addressed such issues as teacher stability, effective leadership, or curricular issues that met the specific needs of students in that geographic region. By thinking systemically and identifying the needs of these children as a system-wide priority, they were able to demonstrate steady improvement of students in the identified areas (Montgomery County Public Schools, 2009).

In various forums, former school superintendent Jerry Weist and colleagues discussed several key principles and strategies for creating a systems-level policy climate that would foster an environment enabling even the most vulnerable students to thrive. Derived from these discussions are five principles:

1. **Focus on collaborating rather than blaming**. Adapted from the Comer School Development Program model, this principle allows the key leaders to focus on the specific problem at hand rather than shifting the focus to each other or the students. By working together and bringing in different perspectives to address the achievement gap in the district, the leaders could design a differentiated program that helped start the process of closing the achievement gap.

2. **Set common goals and figure out how to reach them**. District leaders agreed that MCPS students should leave high school ready for college. To achieve that goal, they needed to focus not just on the high school but on the early grades as well, in order to establish a long-term process for continuous improvement.

3. **Create a system that helps everyone succeed**. District leaders realized that, although they were recognized for their achievements, they still needed to look at performance profiles across the entire district and ensure that all students had the resources—human, fiscal, and material—to achieve their goals.

4. **There is more to equity than equality**. What is important to note here is the recognized need, and subsequent actions employed to level the playing field for all students. Treating all students the same when their needs are vastly different does a disservice to the students, teachers, and support personnel who serve those students. Processes that were implemented to help get to the root of problems of variability in student performance also shed light on ways to identify issues causing high teacher turnover.

5. **Dispel the culture of low performance and low expectations**. The culture of low expectations is often subtle, but its effects are tangible. In an effort to understand the barriers and challenges that students from low-income homes may encounter, school systems can establish processes to reduce the impact of the barriers rather than raising the bar so the barriers are even more difficult to overcome. In this instance, paying attention to the sorting mechanisms for assigning programs and identifying curricula and services that reinforce low expectations enabled the school system to put in place evidence-based practices that give students a true opportunity to learn and achieve at optimal levels. (Montgomery County Public Schools, 2009; National Public Radio, 2010)

Similarly, at the state level, policies that give local districts a framework within which they can provide a comprehensive educational program responsive to the diverse student needs can very effectively facilitate achievement of positive student outcomes. Here, too, the state's policies are a reflection of their vision for students and the value placed on equity of experience and opportunity to learn. What a state chooses as its priorities—what it chooses to measure and to manage—is a reflection of its values and a vision statement for the students under its jurisdiction.

The comprehensive early childhood programs in the state of New Jersey provide an example of setting such priorities. The impetus for the state's reforms was *Abbott v. Burke*, a case in which the Supreme Court ruled on the need to provide educational equity and level the playing field for New Jersey's under-resourced urban districts. According to the Education Law Center, which litigated the case on behalf of the state's poor urban school district, this litigation launched one of the nation's most ambitious and far-reaching efforts to improve public education for poor children and children of color. The Abbott decisions have been called the most important equal education rulings since *Brown v. Board of Education* (Education Law Center, n.d.).

The rulings covered 31 low-wealth, urban school districts, some of which, like Camden and Newark, are among the poorest in the United States. To ensure the children in these schools a "thorough and efficient" education as required by the New Jersey constitution, the Abbott rulings directed implementation of a comprehensive set of improvements, including adequate K–12 foundational funding, universal preschool for all 3- and 4-year-old children, supplemental or at-risk programs and funding, and school-by-school reform of curriculum and instruction (Education Law Center, n.d.).

The Court's ruling directed the legislature to amend or enact a new law to ensure funding for the urban districts (1) at the foundation level "substantially equivalent" to that in the successful suburban districts, and (2) "adequate" to provide for the supplemental programs necessary to address the extreme disadvantages of urban schoolchildren. The Abbott remedies were detailed and comprehensive and broke new ground in school finance and education policy in the United States. According to the Law Center, no other state had equalized or assured parity between educational resources provided to children in its lowest-wealth communities and those provided in more affluent communities. Reportedly, New Jersey was the first state to mandate early education, starting at age 3, for children "at risk" of entering kindergarten or primary school cognitively and socially behind their more-advantaged peers. The Court's "needs-based" approach to supplementary programs and reforms was an unprecedented effort to target funds to initiatives with the goal of improving the educational outcomes of low-income schoolchildren. Finally, New Jersey undertook the most extensive construction program in the United States designed to ameliorate the severely deficient condition and quality of school buildings in low-wealth neighborhoods (Education Law Center, n.d.).

Promoting Hope for the Future

I started this chapter recalling the story of famed neuroscientist Ben Carson. He could have been lost due to the challenges confronting so many young children who experience similar adversities. These include underachievement, economic disadvantage, single-parent head of household, and behavioral problems. However, the active engagement and intervention of Carson's mother inspired a sense of academic self-efficacy and gave him a vision of himself as a learner. Subsequent successes allowed Carson to bring that vision to fruition and to achieve academic and social goals that changed the course of his life, as well as that of his family and the many patients he has treated.

While not all children will become neurosurgeons, ideally, the schooling pro-cess should yield life-changing outcomes—economic disadvantage notwith-standing. Schools provide routine, structure, and opportunities to plan and think strategically. As discussed in Chapter 4, such opportunities are especially impor-tant for children whose home or community environment may be chaotic and unstructured. The predictable school environment may constitute part of a cop-ing strategy for these children, distracting them from the stresses of everyday life and giving them opportunities to redirect their energy in more productive and psychologically beneficial ways. For these children, the schooling process culti-vates not only the cognitive skills necessary for learning but also the psychosocial skills such as persistence, focus, and perseverance that will yield benefits for them long after their formal education ends. Schools also expose children to a range of experiences that develop their sense of the world around them, so they begin to see themselves in a broader context and establish a vision for what they can be and do in life. Children have opportunities to assume leadership roles in school clubs, sports, and student government and leadership organizations, which cul-tivate cognitive and noncognitive skills that will prove useful throughout their educational experience.

It is important to note here that education, in and of itself, is not the great equal-izer. Rather, it is the quality of the educational experience that levels the playing field and makes a difference for children. Having a school with resources that pro-vide stimulation that may be lacking at home is absolutely essential for enhancing children's cognitive capacities and inspiring them to learn. Positive relationships in the school are predictive of positive student outcomes, and for poor children and vulnerable groups like African American males, these relationships have far-reaching effects. Children learn to evaluate who they are in relation to others and to sense whether they are respected as individuals with unique contributions to make. Students who internalize these values and persist through elementary and secondary schools to pursue postsecondary education increase the likelihood that they will have a better quality of life as adults.

The hope-promoting concepts discussed in this chapter are important correlates of educational attainment and achievement. These elements of hope matter because they give children a chance to conceive of and aim for a different future. That sense of expectation and future orientation may help to reduce unintended teenage preg-nancies, substance use and abuse, and other behavior patterns that perpetuate the cycle of poverty. It may also lead to higher graduation rates, and ultimately to preparation for better employment opportunities that will enable adults to care for themselves and their families. In addition to affecting the students, a school climate focused on hope and optimism has reciprocal effects. Teachers and school personnel experience greater work satisfaction, which, in turn, may increase systemic efforts to institutionalize the learning opportunities that help children achieve. Policies that facilitate a sense of personal agency for school staff can also help to ensure that good promoting practices are perpetuated and sustained. The experiences of the Montgomery County Public Schools is just one example that shows the benefits of a system taking an in-depth look at their issues and providing the resources necessary to address them. Most importantly, their model inspires and sustains the belief that, if given the opportunity to learn, every child can succeed.

6

Friends and Mentors

The Protective Power of Relationships

Hope is like peace. It is not a gift from God. It is a gift only we can give one another...Just as despair can come to one only from other human beings, hope, too, can be given to one only by other human beings.
—Elie Wiesel (1986)

Nobel Laureate Elie Wiesel once described hope as a gift that we give to one another. What is most profound about his statement is that he characterizes hope as a gift to be given. In the context of adversity, a helping hand that guides toward an illuminating path from despair is indeed a gift. But how does one give this gift? How is hope conferred by one person upon another? We discussed in earlier chapters how parenting and parenting styles can give rise to hope by fostering positive relationships and bonds of attachment. We have also discussed the idea that hope may be more a cognitive process than an emotion. There may also be innate capacities that enable individuals to be positive and optimistic, even in the midst of circumstances that theoretically should engender hopelessness or despair. The gift of hope is given when parents, friends, or mentors help someone recognize and call upon these innate abilities to achieve their goals and realize their highest potential in life.

This was the case for the three doctors referred to in Chapter 1 who, as youth, made a pact with one another to be accountable and to provide support for each other so that they could accomplish their dreams of becoming doctors. These young men were youth whose demographics suggested that they would be at risk for poor outcomes—high school dropout and susceptibility to street life. However, the strength of their friendship and their motivation to achieve helped them to overcome the many obstacles confronting them. They graduated high school, completed college and medical school, and are now practicing physicians. When asked what contributed to their success and their ability to resist temptations that entice so many young men to take a life path that is less productive, they attributed it to the friendship they have, to mentoring, and to having a goal they could work toward.

In their book, titled *The Pact* (Davis et al., 2003), one of the three friends recalled strategies he used to stay away from the kinds of activities that would mean trouble for him. He also talked about the important role of friendships in helping the three friends achieve their goals:

> *I'm not foolish enough to believe that I was able to avoid negative peer pressure alone. In the kind of neighborhood where I grew up, it would have been easier to believe that what I saw was all there was to life. But I had a third grade teacher who taught me to dream and think for myself. I had a friend whose father spent good time with me and made me feel I was worthy of a father's love. And most of all, I had a mother who worked hard and managed to keep things straight at home...*
>
> *It's hard to have the confidence, especially in the teen years to stand up for what you believe is right when people all around you are pulled in another direction. That's where having positive friendships can really help. If you find the right guys to hang with—guys you trust, who can share your values and your friendship, you'll find that you can stand up to almost anything.* (Davis et al., 2003, pp. 109–110)

Defined as a reciprocal, affective bond between individuals who affirm the relationship and participate willingly, friendship is a give-and-take relationship that provides mutual benefit to both parties (Rubin, Bukowski, Parker, & Bowker, 2008; Hartup & Stevens, 1999; Howes, 1989). Friendships also provide a context within which individuals can display their feelings and emotions (Howes, 1989); thus, researchers believe that individuals with friends are more likely to have a greater sense of well-being than individuals without friends (Hartup & Stevens, 1999).

Indeed, friendships play an important role throughout development. As children grow and mature, close friendships help promote the development of such competencies as interpersonal intimacy and communication, empathy, loyalty, and perspective-taking (LaGreca & Harrison, 2005). These and other sociocognitive abilities take shape at different stages of development (Hartup, 1989: Newcomb & Bagwell, 1995).

During infancy, the attachment bond between parent and child and positive early interactions help lay the foundation upon which later friendships can build. An infant learns the bases of social and emotional reciprocity through the responsiveness of a caring and nurturing parent (Bowlby, 1969; Ainsworth, Blehar, Waters, & Walls, 1978). The quality of this relationship and responsive interactions foster within the child implicit expectations about the interactions with peers and other adults that will occur as the child grows and develops (Rubin et al., 2004).

During early childhood, however, children have the ability to make friends on their own and, most importantly, to have friendships of high quality. Due in part to their developing emotional maturity, as well as social and cognitive skills, young children have the ability to make friends and to sustain them (Rubin et al., 2008; Howes, 1989). Notably, children at this stage can differentiate between friends and playmates. They befriend peers whose behavioral tendencies resemble their own, and these friendships can provide young children with emotional security and serve the purpose of companionship and playful fun (Howes, 1989).

As children enter middle childhood, concerns about social relevance and peer acceptance take center stage in their lives. Inasmuch as their cognitive and social skills are more developed, children at this stage have a greater ability to attain mutuality and give-and-take in their relationships (Erikson, 1968; Eccles, 1999). The nature and quality of their friendships range from appreciating the rewards and pleasures of friendships, to recognizing the mutual benefits and conveniences of friendships, to acknowledging the importance of shared values, to expectations of loyalty and support, and, finally, to having a willingness for self-disclosure (Howes, 1989; Bukowski, Newcomb, & Hartup,1998; Rubin et al., 2008).

Of course, during adolescence, peer relationships become even more central as youth rely less on parents as a source of social and emotional support. While adolescents tend to gravitate toward other youth with similar interests and social and behavioral characteristics, they also show more affective reciprocity and more emotional intensity, and are more likely to behave in positive ways with youth who are friends as opposed to youth who are non-friends (Rubin et al., 2008). As youth at this stage develop their abilities for more complex thinking and capacities for intimacy, friendships provide a positive relational context for both the expression and regulation of affect (Rubin et al., 2008). Mutuality increases, as does the ability to resolve conflicts within the context of a friendship (Hartup & Stevens, 1999; Collins & Steinberg, 2008). Social competencies and other interpersonal skills give rise to feelings of self-esteem as well as identity development (Erikson, 1968).

During this stage of development, youth also form romantic relationships— thus differentiating social friendships from romantic partners. While the capacity to form romantic relationships originates with biological and cultural influences, these relationships become central to group affiliation and belonging as well as to social status (Furman, Brown, & Feiring, 1999; Collins & Steinberg, 2008).

Friendships and Development

Across the stages of development, friendships are associated with a host of psychological and health-related benefits, including overall well-being (Hartup, 1989;

Stephanou, 2011). In general, children value and gravitate toward friendships having positive features that allow them to express their feelings without fear of judgment or retribution (Berndt, 2002). Friendships provide a forum for self-expression and for building self-esteem, social competence, and self-awareness. However, not all friendships are created equal. It is not enough to simply have friends. What is most important is having *high-quality* friendships, and these are essential to achieving psychosocial and health benefits. A high-quality friendship is characterized by high levels of intimacy and low levels of conflicts, or rivalry (Berndt, 2002). These friendships tend to have far-reaching developmental benefits, especially for adolescents.

As discussed earlier, some adolescents are particularly at risk for poor outcomes because they are often exposed to negative peer influences. These influences may lead to health risk behaviors such as substance abuse, early sexual debut, delinquency, and poor academic performance (Bukowski, Hoza, & Boivin, 1993; Eccles, 1999; Steinberg, 2007). In contrast, high-quality friendships are, by definition, positive and may protect against negative influences while encouraging greater prosocial behavior and positive affect (Hartup & Stevens, 1999). Research conducted by Berndt (2002) revealed that adolescents characterize high-quality friendships among best friends as being able to "tell each other everything" or "stick up for one another in a fight" (p. 7).

Hartup and Stevens (1999) linked good, high-quality friendships to having social capital—benefits available through the social networks and relationships that can serve to meet one's needs. This link exists, they argue, because such friendships can be called upon for support and relief in the midst of everyday challenges or, in times of distress and adversity. Financial or residential support and other types of needs-based remediation are benefits as well. High-quality friendships with positive characteristics such as warmth, acceptance, and validation have been associated with lower levels of social anxiety and other internalizing problems and may serve protective mental and behavioral health functions (LaGreca & Harrison, 2005; Rubin et al., 2004). Furthermore, the fact that children often select friends with similar behavioral, cognitive, and physical characteristics may foster a sense of belonging and protect against feelings of isolation and loneliness (Bukowski, Hoza, & Boivin, 1993). In contrast, Hartup and Stevens (1999) argue that low-quality friendships can be a drain on the relationship. Rather than promoting positive affect and mutuality, the researchers assert that low-quality friendships can often be associated with stress and anxiety and may have harmful effects.

Friendships also play an important role in academic contexts. Friends, especially at the high school level, view each other as trustworthy information sources from whom they can seek advice (Riegle-Crumb et al., 2006). As previously noted, peer relationships and the need to be perceived favorably by peers are paramount during this stage of development. Youth have a great deal of influence on their friends in matters of learning, academic persistence, and value of education. Friends can establish norms that legitimate such positive academic behaviors as studying hard and taking challenging and advanced courses (Riegle-Crumb et al., 2006). In so doing, they provide a positive endorsement of the value of education and make it "culturally" acceptable to stay in school and achieve. Adolescents who describe their friendships as having more positive, affirming features are likely to be more involved and actively engaged in school (Berndt & Keefe, 1995). These kinds of positive, high-quality friendships can make a crucial difference for youth who need peer validation to engage academically and do well in school. This issue is particularly important for low-income African American students, especially males. It has been established in the literature, and is an emerging debate in policy arenas, that educational disparities may reflect students' attitudes about academic engagement being perceived as "acting White" and not relevant to the lives they expect to live in their communities (Fordham & Ogbu, 1986; Tyson, Darity, & Castellino, 2005). While friendships are not a panacea for these types of attitudes and behaviors, we can see from examples—like the three young African American men whose pact to help each other enabled them to stay the course academically—that friendships do matter and can make a crucial difference in outcomes for these youth. The old adage *"There is strength in numbers"* takes on added significance for youth when viewed in the context of the important role of friendships.

The Buffering and Protective Role of Friendships

Positive early parent-child attachments and later high-quality friendships are important bedrocks of positive development (Hartup, 1989; Feeney, Noller, & Roberts, 2000). Their buffering and protective qualities have enduring effects and are particularly important for children living in environments that may threaten the development of such personal assets as self-confidence and self-esteem (Garmezy, 1991). However, not all children experience the benefit of a warm, nurturing parenting style. The stress associated with poverty may be overwhelming for some parents, affecting their ability to engage with their children in ways that promote optimal development. These children are often at risk for poor social relations as they begin to engage with peers in contexts of play, in early child care and development settings, and in formal educational contexts and, as a consequence, are subject to a cycle of poor outcomes (Garmezy, 1991; Aber et al., 1997; Anderson-Moore et al., 2009). In light of these potential risks, several questions arise:

- Are there opportunities during development to help redress these early adverse experiences?
- Can high-quality friendships ameliorate the effects of early adversity or poor parenting relationships with the child?

- What role, if any, can friendships play in impacting the associations between exposure to harsh parenting and susceptibility to peer victimization?

These questions have been explored by researchers, with some studies showing promising results while others raise more questions. Examining the relationships among parent-child attachment, friendship quality, and child psychosocial competencies, Rubin and his colleagues (2004) asked whether high-quality adolescent friendships would buffer the effect of insecure attachment or less supportive parenting relationships. They found important gender differences in terms of adjustment, friendship quality, and perceived parental support. Girls with close, supportive friendships had fewer problems such as being anxious, depressed, and withdrawn, even when they perceived maternal support to be low. However, for boys, having a supportive mother protected them from the negative effects of low-quality friendships on their perceived social competence. Overall, the study suggests that warm, validating, high-quality friendships are the key to adjustment, but the question still remains as to whether, in the adolescent years, these friendships can compensate for insecure parent-child relationships.

While Rubin's work looked at aspects of adjustment of school-age youth in the context of parent-child relationships, Schwartz and colleagues (2000) examined the ways in which early friendships might be related to later victimization by peers. They theorized that children who have numerous friendships develop more engaging ways to interact with their peers, thereby encouraging more prosocial and supportive interactions rather than provoking aggression and victimization. Thus, friendships serve an ameliorative function by mitigating the influence of risk factors such as a difficult home environment. The researchers also observed moderately strong associations between early exposure to a harsh home environment and later peer victimization of children who did not succeed in establishing friendships. The relationships among home environment, interpersonal competence, and vulnerability need to be more fully understood. It may be the case, as Schwartz and colleagues suggested, that friendships play a critical role in facilitating the development of important social and interpersonal competencies, as well as the emotion-regulating capacities that help children compensate for risks associated with harsh parenting and difficult home environments. If so, such friendships—presumably high quality—may be considered an important marker of resilience in children and youth (Schwartz et al., 2000).

Research by Criss and colleagues (2003) corroborated these ideas. They, too, studied how positive peer relationships could serve as protective factors against negative family experiences. Looking more broadly at family context, they focused on ecological disadvantage, violent marital conflict, and harsh discipline as three indices of adversity. They also differentiated between peer relationships and friendships in young children and found that peer acceptance was a protective factor overall in that it moderated the impact of all three indices of family adversity. Although this study found that friendship influenced only the impact of harsh discipline, the findings suggest that simply having a friend—and the esprit de corps that accompanies such a friendship—may be the essential requirements for helping young children overcome early family disadvantage.

In summary, positive and enduring friendships, especially in early and middle childhood, may have the potential to ameliorate the effects of harsh parenting and difficult home contexts experienced by youth during these critical times in their development. High-quality friendships help youth to build their capacities to navigate through the difficult waters of childhood and achieve positive youth development outcomes (Lerner et al., 2010; Theokas & Lerner, 2006; Urban, Lewin-Bizan, & Lerner, 2009). Efforts to foster high-quality friendships among children and youth should strive to achieve such outcomes so that children who stand to gain the most from friendship's ameliorative and protective effects may benefit from these relationships and increase their chances of having a brighter, more hopeful future.

The Role of Mentoring on Youth Outcomes

In Chapter 4, I discussed how the extended family and associated social networks play important supporting roles when parents are under duress or need help monitoring and protecting their children from the negative influences of the contexts in which they live. Similarly, mentors can provide support by guiding and directing children who lack positive influences and prosocial role models. The mentoring process, which typically involves a caring and supportive relationship between a youth and a nonparental adult, has been shown to have positive effects on children across multiple developmental domains and to help foster self-sufficiency and autonomy as youth mature into early adulthood (Rhodes et al., 2006; Jekielek et al., 2002). Support, guidance, and encouragement are central components of a mentoring relationship; to yield effective outcomes, the relationship should be consistent and sustained over time.

During preadolescence, youth are particularly susceptible to negative influences as they seek to understand the circumstances around them. In the absence of effective, trustworthy, and prosocial adults, youth may be attracted by high-risk activities observed in their schools and communities. Without a responsible adult to help the youth interpret what they see and experience, some youth may be drawn into relationships that provide alternative, albeit less optimistic, explanations of their experiences and of their future. This was the case with Ashante. When I met him, he was in graduate school working on an advanced degree. However, his journey toward this lofty goal was circuitous to say the least. Growing up in an inner city with a substance-abusing parent and disenchanted with school, Ashante found himself drawn to the streets. In this situation, he was highly influenced by the social and "familial appeal" of gangs and deviant peer groups. They filled information gaps and answered questions for him in ways that prosocial youth and adults could not:

> *The reason why gangs are so successful in inner city areas is because…gangs hone in on talent. Someone has to explain why [they] were in the position they're in. The gang did that. The gang used to speak of education…I didn't understand it back then. The gangs were speaking all the 'isms about uplifting Black people and that influenced me. I had leadership qualities already. I was somewhat educated and I had likeability factor that got me in good positions [with the gangs].*

Ashante's story sheds light on the critical needs for prosocial, adult mentors. In the absence of responsible adults who can steer youth in positive directions, other influences readily fill the void with enticements that appeal to the youth's state of mind. Jekielek and colleagues (2002b) summarized succinctly why mentoring is needed, especially for vulnerable youth:

> First, some features of contemporary society limit young people's access to adults: the growing isolation of many youth in poor communities; high rates of divorce and single parenting; and, in some communities, few institutions and activities to support youth and their families. Second, youth who experienced unsatisfactory or rejecting parental relationships may develop fears and doubts about whether others will accept and support them—fears and doubts that a successful mentoring experience might allay (Bowlby, 1982, cited in Jekielek, 2002b). Finally, even youth with strong positive parental relationships experience the typical "stress and storm" of adolescence and may potentially benefit from the support of another caring, concerned adult. (Jekielek, 2002b, p. 2)

Mentoring, under the right conditions and with the appropriate adults, can help redirect youth, help them overcome internal struggles, and alleviate some of the psychosocial tensions of adolescence. Rhodes and colleagues (2006) asserted the benefits of mentoring in three domains of development: (1) social and emotional, (2) cognitive, and (3) identity development. They suggested that mentoring relationships may provide youth with positive experiences in social relationships, potentially leading to improvements in other important relationships with adults and with more prosocial peers. In providing these experiences, mentors can challenge negative views that youth may have of themselves, their relationships with adults, or even their life circumstances. As a result, mentoring relationships can become what Rhodes and other researchers refer to as a "corrective experience" for youth who may have had difficult relationships with their parents or other important adults in their lives.

The earlier these corrective experiences occur in the life of youth, the greater the likelihood that the youth can be redirected toward more positive social and emotional pathways, thus engendering a greater sense of optimism and hope for the future.

Regarding cognitive development, Rhodes and colleagues (2006) said that mentoring relationships may involve giving youth new opportunities for learning and may also provide the kinds of intellectual challenge and stimulation that promote academic success. Achievement motivation, increased engagement in academic tasks, and support in achieving mastery of difficult academic concepts are all important goals to work toward in a mentoring relationship. As discussed in the previous chapter, success in difficult academic tasks may encourage greater academic self-efficacy and more effort in the pursuit of academic goals. These successes may, in turn, encourage persistence through school and pursuit of higher educational goals. More fundamental than the learning and academic tasks are the basic neurological processes that are fostered in mentoring relationships. Historically, social and developmental psychologists have theorized about mastery and learning through such processes as cognitive apprenticeships, or the zone of proximal development and scaffolding, whereby the child develops competence in mastering a task through the guidance and assistance of a competent, more capable individual, often an adult (Vygotsky, 1978; Rogoff & Wertsch, 1984). More recently, however, researchers have begun to theorize about the biological underpinnings of the mentor-mentee relationship. Southwick and colleagues (2007) assert that resilience is enhanced through learning, particularly when the mentee imitates the more resilient mentor. This happens through the mentee's repetitive imitation of a mentor's cognitive strategies and behaviors. As a result, specific areas of the brain become activated, new neuronal pathways and connections are formed, synaptic transmission increases, and the size and shape of stimulated cortical areas change (Southwick et al., 2007). Most importantly, if the mentee imitates the desired behaviors and cognitive strategies for a long enough period of time, the behaviors can become habits. This observation lends credence to the argument that mentoring relationships need to be long-term for their benefits to be realized.

Finally, by serving as role models and advocates, mentors may contribute to youths' positive identity development (Rhodes et al., 2006). The youth "see what they can be" through the examples of their mentors and formulate an identity that transcends stereotypes or preconceived notions regarding what their future holds. Identity is shown in the literature as an important asset for youth (Erikson, 1968; Hurd, Sanchez, Zimmerman, & Caldwell, 2012). Identity development played a large role in Ashante's transformation. Here he reflects on the tensions between his self-identity and the identity his grandfather hoped to confer upon him:

> *My grandfather said I would be a doctor. I never really believed it. Doctor? Doctor of what? With youth, there's this false identity and this invincibility and*

*all these other things. I was like a doctor? A doctor of what—cooking crack?
Stop it. I'm not going to be a doctor. My grandfather would just laugh at me.
I think because he believed it and spoke it in the universe it eventually came to
fruition. So many prayers of my people, they just guided me. I'm part of that
continuity. I'm an extension. Every time I take a test or read a book I think wow,
I'm going to be a doctor. My grandfather peered into the darkness that would be
my light in order to perceive something for me.*

The more diverse the mentoring models and experiences, the more options
youth will perceive within reach for them to pursue. This is important for many
lower-income youth, who may have few positive role examples at home or in the
community.

Clearly, mentoring plays an important role in the cognitive and psychosocial
development of youth, and it has been found to have health and safety benefits like
preventing youth from engaging in risky behaviors such as substance use and abuse,
violence, and other delinquent behaviors (Jekielek et al., 2002a). Evaluations of
mentoring programs that target these outcomes show that youth were 46 percent
less likely than youth in a control group to initiate drug use during the period of
study (Jekielek et al., 2002a). Notably, the impact was even stronger for minority
youth, who were 70 percent less likely to initiate drug use than similar youth who
were not in a mentoring program (Jekielek et al., 2002a). Similarly, Beier and colleagues (2000) found that adolescents in their study who had adult mentors were
less likely (compared to those who had no mentor) to engage in risk behaviors,
including carrying a weapon, using illicit drugs, excessive smoking, or having more
than one sexual partner over a six-month period. Taken together, these findings
demonstrate a relationship between having a mentor and less participation in some
risky behaviors.

Thus, mentoring as a preventive intervention is particularly critical during early
and late adolescence, as youth are at the developmental stage in which they struggle
with issues of self-identity and acceptance and, most especially, transition to adulthood. Mentoring relationships can be either naturally occurring (informal relationships established with known adults) or formal (a systematic program with adult
volunteers matched on certain characteristics).

Natural (Informal) Mentors

Natural mentoring relationships are typically formed between youth and nonparental family members, or a community member from a youth's pre-existing social network, rather than being structurally introduced through a formal program. These
natural relationships may be more enduring than formal mentoring relationships,
and youth may feel that they are more authentic. As a result, natural mentoring
may yield more positive benefits to youth in the long run. According to Rhodes

and colleagues (2002), the natural mentor bond is characterized as the ideal relationship between youth and nonparental adults who not only provide guidance, encouragement, and emotional support but often have a hybrid role, functioning somewhat like parents or peers.

Natural mentors tend to be more concerned with the nature of the relationship bond and maintaining its authenticity and "realness" than with the formality or structure of the relationship (Rhodes et al., 2002). An important but understudied aspect of the natural mentor-mentee relationship is how it lends credibility to the formation of racial identity—an important developmental asset in adolescence. Hurd and colleagues (2012) conducted one of the first studies that showed connections between natural mentoring relationships and African American adolescent outcomes as a byproduct of racial identity development. Their work suggests that relationships between youth and natural mentors foster academic resilience by strengthening racial identity beliefs as well as beliefs in the importance of school as a means toward future success. Ashante's reflections below, as well as his earlier insights, provide insight into this phenomenon as he describes an informal relationship with his faculty mentor:

> When I got to [my school], I seen different black males that I wanted to "sharpen iron" with. I used to sit in [my professor's] office and talk. He was fascinated by what I told him. I told him how I was 13 years old selling crack. The way I had seen the world. A lot of us as kids were already men, 'cause we had to be men. We grew up at an earlier age and a faster age. The brother was helping me with this dialogue and was exposing me to the other side. A lot of individuals in the inner city, we don't get exposed to the other side.... Being the first individual in my family to receive a high school equivalency diploma. First one in the college sometimes—I would get down because my family ... because a lot of them didn't understand. I would talk to one of my favorite professors.... He said whenever you feel down find solace in what your ancestors did—the slaves. They did so many things in order for you to be here in this classroom. Their resiliency and their strength—find strength in that. You're a product of that. Even if your immediate family is crazy and they're not trying to [help you]—it's ok. Love them. You're a part of sacrifice. You're a part of strength. You gotta keep progressing....

From Ashante's example, we see that the need for authenticity, understanding, and acceptance is tangible. As youth transition to adulthood, they need support not only with identity development but also with regulating emotions and making important decisions that may affect their future directions. Hurd and Zimmerman (2010) studied these ideas and found that natural mentors exert potentially long-term promotive effects on depressive symptoms and sexual risk behaviors, suggesting that natural mentors are an important resource in helping youth to overcome the risks faced as they transition into adulthood.

Adolescent pregnancy is a critical concern during this phase of development. According to the Centers for Disease Control and Prevention (CDC), the socioeconomically disadvantaged youth of any race or ethnicity experience the highest rates of teen pregnancy and childbirth, with black and Hispanic youth comprising 57 percent of U.S. teen births in 2011 (CDC, 2012). Unfortunately, the prevalence of teen pregnancy among these groups may lead to school dropout, underemployment, and other public health concerns. Asserting that natural mentors may play important mitigating roles in the lives of adolescent mothers, Klaw and her colleagues (2003) examined the role of natural mentors in promoting academic attainment by African American adolescents as they made the transition from pregnancy or recent delivery to two years postpartum. The purpose of the study was to examine the effects of enduring relationships: comparing young mothers whose relationships with natural mentors were still intact after a two-year period with young mothers having no mentoring relationships or whose relationships had terminated. The researchers wanted to gain a deeper understanding of the mentoring relationship ties in order to better understand ways in which mentoring might improve outcomes for these youth. The study found that young mothers whose mentor relationships continued for at least two years were 3.5 times more likely to have remained in school or graduated, underscoring the importance of the enduring support of mentors. In fact, some participants in the study indicated that they knew their mentors for an average of 14 years, constituting most of their lives. Thus, guidance and support from an adult outside the home can strongly influence the lives of young mothers, especially if a long-term relationship is established (Klaw et al., 2003).

Transition to adulthood takes on a different and more complex meaning for adolescents who are transitioning out of foster care. Just by entering foster care, these youth have experienced the kinds of stressful life events that put them at greater risk for difficulty in mastering the development tasks of emerging adulthood (Ahrens et al., 2008; Munson & McMillan, 2009). Thus, Munson and her research team asked whether the presence of naturally occurring relationships with non-kin mentors would be associated with positive psychosocial outcomes. As expected, they found that mentoring was related to important psychological and behavioral outcomes such as fewer depressive symptoms, less perceived stress, and greater satisfaction with life when assessed six months later (at age 18½). While much more needs to be done to support this highly vulnerable population of youth, these findings provide hope that the sustained presence of a natural mentor may lessen the effects of such stressful and potentially deleterious life experiences.

Participation in postsecondary education and in the workforce is a major task of emerging adulthood and a marker of independence and autonomy. This is an ideal point at which natural mentors can help youth develop the competencies to smoothly transition into roles and relationships requiring persistence and perseverance as well as good decision making. Dubois and Silverthorn (2005) investigated the impact of natural mentoring relationships on outcomes in education, work, problem behavior, psychological well-being, and physical health. The youth in their study who reported having a natural mentoring relationship were more likely to report high school completion, college attendance, or working at least 10 hours a week. In terms of behavioral outcomes, these youth reported reduced risk of gang membership and hurting others in physical fights, and they also reported decreased risk taking. With respect to psychological well-being, youth with natural mentors were observed to have heightened self-esteem and life satisfaction. Finally, a higher level of physical activity and greater use of birth control were also observed as indicators of positive behavioral outcomes. This study further confirmed that mentoring has the potential to positively affect a broad range of outcomes across important domains of development. As with other studies discussed in this chapter, a compelling take-home message of the Dubois and Silverthorn study is that these outcomes hinge on long-term ties with mentors. Youth need to experience the stability of the relationship in order to establish the type of bond that will yield desired benefits. Mentors known to youth—such as extended family members, employers, or school personnel who have access to youth, presumably for extended periods of time—are well poised to engage youth in meaningful ways over time. Students participating in the Comer youth leadership academy confirm this idea. When asked whether they had a mentor at school, the students shared their stories of meaningful relationships with school staff:

> **Student 1**: *Well, I actually had a mentor for about five years. I met her even before I got to middle school, because my sister went to the same middle school and she was taught by her and she was just so wonderful. I loved her so much. And she was my mentor not only because she was my teacher, she was my mentor because she was a coordinator of a club we had at school…it was a mentoring group for all students who wanted to join, and we would help the ones who were struggling and the ones who were interested in this or that, you know things like that. And she was a math teacher and the sub-coordinator was a science teacher. So they had math and science and it was just wonderful. She was my mentor and she was the one that got me talking in front of people and going to meetings and things like that. And she definitely turned my life around because before this I was a very, very shy person…I wouldn't get in front of anyone and talk. And she was the one that pushed me and she was the one that stayed after school and did all that stuff. She was the one that took us to incredible field trips. Unfortunately, she passed away…but she left a definite footprint in my life and I will never forget that. I mean, I'm here and I do this in her memory, I know I have to go on and work and prove no matter how proud of me she was before she left that I still have to work and make her even prouder. So definitely people like that are the ones that leave the impact in your life. And she definitely did with me.*
>
> **Student 2**: *During basketball this year, I was having a good season. And in the middle of the season, I started doing really bad. I was ready to quit because it was*

just embarrassing going out there every night. So I was about to quit and then
the coach, he's my science teacher too, he really encouraged me and he wouldn't
let me quit. Like if I didn't come to practice he would come find me and make me
come to practice. So he taught me to not give up and I finished the season. It was
pretty good.

Student 3: *My fourth grade teacher, she was really supportive, because at the*
time I was going back and forth because of my ulcer. And she was always there,
she helped me get back up my grades, so that whenever I was missing or at the
hospital or something, she always saved my work and then she would always help
me with my work. She'd always talk with me and help me through those times
when I didn't feel like there was anywhere to go. She just was always there for me
to talk to and I really appreciate that.

Relationships between adolescents and parents can be rocky at times, especially as adolescents strive for autonomy and independence. Thus, it might seem counter-intuitive that having a mentor would strengthen the parental relationship. However, Rhodes, Grossman, and Resch (2000) put forward the idea that, for some adolescents, a nonparental mentor relationship can relieve some of the relationship tensions and conflicts that naturally arise between parents and adolescents. This may be true even for adolescents who generally perceive parental support as available. The researchers suggest that the nonparental mentor relationship is an alternative source of adult support and as such can mediate adolescents' paradoxical and simultaneous needs for both autonomy and adult guidance. In doing so, the mentors help adolescents cope with everyday stressors and serve as models for conflict resolution. This can help reduce parental stress, improve parent-child interactions, and ultimately promote improvements in a range of adolescent psychosocial and academic outcomes (Rhodes, Grossman, & Resch 2000).

Formal Mentoring

Formal mentors, sometimes called volunteer mentors, are often engaged through structured programs for youth. A variety of such programs have proliferated over the past few decades to provide social support for youth, especially those from disadvantaged backgrounds. Big Brothers Big Sisters of America is the oldest and perhaps the most well-known formal mentoring program (Thompson & Kelly-Vance, 2001). The hallmark of these programs is that they are systematically implemented and call for a match between an appropriate adult mentor and youth. Such programs are thought to ensure that youth will obtain the intended benefits, including improved academic achievement and school performance, prosocial behavior, and the opportunity for socialization in a positive, affirming context. Unfortunately, many of these programs have not been systematically evaluated, and those that have been evaluated show varying results. However, programs that are evidence-based or founded on a strong theoretical framework are thought to provide the greatest benefit to youth.

Thompson and Kelly-Vance (2001) conducted an evaluation of a regional Big Brothers Big Sisters agency and found positive effects of formal mentoring on academic achievement of at-risk youth participating in the program. While academics are not a primary program emphasis, participants in their study performed better than their counterparts in the control group in reading and in math, suggesting that under the right conditions, the one-on-one relationship can produce a range of positive outcomes for youth.

Formal mentoring programs categorized as having either a school-based or community-based locus of mentoring activities are deemed more effective in influencing their mentee's social behavior by improving social skills, self-esteem, relationships with family members, and showing concern for others (Hererra et al., 2000). The Family Mentoring Program, a community-based mentoring program, targets young children and explicitly includes parents in some activities as part of its theory of change. As described in a study by Barron-McKeagney and colleagues (2002), the program targeted what the researchers describe as an identified transitional, at-risk neighborhood that had been underserved by community programs. In addition, the program focused on a community partnership rather than schools, and served primarily Latino youth whose parents were often recent, non-English-speaking immigrants. The goals of the mentoring program were to increase children's effective participation in positive community activities, including school life, and to increase parents' participation in the types of community services that would improve their parenting abilities. These goals, the researchers assert, were based on the assumption that, beyond mentoring as an end in itself, participation in community life offers protective factors that can decrease risk for delinquency and health-risk behaviors, paving the way for a more hopeful and optimistic future. In addition to individual mentoring for the children, the program sponsored group activities for both youth and their parents and offered referral and case management as needed. The results of the study seemed to suggest that, for a program to be effective, a strong parental component must go hand in hand with the youth component.

Faith-based organizations are also important resources for providing relationship-based mentoring and support to youth and their families. Motivated by their spiritual commitment and calling to serve humanity, more individuals volunteer through these organizations than through any other institution, with nearly 60 percent of the members of religious congregations engaging in some type of volunteerism (Rhodes & Chan, 2008). Mentoring in these contexts can have both natural and formal approaches occurring either through formalized activities that engage highly vulnerable youth or through informal, compensatory activities mirroring family life and engagement (Rhodes & Chan, 2008). As will be discussed later in this volume, faith-based organizations are typically one of the most stable institutions in some communities and can provide the continuity of relationships needed to bring about positive youth outcomes.

While formal mentoring programs in general provide the critically important foundation for learning, the outcomes of mentoring activities often yield very modest academic differences for participants, primarily because that is not their primary aim. In contrast, school-based programs have a direct focus on academic success. These programs were born out of the school reform movement and education policies that advocated stronger linkages between social support programs and academic achievement (Wheeler et al., 2010; Hererra et al., 2000). Such formal mentoring programs call for a strong relationship between the youth and the teacher, in contrast to community programs in which parents were the main point of connection. By focusing directly on student achievement, teachers and school personnel have greater control over specific academic content and have more leverage for promoting achievement motivation, personal agency, and pathways thinking—elements of hope theory that give rise to academic success.

In summary, formal mentoring programs hold a great deal of potential for promoting optimal youth development. Both school- and community-based contexts are well suited to help ameliorate some of the issues and challenges of economically disadvantaged youth. School-based programs often serve more academically troubled youth from underperforming and under-resourced schools, while community-based programs typically serve youth who are at risk for delinquency, succumbing to negative peer pressure, neighborhood dysfunction, or interaction with the juvenile justice system. Such programs with a solid evidence base have shown positive results for these youth.

It is important to point out that having a mentor, in and of itself, may not yield results that give rise to the critical aspects of hope or foster resilience. To be effective, formal programs must include the following: (1) standards and procedures for screening the volunteers and youth, procedures for the creation of the relationship, and ongoing supervision of the relationship; (2) clearly defined expectations for all parties; (3) consistent contact between the youth and the adult; and (4) ongoing training for volunteers and program staff to operate and oversee the program (Thompson & Kelly-Vance, 2001). Volunteers and youth cannot simply be matched together and left to their own devices. Instead, programs need to provide an infrastructure that fosters the development of meaningful and effective relationships with responsible adults (Sipe, 2002). These relationships need to be sustained and nurtured over time. A review of programs that meet these standards can be found at http://www.nrepp.samhsa.gov/.

Challenges and Opportunities for Programs and Policies

Formal and natural opportunities for relationships must have important processes in place for youth to benefit maximally. Among the most salient opportunities are programs specifically tailored to the needs of the youth as opposed to the desires of the adult mentor. Programs based on a flexible and adaptable approach to mentoring, rather than a prescriptive approach, tend to last longer and be more satisfying for both mentors and mentees (Jekielek et al., 2002a).

As discussed earlier, mentoring programs and relationships that extend for longer periods of time ensure better outcomes for youth. This characteristic is particularly important for youth who may lack stability of relationships in their home or neighborhood environments. Programs with short duration or those having inconsistent participation by the mentors run the risk of reinforcing youths' negative perceptions about adults and may yield unintended consequences rather than the desired ameliorative effects. Toward this end, Langhout, Rhodes, and Osborne (2004) examined the interactive nature of the mentor-mentee bond to determine the relationship conditions under which low-income urban youth benefited most. Their analysis categorized four types of mentor-mentee relationships: moderate, unconditionally supportive, active, and low-key. They found that mentoring relationships characterized by conditional support with structure, activity, and expectations are more beneficial than relationships characterized by little structure, low activity, and unconditional support. Interestingly, this finding is consistent with the documented benefits of authoritative parenting styles versus the problems of permissive parenting. In both cases, clear goals and shared understandings about the nature of the relationship are most effective in producing positive outcomes, both short and long term.

Another important challenge for programs will be to achieve more precision in matching adolescents' needs and risks to the appropriate level of intervention. Certain adolescents might respond only to highly structured, one-on-one relationships, whereas others may be skilled and at ease with asking for help or support and require less structure. Thoughtful attention to these behavioral elements may make the difference between a successful and affirming mentor-mentee relationship and one that is strained and counterproductive (Rhodes et al., 2002).

Significantly stronger positive effects on youth are obtained from programs that have incorporated a range of practices that are expected to promote the types of close, enduring, and developmentally enriching relationships highlighted as desirable by the research discussed in this chapter. These practices include training and ongoing supervision of mentors, clear goals and expectations, and, most importantly, long-lasting relationships between mentors and youth. Activities to enhance the development of mentoring relationships are also important. Even in the context of a long-standing relationship, a mentor and mentee should not always be assumed to be in sync with respect to their needs and expectations. Support should be provided to ensure that the mentor-mentee relationship stays intact. Finally, whenever possible, it is vitally important to provide opportunities that encourage parental involvement in the mentoring intervention to ensure continuity of practice, values, and ideas. Such efforts strengthen not only the mentor-mentee relationship but the parent-child relationship as well.

As discussed earlier, the success of mentoring is contingent upon the structure of the mentoring relationship and the effectiveness of the mentor. In addition, a mentor's trustworthiness is an important consideration in terms of the design of the mentoring intervention as well as the mentor's ability to connect with participating youth. It is imperative that youth deem the mentor a person with whom they can share their concerns as well as their aspirations. Mentors who focus first on building trust and becoming friends with their youth tend to be more effective than those who are overly goal-oriented and immediately try to change or reform their mentees (Herrera et al., 2000; Jekielek et al., 2002b; Rhodes, 2003). Sipe (2002) warns that adults whose attention is concentrated solely on reforming youth are often frustrated by what might appear to be apathy or lack of receptivity. It may be that these volunteers are overzealous in pressing youth too hard and too quickly to talk about sensitive issues before they are ready and before trust and confidence in the relationship are established (Sipe, 2002). To foster the protective benefits of the mentoring relationship, it is necessary for youth to have a stake in the mentor-mentee relationship as well as some degree of ownership and responsibility for how the relationship unfolds over time. In addition to the issues noted earlier, Herrera and colleagues (2000) suggested the importance of mentors being acquainted with the youth's family and pointed out that nonsupportive parents can sabotage these programmatic relationships.

Why Relationships Matter

Clearly, relationships are vitally important for enhancing the well-being of all children, especially those most at risk for negative outcomes. Friendships may fulfill a child's basic need for a sense of belonging, interpersonal connection, identity development, and social support—all of which are essential for psychological adjustment and help to buffer against the development of internalizing problems (e.g., depression and anxiety) and externalizing problems (e.g., aggression). Indeed, high-quality friendships can have ameliorative effects and could be a marker of resilience.

Mentors, both formal and natural, play a critically important role in promoting positive outcomes in several domains of development, including cognitive, social, and biological. Mentors who have long-term, supportive relationships exert a significant impact on a youth's sense of self-efficacy, social identity, and future orientation. Formal mentoring programs that expose youth to broader and more stimulating environments help to expand their social network and social capital. Fascinating work by Southwick and fellow researchers has helped us understand the biological underpinnings of what they call "mentor-enhanced resilience," a process that involves activation of complex neurobiological circuitry associated with reward, attachment, learning, and memory (Southwick, Vythilingam, & Charney, 2005). These factors contribute to important regulatory processes leading to competence, confidence, connection, character, and caring that will enable the youth to overcome adversity and, one day, become a model for other youth to emulate.

As a practical matter, faith-based and other social organizations, businesses, and supportive families can create opportunities for positive high-quality friendships and natural mentoring relationships to flourish. The major costs are time and the willingness to extend personal resources and social capital to help youth learn to negotiate the challenges they encounter daily. However, as a matter of policy, we must recognize that although mentoring and friendships are necessary, they are not sufficient to compensate for the depth of adversity that engulfs many poor children and families. These meaningful processes must be accompanied by supportive policies that enable formal programs to exist in school and community contexts and that ensure easy access to the resources provided. In addition, evidence-based programs need sufficient funding to sustain the long-term relationships required for programs to be effective. Resources are also necessary to deliver high-quality programming, trained mentors, and research-informed curricula.

We know intuitively that nurturing and supportive relationships with responsible adults can have a transformative influence in the lives of vulnerable youth. Positive models and prosocial friendships also have protective effects. The pact formed by three inner city youth—now doctors—is a testament to these effects. Yet, in addition, there must be the willingness to invest in these youth and to provide safe spaces, both physically and psychologically, for influential relationships to take hold and flourish. Most important is the willingness to stay the course—to maintain the connection so that youth can feel confident that responsible adults do indeed care and that the gift of hope can be conferred. As Ashante's insightful words confirm, one caring adult can make the difference between a youth finding their truth in the wisdom of the streets or finding meaning and purpose via the guidance of adults who provide safe passage from childhood, through adolescence, and on into adulthood.

7

Empowering Neighborhoods
and Communities to Foster Resilience

We dream of a city in which all families are housed, intact, growing stronger, and giving life to themselves, their children, their neighbors and their communities.

—Hope and a Home (www.hopeandahome.org)

The old adage "It takes a whole village to raise a child" has been bandied about as an African proverb suggesting that raising children is the collective responsibility of all the members of a community. A child is a special gift to a particular community and should be nurtured, so that he or she has the opportunity to grow into a productive adult who can contribute to the community and, in turn, share in rearing and nurturing another child. The community places its hopes and dreams in a child, expecting that, with proper grooming for leadership, nurturing, mentoring, and support, the child will fulfill these dreams and carry on family and community traditions in some appropriate capacity.

The adage also suggests that, while the primary locus of childrearing is within the family, parents are not alone in that process. Community members play important roles, including the role of "community disciplinarian"—with children aware that a community elder can inform parents about misbehavior or can discipline a child directly. Another role is that of educator—one who passes on oral traditions and customs, tells stories of family history, and gives children a sense of place and belonging. Implicit in this adage is a general consensus among community members regarding shared values of the community, cultural practices, and expectations for interaction and communication among its members. These shared values and goals also give community members a sense of place, of belonging, and of social order. In addition, extended family and community members can provide support and share resources to help the parents, especially when difficulties arise. The displays of collective responsibility for community well-being not only are helpful to families in need but also demonstrate

117

to young, impressionable minds how to value and be a contributing member of one's community.

Perhaps the notion of collaborative childrearing reflects the desire for a higher consciousness regarding community well-being. Shared responsibility for one's social, emotional, physical, and spiritual health makes a community cohesive and provides a community identity. This is what members of the community rely on during times of adversity and distress, and it is what children recall and try to emulate when they mature and are in a position to reciprocate. If it *does* take a whole village to raise a child, then it also takes a *whole* child to raise a village. As the community nurtures a child to achieve his or her full potential, the child now has the psychological resources and spiritual consciousness to contribute to the community as a fully functioning human being, rather than being a drain on community resources.

This view of child and family in the context of an entire community is protective. As discussed in previous chapters, nurturing, warmth, and caring are essential for fostering a child's sense of self-worth, belongingness, and well-being—all important factors that promote hope and foster resilience. Children and youth envision a future for themselves, are motivated to set goals, and—with the guidance of family and community—develop psychological processes to carry out the goals and achieve positive outcomes.

In recent years, people have debated whether this saying is indeed an African proverb or perhaps a sentiment that, over the years, has been attributed to African culture and communal ways of life. Regardless of its origin, the saying bespeaks a human desire to be part of a caring community, one that embraces its young and ensures that the resources—human, material, and fiscal—are there to ensure that a child grows to reach its full potential. Toward that end, this chapter will elaborate on the hopeful factors that empower communities to be supportive, as idealized in the African proverb, and will shed light on processes through which neighborhoods enable children to feel a sense of safety, nurturing, and belonging.

What Constitutes a Neighborhood?

Neighborhoods are commonly thought of as physical locations or geographic boundaries within which individuals and families reside. They also have distinctive characteristics, often demographic, by which they are identified. These characteristics give rise to the formation of communities that typically reflect more of the sociocultural aspects, common interests, and shared values of groups of people within the neighborhood (MacQueen et al., 2001). It goes without saying that most families want to live and raise their children in neighborhoods that are safe, supportive, and in harmony with their personal and cultural values. They prefer to dwell in or near a place with resources that meet their daily living needs and allow their children to grow and develop optimally. However, children and families living in economic disadvantage all too often reside in neighborhoods with higher levels of crime and violence, limited social and recreational resources, and fewer services and basic resources for daily living (Morenoff, Sampson, & Raudenbush, 2001; Harding, 2009). This lack of resources was pointed out during my interview with Carlton:

> *I don't particularly like the way the bus runs. There is a corner store right here. The bus don't come back up the street. If you have bags and stuff there are people at the store that will run you home for $5.00. [There are] no other resources around here.*

The structural and physical aspects of a neighborhood speak volumes regarding the well-being of its residents. Decayed and abandoned buildings fuel more crime and delinquency, giving rise to feelings of insecurity, anxiety, and hypervigilance (Evans, 2004). Neighborhoods with easy access to alcohol and drugs have more problems with substance use and abuse, injuries, and vagrancy and homelessness (Komro, Flay, & Biglan, 2011). Moreover, these aspects of a neighborhood affect social relations among its residents and impede important activities that promote child development, such as opportunities to play and engage in physical activity. Such conditions send a message to children and the community about their perceived value and worth to the larger society. Consequently, poor neighborhoods exert a tangible influence by their effects on children's mental and physical health and psychosocial development (Evans, 2004).

Families are affected not only by their immediate surroundings but also by areas not in the immediate vicinity of their homes (Caughy, Hayslett-McCall, & O'Campo, 2007; Harding, 2009). Spillover of crime and violence into an otherwise supportive neighborhood might engender feelings of uncertainty and unpredictability in the community. In contrast, disadvantaged neighborhoods abutting communities with more resources, lower crime, or better schools might provide opportunities to extend families' abilities to promote safety and well-being for their children. Caughy and colleagues (2007) pointed out that neighborhoods are not independent, especially in densely populated urban areas, but function interdependently with surrounding neighborhoods, either promoting well-being or exacerbating disadvantage.

Despite neighborhood risks, not all families succumb to the challenges inherent in these contexts. Some families manage to maneuver around the obstacles, find ways to make the community livable, and, through their actions, redefine the meaning of neighborhood. These families interact frequently with neighbors and neighborhood institutions, creating their own psychosocial ecology. In these contexts children are educated and receive social, health, and other important services. Most importantly, familial and cultural values are inculcated, and children develop a sense of belonging, of safety, and of expectations of others (Ingoldsby & Shaw, 2002).

Thus, researchers studying neighborhood and community processes (Sampson, Morenoff, & Gannon-Rowley, 2002) say that social processes and spatial neighborhood interdependence provide a broader lens through which to identify protective assets as well as the adaptive processes families employ to manage the complexities of their surroundings. Families are keenly aware of the local pockets of crime, areas of potential danger, and hidden havens of safety in the vicinity of their homes. This awareness influences their patterns of movement in and out of the neighborhood and informs the choices made and monitoring strategies employed to keep their children safe (Sampson, Morenoff, & Gannon-Rowley, 2002). Carlton explains how he allows his daughter to play but monitors her safety:

> Guys are here selling drugs. So I don't let her run wild. There is a girl across the street that she went to kindergarten with. I met her father and so I let her go with her friend or her friend comes here. They play together....I walk outside to make sure she gets across the street and into the building. I won't trust her to walk way down the street or up to the corner or anything like that.

Thus, parents actively identify families and individuals in the community with whom they can trust their children for monitoring or "child keeping" during particularly stressful times (Howard, 1996; McLoyd, 1990). In so doing, parents are intentionally engaged in defining their own community and creating spaces of engagement that foster well-being. For example, parents who send their child to play with friends in a nearby neighborhood, where residents tend to engage in collective supervision and monitoring, create their own community of caregivers and derive a spatial advantage in much the same way that they would benefit from living near a park or a good school (Sampson, Morenoff, & Gannon-Rowley, 2002). In doing so, families extend their neighborhood beyond its geographic boundaries, broadening its assets and bolstering the protective elements that help promote hope and foster well-being in children.

Fostering Resilience: Identifying Neighborhood Assets

Research on neighborhood assets provides a promising way to understand how the protective factors operating within families can be strengthened. For families in which adversity and toxic stress have taken their toll, compensatory resources may be available in some neighborhoods to help them recover from these challenges and provide families with strategies to map out hopeful and optimistic paths for their children. In an effort to capture a broader set of ecological assets for children and youth, Theokas and Lerner (2006) identified four categories of neighborhood assets: human resources, physical and institutional resources, collective activity, and accessibility. Subsumed under these are resources and competencies that further explicate the neighborhood assets:

1. **Human resources** are the strengths, skills, talents, and abilities of people in the neighborhood. These include the percent of college-educated residents, the percent of employed adult males, and the presence of at least one nonparental adult mentor (Urban et al., 2009).
2. **Physical and institutional resources** in the neighborhood range from the presence of health services to the availability of transportation; from parks and recreational opportunities to after-school programs and clubs. The ability to engage with the physical and social world through libraries, museums, or other facilities provides routine and structure for youth and families, thereby establishing expectations for engagement with their social environment.
3. **Collective activity** involves the relationships and connections among institutions, youth, and community members, through neighborhood groups and youth coalitions. Mutual engagement among these entities, and the resultant formal and informal programs, reflect the depth and breadth of social ties and connections among community members.
4. **Accessibility** refers to opportunities for people to *utilize* the human resources elaborated above. Factors such as neighborhood stability allow youth to interact with adults who may be long-time residents of the community and who could play a consistent and meaningful role in their lives. Physical ease of access to the various resources is also an important aspect of accessibility.

Taken together, these assets create opportunities for both social and cognitive enrichment of children and youth. These are especially important resources because, where multiple risks are present in the lives of children, multiple assets are needed to ameliorate their effects and buffer children against additional adversity.

In another study, Urban, Lewin-Bizan, and Lerner (2009) assessed whether collective activity (represented by participation in extracurricular activities) had a more positive effect on outcomes for youth living in asset-poor neighborhoods than on youth living in asset-rich neighborhoods. They theorized that as children mature and become adolescents, they spend less time in their families and more in the neighborhoods. As a consequence, the extent to which these resources are available may prove influential in strengthening youth adaptive processes. These include providing youth with the organizational structure and psychological wherewithal to resist the peer pressure to participate in unhealthy risk-taking behaviors. Ideally, this would enable them to engage in positive youth development activities that foster hope and resilience (Urban, Lewin-Bizan, & Lerner, 2009).

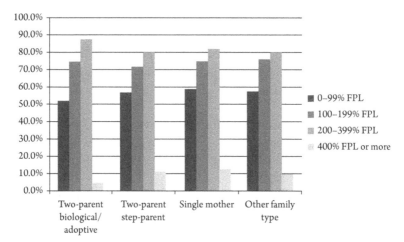

Figure 7.1 PARTICIPATION IN EXTRACURRICULAR ACTIVITIES BY INCOME AND FAMILY TYPE. National Survey of Children's Health, NSCH 2007. Maternal and Child Health Bureau in collaboration with the National Center for Health Statistics. Technical Assistance provided by the Data Resource Center for Child and Adolescent Health, Child and Adolescent Health Measurement Initiative, www.childhealthdata.org.

Data from the NSCH 2007 show that 50 percent or more of children and youth, across the income groups and family types, report participation in organized activities outside of the school (see Figure 7.1).

On average, slightly more than a third of children and youth for most of the income groups and family types report participation and regular involvement in community service or volunteer work (see Figure 7.2).

These data, while largely descriptive, may suggest the desire of families to have their children meaningfully engaged in such prosocial activities. Whether this involvement translates into positive adaptation cannot be determined from these data. However, the data appear to dispel the notion of disengaged poor youth and provide a useful starting point for engaging youth in collective activity. Such engagement should occur not just during adolescence but as early as possible, continuing throughout the course of development.

Hope and Optimism: The Power of Social Relationships

Collective Efficacy and Social Control

The social fabric of any community is only as strong as the trust among its members. Community members may have implicit understandings about the ways they can live together without disrupting their quality of life. They go about their day-to-day

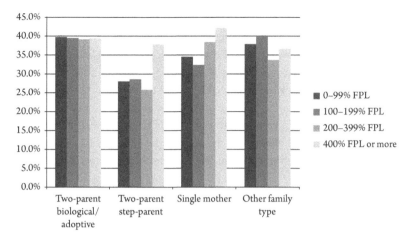

Figure 7.2 MONTHLY PARTICIPATION IN COMMUNITY SERVICE BY INCOME AND FAMILY TYPE. National Survey of Children's Health, NSCH 2007. Maternal and Child Health Bureau in collaboration with the National Center for Health Statistics. Technical Assistance provided by the Data Resource Center for Child and Adolescent Health, Child and Adolescent Health Measurement Initiative, www.childhealthdata.org.

lives trusting that neighbors will not violate these understandings. Where communities have explicitly stated codes of conduct through neighborhood councils or other organized groups, the social relationships are strengthened through this mutual agreement and community consensus (Chavis, Hogge, McMillan, & Wandersman, 1986). This gives rise to an environment that fosters collective efficacy or "the linkages of mutual trust and the shared willingness to intervene for the common good of the community" (Sampson, Raudenbush, & Earls, 1997, p. 919) in much the same manner implied by the African proverb.

Nevertheless, a major concern in many poor neighborhoods is the occurrence of violence and crime and children's exposure to violence. This situation violates trust, disrupts social order and cohesion, and undercuts a family's ability to protect their children from negative influences. It has the potential to challenge a community's efforts to intervene for the common good because the consequences of doing so may be detrimental to their well-being or, worst of all, fatal. How, then, are communities to be protective and maintain control against such disruptions? Sampson, Raudenbush, and Earls (1997) studied neighborhoods where the occurrence of violent crimes was high to determine whether their neighborhood collective efficacy could explain variations in the levels of violence in the community. The authors drew comparisons between individual or self-efficacy (as discussed in Chapter 2) and neighborhood collective efficacy, in the sense that both are active processes that seek to achieve an intended result. At the individual level, efficacy may be situational and fostered through opportunities to have success at particular tasks, so that competencies are developed in a specific domain; in neighborhoods, however, collective efficacy is contingent upon the willingness and capability of a critical mass of families to stand in solidarity and intervene on behalf of neighborhood residents to maintain social control (Sampson, Morenoff, & Gannon-Rowley, 2002). In neighborhoods where people know and trust each other, collective efficacy is high—the benefits of which often include reduced crime and juvenile delinquency (Harding, 2009). Neighbors, through associations or neighborhood watch efforts, agree on norms for behavior in the neighborhood and in so doing encourage the sense of agency and confidence in neighborhood leaders to take action when those norms are violated.

Social control is an important component of collective efficacy. This refers to the capacity of a group to regulate its members according to desired principles, such as valuing each others' property, respecting family status in the community, behaving in ways that promote safety and security, being willing to intervene to prevent acts such as truancy and street-corner "hanging" by teenage peer groups, and confronting persons who exploit or disturb public space (Sampson, Raudenbush, & Earls, 1997). Ultimately, social control allows the members of a community to realize collective goals—again underscoring the active process of defining community culture. Residential stability plays an important role in a community's ability to maintain social control (Sampson, Raudenbush, & Earls, 1998). Low-income families often move from neighborhood to neighborhood to find safe havens for their children, to afford housing, or to stay a step ahead of possible eviction. Such instability hampers a community's ability to maintain its asset base and potentially erodes efforts to maintain social control.

In addition to its noted social benefits, collective efficacy is also associated with positive mental health outcomes in children (Xue, Leventhal, Brooks-Gunn, & Earls, 2005). This may be due to reduced exposure to violence and perhaps an emerging awareness that caring adults are available to provide support when needed. This is important for children who experience a high degree of instability and chaos within the family. Children who have friends both in the neighborhood where they reside and also in adjacent neighborhoods may find comfort in having access to more stable and nurturing home environments. Amanda recalls how she found ways to compensate for the dysfunction she experienced in her family:

> I volunteered in all sorts of clubs in my public high school. I would listen for how they did things and would try to emulate that. When I was a kid instead of playing [with other kids], I would follow the parent around. When I found a parent I liked I watched what they did so that I could know how families are supposed to function.

In addition, children whose parents are the neighborhood leaders and are involved in various or collective activities observe firsthand in their parents the problem-solving strategies, positive social interactions, help-seeking behaviors, and advocacy skills that help promote collective efficacy within their communities. These interactions and leadership skills are important models for children to emulate in their social environment and in their relationships with peers. Ramona, a family support worker introduced in Chapter 1, shares the story of a participant in her program who learned how to advocate for herself and her family after having a negative experience with her landlord regarding substandard housing conditions:

> She has been through so much. Her husband passed away, and she has two young boys in elementary school. The whole family has gone through a lot of pain. She started coming here. Bright, beautiful woman with an infectious laugh. Well, she had a problem with her landlord. She had lead poisoning problems, bed bugs and so forth. The landlord tried to exploit the fact that she didn't speak English well and take advantage of her. She didn't keep quiet about it. Her showing that she had this greater network and support system led to our staff asking how we can boycott this landlord [for future program participants] so that it doesn't happen again. She is now helping other women. She has a greater sense of purpose. She tells her story in class. She moved from that place, but there was this feeling of "I didn't just walk out quietly. I put up a fight so he knows he can't mess with Latina women." She's very grateful for being here and being part of this family—"I'm a mom, I'm a strong mom, I stood up for myself."

The woman's recognition of her own personal strengths resulted in a collective effort to call attention to and stop a situation that could have significantly affected the well-being of children and families living in that housing context. Children observing their mothers' courage to advocate for themselves and the landlord's response to their advocacy will undoubtedly be bolstered in their developing sense of pride, self-efficacy, and social competence.

Finally, children benefit from having access to parks where they can play safely, fostering positive mental health and other developmental outcomes. Parents may be willing to allow their children to take advantage of these neighborhood assets if trusted and responsible adults are willing to share in monitoring children in these spaces (Sampson, Morenoff, & Earls, 1999). Thus, having access to recreational facilities, family support centers, libraries, and other spaces where people can gather in supportive ways is also important for promoting children's well-being and for engaging parents in ways that extend goodwill and the benefits of collective efficacy. Data from the NSCH 2007 show that a significant percentage of the respondents across income groups and family types indicated that they live in neighborhoods containing parks, a recreation center, and other amenities. (see Figure 7.3).

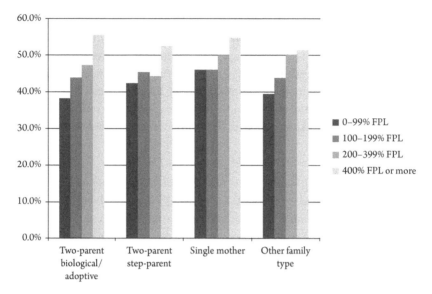

Figure 7.3 NEIGHBORHOOD CONTAINS ALL 4 AMENITIES BY INCOME AND FAMILY TYPE. National Survey of Children's Health, NSCH 2007. Maternal and Child Health Bureau in collaboration with the National Center for Health Statistics. Technical Assistance provided by the Data Resource Center for Child and Adolescent Health, Child and Adolescent Health Measurement Initiative, www.childhealthdata.org.

Whether and to what extent these resources are utilized is an important consideration for neighborhood policymakers and practitioners working with disadvantaged families. Also important is the extent to which these amenities and resources are accessible and whether they are of such quality that the families will want to use them. Assessing the utility of these resources, and the perceptions of safety in neighborhoods where these amenities exist, is an important step in increasing the use of these neighborhood assets and in linking them to positive outcomes for youth.

Psychological Sense of Community

An indicator of the quality of community life, *psychological sense of community* reflects community members' feeling of belonging and interdependence with each other—that they matter to one another and to the group, and their shared faith that members' needs will be met through their commitments (Sarason, 1977; Obst, Smith, & Zinkiewicz, 2001; Perkins & Long, 2002). McMillan and Chavis (1986) identified four components of psychological sense of community:

1. Membership—the feeling and psychological rewards of belonging. The identification with and being part of a community.

2. Bidirectional influence—speaks to community cohesiveness. The community influences its individual members and at the same time allows them to feel they have some control and influence over community functioning.
3. Integration and fulfillment of needs—involves a positive sense of togetherness. This is maintained as the individual-group association as long as it continues to be rewarding for the individual members.
4. Shared emotional connection—fosters a bond among members. The more people in the community interact with each other, the stronger the bonds between them, and these bonds then develop into a community spirit.

Taken together, these elements not only create but help to maintain an overall sense of community (Obst, Smith, & Zankiewicz, 2001).

In other conceptions of this community asset, psychological sense of community is thought to be a protective factor against mental health risks stemming from early adverse experiences (Greenfield & Marks, 2010) and a motivational factor promoting hope (Harley, 2011). In their study of the relationship between childhood exposure to family violence and mental health risks as adults, Greenfield and Marks (2010) suggested that having a strong sense of community might be protective against future psychological problems and asserted that individuals with strong positive attachments to their community might derive a sense of mastery or the feeling that they can overcome obstacles because they perceive themselves as part of a cohesive social network. This sense of mastery, in turn, can help foster resilience and positive adaptation despite early exposures to adversity. Harley (2011), drawing upon hope theory, described how participants in her study found neighbors to be sources of support and hope even when other aspects of the neighborhood were viewed as hopeless. Youth in her study described this caring connection among neighbors and how they served as surrogate parents when the youths' own parents were working or otherwise unavailable, ensuring that the youth kept curfews or stayed away from peers who could lead them into trouble. These caring neighborhood connections inspired hopefulness among the youth by motivating them to engage in prosocial behavior.

Parental Monitoring, Social Networking, and Resource Utilization

In Chapter 4, I discussed the important role of parents and extended family networks in promoting hope and fostering resilience in children and youth. It is also an important asset in disadvantaged neighborhoods and communities. While collective efficacy involves the willingness to intervene in social problems in the community, parenting and the shared responsibility for childrearing may not necessarily involve a formal or organized intervention. Instead, they may reflect a kind of proactive interruption of negative events by actively monitoring, seeking resources, and problem solving with other parents regarding ways to separate children from the strong attraction of street life (Letiecq & Koblinsky, 2004). Jarrett (1999) refers to these kinds of actions as community-bridging and resource-seeking strategies. Parents employ these methods strategically to help avoid the additional challenges and stressors associated with living in inner-city or low-asset neighborhoods (Jarrett, 1995). Parental competencies in child monitoring and communicating family priorities are essential, as are effectiveness in seeking help and in identifying and using resources within and outside the immediate vicinity of their homes. These skills are especially important for parents of adolescents who may be challenged with making decisions and engaging in behaviors that could place them at risk for poor outcomes. Adolescence is a time of development when youth experience a variety of changes and life transitions. Social relationships are central to an adolescent's sense of self, social identity, and decision making. As Urban and colleagues (2009) pointed out, adolescents gravitate toward peers, establish new friendships, and are less likely to seek advice from parents or spend time at home. By such behaviors, adolescents seek to become independent and establish their own identities—which can cause conflict in the home. Community-bridging and resourceful parents want to protect their adolescents from negative neighborhood influences (Jarrett, 1995). However, they must also be skillful at balancing the desire to keep their adolescents safe by maintaining an open and communicative relationship while, at the same time, actively discouraging potentially harmful friendships and social activities. The degree to which parents establish a secure attachment bond and supportive relationship will play a role in how well they are able to monitor behavior and encourage adolescents to engage in collective activities that contribute to social cohesion and support, and that also promote positive youth development. Therefore, parents must be adept at finding compelling activities in which their child will want to participate. Parents' connections through their extended families or other kinship ties, neighborhood associations, or churches can be leveraged to keep children occupied and supervised during after-school hours—a time when children and youth are likely engage in risk behaviors.

The efficacy of parents, in conjunction with the collective efficacy of the community, can help buffer children and adolescents from the negative influences of disadvantaged neighborhoods and also enable them to be resilient despite the challenges of this environment. Most importantly, access to these human and institutional resources can be a source of motivation for children and youth, giving them enough psychological distance from the stressors of their environment to envision a positive future and to set goals for bringing that vision to fruition.

Social Capital—Strength in Numbers

People who participate on teams—whether through sports and athletics, professional associations, business models, or social clubs—recognize the value of working together to solve common problems or achieve goals. The organizational and business community uses TEAM as an acronym for the phrase "Together Everyone Achieves More." This is used as a motto in schools and in places where the goal is for members of a particular group to recognize and celebrate their interdependence. The same principle applies to neighborhoods and communities. Each family brings something to the culture of their community that can be socially and psychologically enhancing. In many ways, "TEAM" is analogous to social capital. Social capital is believed to promote a variety of outcomes by increasing access to social support, including emotional support and information, social influence on behavior and coping, engagement and attachment, and access to shared resources and material goods (Taylor, Repetti, & Seeman, 1997). Social capital is characterized by participation in networks, reciprocity (members can expect to give and to receive), mutual trust, shared recognition of social norms of behavior, shared ownership of common resources, and collective efficacy (Coleman, 1988; Sampson, Morenoff, & Earls, 1999). Social capital exists when relationships among people enable individual or joint achievements that otherwise would not be possible. It involves parents and children in friendship networks and community organizations, both formal and informal, characterized by a set of obligations, expectations, and social ties (Runyan et al., 1998; Dorsey & Forehand, 2003). Information is exchanged, and norms and informal systems of social control are established. In much the same manner as the idealized African proverb, where social capital exists a child is raised in a neighborhood environment with norms and behavioral expectations that are not, or cannot be, brought about by a single individual or isolated adult (Taylor, Repetti, & Seeman, 1997).

According to Runyan and colleagues (1998), social capital is a manifestation of the benefits derived from personal social relationships within families and communities, and their respective social affiliations. They examined the extent to which social capital is associated with positive developmental and behavioral outcomes in high-risk preschool children and found impacts on children's well-being as early as the preschool years. The researchers concluded that parents' social capital confers benefits on their children in much the same way as benefits conferred from the parents' financial and human capital because families and, by extension, children have access to resources and support not otherwise available to them (Taylor, Repetti, & Seeman, 1997; Runyan et al., 1998).

Neighborhoods in Action

The assets described in this chapter are important for fostering parental competencies and creating micro-ecologies of safety that can buffer children against negative influences of disadvantaged neighborhoods. However, having these assets in communities is of little value unless they can be translated into active processes that will help empower residents to transform their environment into safe, stable communities where every child has the opportunity for optimal growth and development. As discussed earlier, many disadvantaged communities are torn by high levels of violence and crime that make it difficult to maintain cohesion and a sense of social order. Interventions and programs are needed that build on communities' strengths and assets to leverage their individual competencies, collective efficacy, and social capital in ways that will help regain social control and strengthen the social fabric of the community.

Thus, comprehensive interventional approaches to problem solving in these communities must involve multiple agencies and individuals throughout the community. This is important because the level of disadvantage and chronicity of violence and other social problems may make it difficult for any one group, institution, or family to have an impact on the community. By bolstering networks of people who care and have the wherewithal to intervene, community supports can help children and families feel less isolated and overwhelmed, and more capable of coping with the daily challenges of living in a disadvantaged community (Osofsky, 1999).

Comprehensive Community Approaches

Indeed, interventions programs are needed to help promote collective efficacy and social capital in low-asset, under-resourced communities. However, these programs must be comprehensive and should be informed by and responsive to a community's hierarchy of needs. Recall that in Chapter 2 we discussed Abraham Maslow's classic theory of the *Hierarchy of Needs* as it relates to mechanisms of hope. This theory suggests that in order for individuals to achieve the ultimate goal of self-actualization, basic needs must be addressed. When one level of needs has been "satisfied," the individual can be open and receptive to managing the needs at the next level and so on. Applying this hierarchy to interventions designed to promote collective efficacy may benefit from the ideas underpinning this theory. It stands to reason that communities will have difficulty achieving the idealized goals if a strong foundation of support to first motivate and then sustain these goals is absent. Interventions shown to be effective need to be sustained over time so that communities can enjoy the long-term benefits of collective efficacy and social capital, and also so that children have the opportunity to observe the adults in their community functioning collaboratively and using effective problem-solving approaches. In many ways, Josephine's individual experience exemplifies the importance of this comprehensive approach and parallels the kinds of interventions and policies that are needed at the community level. You may recall from her introduction in Chapter 1 that Josephine, a mother of five children, lost her home because of an inability to pay the water bill despite the fact that she was working two jobs. She found herself in the shelter system, and because of the system policies in her community she could not keep her family together. These setbacks led to a cascade of other problems, challenging her sense of efficacy as a parent and making it difficult for her to draw upon her strengths to rebound from this adversity. However, once she was able to meet her basic need of shelter through the intervention of a transitional housing program and to have a sense of security that the housing program provided, she then was able to re-establish social networks and take advantage of opportunities in her community for herself and her children, thereby reaffirming her efficacy as a parent and becoming in tune again with her strengths:

> *Having this [kind of intervention] takes you out of the realm of the emergency and the immediate. And places you back to a place where you can take some steps and that is what a program like this does. It allows you a place where you can take some steps and if you can begin to take some steps you can begin to dream. You can begin to think about "what is it that I want to do? Where do I go from here?" There are options that become available to you that don't happen to you when you're constantly moving from place to place.*

Of necessity, the transitional housing program required that Josephine develop a strategic plan for how she would sustain the gains she had made, including budgeting and paying bills on time. Through these interventions, Josephine was able to leave the transitional housing program and to purchase her own home. Her children excelled in school, and she was able to help other families achieve successful outcomes:

> *The important thing is that if people are encouraged and feeling good, then we don't want anything [in the system] to keep that from happening. A lot of what we do is try to advocate for the families and, when possible, we have to go with them to help solve problems or we may even do the research and give the information to them so they can go on their own.*
>
> *Sometimes we think people understand. Even with the finances and putting together a budget, people don't understand, so what they do is what they know. We take some things for granted. Depending on where they are and where they come from they have a different understanding about what money is and what values are. Those are the type of things that put people in difficult situations. Where they are is totally different from the world system and how it operates. We're helping them on these goals.*

Josephine's personal example reinforces the notion that a comprehensive approach is needed to help engage individuals in a community to tap into their respective strengths and assets so that the collective benefit can be realized. However, such an approach must begin with the individual's most pressing and fundamental needs and subsequently incorporate broader concerns once the basic needs are met. In Table 7.1, I align examples of intervention programs with Maslow's *Hierarchy of*

Table 7.1 **Hierarchy of Comprehensive Community Program Needs**

Hierarchy of Needs	*Comprehensive Community Program Needs*
Basic Needs: *food, shelter, warmth, clothing; physiological needs*	Programs and policies that provide transitional and long-term housing. Interventions should teach basic skills of home maintenance, budgeting for food, clothing and other important daily needs to promote stability. Programs that provide stress reduction, mental health services, and programming for recovery from addictions and other challenges meet basic needs.
Safety Needs: *protection, security, social order*	Programs and policies that help create safe havens in the community for children to play and for families to establish social and behavioral norms. This may include neighborhood watch and community policing programs. Programs that teach parental monitoring skills also meet these needs.
Belonging Needs: *family, friends, affiliations*	Programs and policies that help promote social cohesion in the community through establishing social networking opportunities. Faith-based programs, community centers, and social, civic, and sports/entertainment organizations help foster these needs.
Esteem Needs: *achievement, status, responsibility, feelings of accomplishment*	Programs that engage community members in their own improvement process, fostering shared goal setting and program planning as well as community redesign. Community development organizations, community councils, and neighborhood advisory boards help to facilitate these needs.
Self-Actualization: *personal growth and fulfillment*	Programs and policies that provide opportunities for higher education and training for parents, as well as opportunities for adult-to-adult mentoring and goal-setting programs. Programs that focus on promoting optimal child development, fostering creativity, and prosocial skills address also these needs. Programs that teach financial literacy, entrepreneurship, and self-sufficiency help meet these needs. Opportunities for home ownership to promote family stability and potential for economic security are appropriate as well.

Needs, starting with the most foundational needs and continuing to needs that promote hope and foster adaptation and community-level resilience.

The policies and programs can target each level of need based on community readiness and capacity to sustain changes once the programs are implemented. To do so, it may be important to identify stable community resources in which a good deal of social capital already exists. Faith-based organizations and associated community development programs are examples of stable entities that can help communities organize to address their own needs. While some of these programs are supported through government funding, many are self-sufficient and rely on the support of parishioners as well as local entrepreneurship. These programs provide an array of resources and may help communities address this hierarchy of needs. They provide resources for child care, as many churches incorporate ministries that address child development. Some churches and faith-based organizations offer opportunities for employment; others provide food, transportation, and basic and safety needs for community residents (Dionne & Chen, 2001; Branch, 2002). Increasingly, churches in urban centers form community development corporations that engage in activities ranging from providing basic food and clothing to building low- to moderate-income housing and schools (Branch, 2002; Anglin, 2004; Owens, 2004). These housing programs provide training to teach families how to purchase homes and maintain them. These corporations allow the faith communities to engage in a range of activities to empower the community residents and to build strengths and assets to transform the communities so that they become places of growth and continuous improvement. However, some researchers call for efforts to build greater capacity so that these comprehensive approaches can achieve their intended outcomes (Dionne & Chen; 2001; Hartman, 2002; Gordon, 2003; Anglin, 2004; Owens, 2004).

More broadly, McRoberts (2001) refers to trans-neighborhood faith-based development. These are coalitions of churches and faith-based organizations that may not be based in a particular neighborhood but unite to address cross-cutting neighborhood and community needs. This kind of collaboration is needed, especially in light of the fact that, increasingly, churches serve diverse populations of parishioners from a wide variety of backgrounds. As well, the small neighborhood church may not be available in some of the neediest and most disenfranchised communities or may not have the wherewithal on their own to address some of the most intractable problems. These coalitions garner broad-based support and pool human and fiscal resources to address common problems across a number of communities. McRoberts highlights the Mattapan-Dorchester Churches in Action and the Ten Point Coalition as examples of trans-neighborhood efforts. These were formed to challenge the presumed power structures preventing the neighborhoods from pursuing their identified goals or achieving their fullest potential (McRoberts, 2001).

The Harlem Children's Zone (HCZ) is another type of comprehensive community development program that has garnered a great deal of attention as an example of a highly effective intervention model, building on the strengths and assets of a community to ensure that children have every possible chance for success in life. The program is designed to address the entire range of community needs, with its focus on changing the outcomes for children growing up in poverty. Focusing on the centrality of education as a means for achieving positive outcomes, the HCZ offers a pipeline of services that can address children's needs throughout the various stages of their development, and it provides a supportive neighborhood environment so children will not get lost in the system or drop out of school (Page & Stone, 2010). These important protective mechanisms diminish children's exposure to negative neighborhood influences and allow them the opportunity to develop personal agency and self-efficacy needed to experience success. Opportunities for parents and communities to develop their competencies are also part of this model, thus ensuring the availability of resources and means to support and nurture children as they grow, developing the skills and resources to transform their communities into nurturing and safe havens. The HCZ boasts impressive outcomes, including improved student academic achievement, thus closing the achievement gap as well as accomplishing important family, community, and health outcomes (www.hzg.org; Page & Stone, 2010).

Building on the success of the famed Harlem Children's Zone, Promise Neighborhoods, a program administered by the U.S. Department of Education, has also received a great deal of attention in recent years. Like the HCZ, Promise Neighborhoods is a comprehensive approach that uses education as the vehicle for community improvement and, most importantly, for positive youth outcomes. The program's vision, as explained by the U.S. Department of Education, is for all children and youth growing up in Promise Neighborhoods to have access to great schools and strong systems of family and community support that will prepare them to obtain an excellent education and successfully transition to college and a career. The purpose of Promise Neighborhoods is to significantly improve educational and developmental outcomes of children and youth in distressed communities, as well as to transform those communities by:

1. identifying and increasing the capacity of eligible entities that focus on achieving results for children and youth throughout an entire neighborhood;
2. building a complete continuum of cradle-to-career solutions of both educational programs and family and community supports, with great schools at the center;
3. integrating programs and breaking down agency "silos" so that solutions are implemented effectively and efficiently across agencies; and
4. developing the local infrastructure of systems and resources needed to sustain and scale up proven, effective solutions across the broader region beyond the initial neighborhood (U.S. Department of Education, 2013).

Several indicators have been recommended for measuring the effect of Promise Neighborhoods on child outcomes: reading and math proficiency, school readiness, improved school attendance, reduced infant and child mortality from violent crimes and child maltreatment, increased civic participation and volunteerism, and improved mental health outcomes including hopefulness and optimism (Child Trends, 2009).

Asset-Based Approaches

An important strategy emanating from the community development literature is the asset-based community development (ABCD) approach. This approach stands in contrast to traditional needs-based approaches in which problems are identified and strategies devised to solve those problems—largely by outside "leaders" or people external to the community (Mathie & Cunningham, 2003). This leads to dependence on the part of the neighborhood residents and, to a large degree, to internalizing the needs and deficits that these needs-based approaches highlight (Kretzmann & McKnight, 1996). Indeed, Kretzmann and McKnight (1996) argue that the key to neighborhood regeneration is to locate all of the available local assets, connect them in ways that multiply their power and effectiveness, and then harness local institutions that are not yet available for local development purposes to maximize the impact of the connected assets.

Toward that end, the ABCD approach is a way to capitalize on communities' strengths to help members empower themselves to strengthen their own communities and, collectively, improve the quality of their lives (Kretzmann & McKnight, 1996; Mathie & Cunningham, 2003). The basic premise of this model, according to Kretzmann and McKnight, is threefold: First, as the name implies, ABCD is asset-based, and the development strategy starts with the strengths present in the community, the capacities of its residents and workers, and the associational and institutional base of the area—not with what is absent, or what is problematic, or what the community "needs." Second, it is "internally focused," meaning that the development strategy is centered on the agenda-building and problem-solving capacities of local residents, local associations, and local institutions. In so doing, the model stresses the primacy of local definition, investment, creativity, hope, and, most importantly, local control. The premise put forward by the researchers is that the model of necessity is relationship-driven. The relationships throughout the community development enterprise must focus on continuous building and rebuilding of the networks between and among local residents, associations, and institutions.

Pan and colleagues (2005) examined the utility of this model for the medical community and outlined five core assets for mobilizing communities and for engaging health professionals in participatory health-promotion efforts. These are quite similar to those outlined by Kretzmann and McKnight; however, these researchers focused on the assets' transformative capacity to improve the health and well-being of the whole community. Pan and colleagues identify the first asset as the skills and capacities of individuals residing in the community. In this way, institutions and outside organizations can be much more efficacious in their intervention efforts, and community members are able to participate in their own improvement process. They identify the second important asset as the "associational life" of community members. This asset encompasses the groups of people who volunteer to come together for a common purpose and form the social fabric of communities. Associations range from informal card-playing groups and walking groups to religious groups, sports clubs, and political action groups to more formal service organizations. Such associations provide forums for networking and social support, and serve as organizing venues where community residents can contribute their gifts, talents, and skills.

Institutions, the third major asset, include such entities as government agencies, businesses, and nonprofit organizations, as well as those organizations that provide employment, goods, and services to community residents. Pan et al. (2005) also refer to "institutional treasures" that promote community-building efforts. These include facilities for meetings, purchasing power, professional expertise, workforce, and connections with key decision makers who control community resources.

The economic development potential of a community is the fourth asset, and the fifth is land and other physical assets. These last two enable leveraging of the economic potential of institutions (e.g., schools and hospitals) and converting physical liabilities such as abandoned buildings and vacant lots into assets (Pan et al., 2005).

Public Health Approaches

Communities That Care (CTC) is a program of the Center for Substance Abuse Prevention (CSAP) in the office of the U.S. Government's Substance and Mental Health Services Administration (SAMHSA). CTC uses a public health approach to prevent youth from engaging in problem behaviors such as violence, delinquency, dropping out of school, and substance abuse (Hawkins et al., 2009). The system is designed to help community stakeholders and decision makers understand and apply information about youth risk, protective factors, and evidence-based programs that have been proven effective in promoting healthy youth development (Arthur et al., 2010; Brown, Feinberg, & Greenberg, 2010). In so doing, communities become more empowered and develop the collective efficacy to address specific issues facing their youth. One goal in CTC communities is to ensure that adults and community organizations provide youth with developmentally appropriate opportunities, skills, and recognition, as well as healthy standards for behavior that promote social cohesion. The CTC guides a community coalition of decision makers through a process of assessment and prioritization to identify the risk and protective factors most needing attention, then links those priorities to prevention programs that have proven effective in addressing them.

Studies evaluating this model have shown CTC's success in changing system outcomes that lead to reduced risk, enhanced protective factors, and improved adolescent health and behavior outcomes, including less delinquent behavior (Hawkins et al., 2008 Hawkins et al., 2009). In addition, Feinberg et al. (2010) investigated whether this model had a positive impact among adolescents with regard to risk and protective factors, as well as academic and behavioral outcomes. The positive findings of the study led Feinberg and colleagues to conclude that the implementation of the CTC model in a community was associated with less delinquency throughout adolescence, better academic performance, and lower likelihood that youth would move to higher levels of risk as they developed through their adolescent years.

Revisiting the Village

Indeed, it does take a village to protect, nurture, and raise a child. Children— especially those living in high-crime areas with chronic violence—need the support of caring adults in order to have a sense of safety, security, and well-being in their neighborhood. This recognition suggests that broader conceptualizations of neighborhood need to be the focus of research, programming, and policymaking decisions, so that children and families may benefit from a broader array of neighborhood assets. Programs that not only foster collective efficacy and social cohesion but also build on those assets to empower residents to play an influential role in transforming their own neighborhoods and communities are absolutely essential.

Most children spend as much time at school as they do at home; therefore, as asset-rich institutions within the community, schools must play instrumental roles in providing human resources and accessibility. Schools not only function as educational institutions but also provide children with opportunities to benefit from the support of teachers, peers, mentors, and other adults—all of whom are instrumental in buffering against cumulative deleterious risks. With the guiding hand of responsible adults, children will be able to envision a bright future for themselves and to engage in activities that will ultimately enable them to bring their vision to fruition. As pointed out in many studies reviewed in this chapter, neighborhood assets *do* help families and children to cope. However, the level and recurrence of violence, chaos, or the breakdown of social cohesion place additional burdens on the families and, by extension, the communities; the challenge of overcoming these burdens hampers their ability to draw on the assets. For this reason, it is vital to have comprehensive, systemic approaches based on a hierarchy of needs that call upon every available resource to help families maintain a level of optimism. In doing so, they participate in their own community's revitalization and renewal.

The challenges of economic disadvantage are complex and formidable, and we must not assume that merely acknowledging the existence of strengths is sufficient to overcome these challenges. There is a desperate need for economic and material resources that can break the cycle of poverty and its associated problems. An assessment of strengths, in order to determine where to apply resources and how to gauge their maximum benefit for children, is an important and hope-promoting place to start. As Josephine wisely offered:

> *Some people have been told they weren't nothing, they'll never be nothing. Or they been told that because of their situation—it's terrible; it's their fault. But if they can grasp that there is a prospect and that they have the capacity to do better—that's what they want. They can do better, they can move in another direction. They have the realization that whatever has happened before, they can be better. They can make changes that will impact their lives and their children. They have hope for their children, even when others say they can't do it.*

8

Hope, Optimism, and Resilience

Cultural Frames of Reference

Optimism is the faith that leads to achievement. Nothing can be done without hope and confidence.
— Helen Keller, *Optimism: An Essay* (1903)

Culture exerts a strong influence on the frames of reference used to characterize day-to-day challenges as well as larger, potentially catastrophic life events (Ogbu, 1994). Even the ways that individuals or families perceive and find meaning in their station in life are filtered through cultural lenses. These perceptions reflect the collective experiences, shared values, identities, and goals of individuals belonging to a particular cultural group and may arise from historical or religious traditions or from socially constructed conditions that unite groups of people in time and place (Gutiérrez & Rogoff, 2003). In this chapter, I explore cultural frames of reference and their important role in shaping individuals' perceptions, explanations for life circumstances, and approaches to managing the challenges of economic adversity. I pose the following questions: How do culture and its influences give rise to the mechanisms of hope and optimism? What role, if any, does culture play in fostering resilient outcomes in children and families? Are there particular perspectives or practices that help children and families cope with their circumstances?

To explore these questions, I'll share insights from my interviews with Sarah, Ramona and Ashante. Recall from Chapter 1 that both Ramona and Sarah provide services to families who have experienced various types of adversity. Through her organization, The Family Place, Ramona works with immigrant women, primarily from Latin America, who want to learn English as a way to gain greater access to resources, education, and jobs. Sarah is an academic professional who works with American Indian families to develop and implement helpful interventions within this community. Ashante, as we learned earlier in this volume, is an African American male who was a troubled youth, spending his adolescence and early adulthood in and out of jail. His pathway toward overcoming the challenges experienced in his childhood and adolescent years was facilitated by his recognition and adoption of his cultural and racial identity. Ashante's story sheds light on his evolving views of race and culture and how they ultimately motivated him (pathways thinking) to make different choices and turn his life around:

> It wasn't until I became aware of my cultural identity that I understood how I was mislead; how I didn't understand who I was, where I was and how got where I was. Gaining that appreciation for myself and my cultural identity made me respect myself and propelled me through my educational process.

Ashante's explanations and thought processes about his experience underscore the notion that the ways in which individuals and members of a group cope with adversity and adapt to difficult life circumstances may be revealed in their explanations of the events that occur in their life. Researchers say these *explanatory styles* reflect the habitual way that people explain the causes of events in their lives and are correlated with a number of psychological processes, including achievement and well-being when the styles are more optimistic, and depression, anxiety, and other internalizing problems when the style is more pessimistic (Peterson, 1991). Explanatory style predicts behavior, problem-solving strategies, and decision-making strategies employed to cope with adversity (Buchannan & Seligman, 1995). A pessimistic style involves a tendency to make internal (something about the self, e.g., "It's all my fault"), stable (persisting or recurring over time, e.g., "It's going to last forever"), and global (affecting many situations, e.g., "This will affect everything I do") attributions for negative events. Alternatively, an optimistic explanatory style involves a tendency to make external (e.g., "God allowed this to happen for a reason"), unstable (e.g., "This too shall pass"), and specific (e.g., "This does not affect everything I do — it's just a temporary setback") attributions for negative events (Oettingen, 1995; Schulman, Castellon, & Seligman, 1989).

Individuals with more optimistic explanations are thought to have better health and psychoemotional outcomes than those with a pessimistic style (Peterson, 1991). Carver, Scheier, and Weintraub (1986) observed the use of active, problem-focused coping strategies among people with optimistic outlooks. They suggest that optimistic individuals tend to reinterpret adverse events positively and accept the reality of a situation, whereas pessimists tend toward denial, substance abuse, or other means in order to lessen their awareness of the problem at hand. Optimists also attempt to make the best of a situation by learning from their adverse experiences. Thus, more optimistic explanations may be associated with better adaptation, greater resilience, and better developmental outcomes for children (Carver, Scheier, & Weintraub, 1986).

An important consideration is whether these explanations are influenced by cultural perspectives. It may be that types of explanations are a means for adults in a cultural community to pass values and culturally informed coping strategies to their children. Parents play a role of fostering optimistic explanations in their children through authoritative parenting approaches (Jackson, Pratt, Hunsberger, & Pancer, 2005; Peterson & Steen, 2009). Children may learn adaptive strategies that may help them rise above the challenges and lead to better outcomes. This is particularly important for children reared in a cultural context of persistent poverty, historical trauma, or marginalization. For example, various racial and ethnic groups in this country have experienced adversities that include both discrimination and issues associated with poverty and economic disadvantage. Children reared in these groups must manage the complexities of growing up in these contexts as well as the inherent challenges of maturation (Boykin, 1986). African American youth face specific challenges during development. For example, Spencer and colleagues (2003) write that African American adolescent boys in particular are treated as "stereotyped miniature adults" (p. 181), often eliciting a great deal of anxiety among adults outside their communities or social networks. As a consequence, these youth frequently experience manifestations of structural racism and racial stereotyping, both overt and subtle. Spencer contends that such experiences pose risks for poor health and problems in adolescent development. However, the effects of these experiences can be mitigated by optimistic explanatory styles as well as by protective factors such as identity development and self-efficacy, which can help promote adaptation in the context of such adverse experiences (Buchanan & Seligman, 1995; Oettingen, 1995).

The Latino population in the United States is rapidly growing, and Mexican Americans are among the largest and fastest-growing Latino subgroup, representing more than half of the Latino population and slightly under 10 percent of the U.S. population (Ennis, Ríos-Vargas, & Albert, 2011). Not surprisingly, youth of Mexican origin face the challenge of adapting to mainstream U.S. culture while also maintaining ties and adapting to the Mexican culture and its permutations in the United States (Knight et al., 2011). Their particular challenges include parenting and socialization practices, and maintaining strong and cohesive social and family support, as the process of immigration often separates and isolates members of the nuclear and extended family (Knight et al., 2011). Overcoming language barriers to secure employment and to facilitate children's education is also a critical challenge that, if not successfully addressed, could lead to increased poverty and poor developmental, behavioral, and health outcomes for children.

Few groups have experienced more kinds of adversity than the American Indian. As noted by LaFromboise and colleagues (1993), American Indians' stressors include balancing the demands of American culture against their own cultural practices and values, as in other racial and ethnic groups. However, their unique life circumstances bring challenges distinct from most other racial/ethnic groups in this country (Gone, 2004; LaFromboise et al., 1993; Graham,

2011). American Indian adolescents, for example, must learn to negotiate the often-changing requirements of multiple social and cultural systems both on and off the reservation as they mature into adulthood (Beauvais, 2000, cited in LaFromboise et al., 2006). Yet youth living in urban areas or outside the reservations may lack access to the social support networks, such as extended family networks, more readily available to youths on reservations. As a result, non-reservation youth may experience additional psychological challenges as a consequence of their efforts to be assimilated into mainstream culture (LaFromboise & Dizon, 2003).

Despite these experiences, members of various racial and ethnic groups have been shown to manage these circumstances in positive, productive ways. The assets and strengths-based coping strategies used to negotiate the challenges of economic disadvantage, as well as issues of acculturation and assimilation, are appearing more prominently in the sociological and psychological literatures, and current research notes evidence of a host of processes that foster resilience in these groups (American Psychological Association, 2008; Claus-Ehlers, 2008; Utsey et al., 2007; Kenyon & Hanson, 2012; Panter-Brick & Eggerman, 2012). As researchers move from deficit and problem-based models toward more positive frameworks for understanding and documenting outcomes for youth in various cultural groups, we gain a clearer picture of how individuals in these groups take steps toward overcoming adversity.

I've drawn four influential strengths-based cultural processes and practices from the literature. These are:

1. *Spirituality and religion*—practices by which individuals and cultural groups transcend their circumstances and give meaning to the nature of their adversity;
2. *Racial socialization and cultural identity*—processes that mitigate against the stresses of acculturation and assimilation by affirming the value and worth of cultural heritage;
3. *Cultural perspective-taking on coping and resilience*—provides a prism through which adversity and challenges are viewed, and the particular perspectives that frame how cultural groups respond and cope in difficult circumstances; and
4. *Cultural traditions and practices*—promote hope among groups with adherence to those traditions; these practices are motivational in that they inspire children and youth with a vision to work toward and encourage goal setting and active strategies for accomplishing those goals.

In the section that follows, I explore in more depth the research on these four processes, enriched by insights from Ashante, Sarah, and Ramona to shed light on the ways that adaptation is fostered by these cultural assets and strengths.

Spirituality and Religion

Religiosity, as reflected in attending religious services and participating in religious activities, has been cited in the literature as an important buffer against stressors brought on by adversity (Peterson, 1990). Beyond the obvious social supports, participation in religious activities enables members of cultural groups to coalesce around common interests and goals, thereby strengthening an individual's resolve to be a fully functioning human being, as discussed by Carl Rogers, humanistic psychologist (1961). He theorized that such an individual lives in the here and now, is open to new experiences, and trusts in his or her own ability to manage life's complexities. Participation in religious activities also helps individuals meet needs along Maslow's classic Hierarchy of Needs. As discussed in previous chapters, this theory suggests that, in addition to basic physiological needs for survival and daily living, we all have needs for belonging, affiliation, and acceptance. As these needs are met, esteem needs emerge in the foreground. These reflect the human need to be respected, valued, and held in high regard by others. The pinnacle of this hierarchy is self-actualization—transcendence—the desire and drive to achieve one's full potential. Often, religious and spiritual orientation to life allows one to strive for transcendence and self-actualization as a life-long process of discovery.

Other researchers say that religion and engaging in religious practices may play an important role in happiness and well-being (Krause, 1992; French & Joseph, 1999; Graham, 2011). The association between religion and happiness may be related to finding purpose in life, and it is generally understood that religious people are more likely to feel that their life has meaning and purpose and is worth living, despite the fact that their circumstances may suggest otherwise (Noddings, 2003; Graham, 2011). These feelings of fulfillment and meaning are often due to a belief in better circumstances in an afterlife. Religious devotion, as it fosters the ability to look past one's circumstances, serves an important adaptive function. Indeed, Tiger (1979) argued that religions arose, at least in part, to tap what he referred to as people's biologically given need to be optimistic. He argued further that religious thought lends itself particularly well to what he termed "big optimism," or dispositional optimism, because of its certainty and the absoluteness of its tenets (Tiger, 1979, cited in Peterson, 2000).

Data from the National Survey of Children's Health (NSCH, 2007) show that, across income levels and family types, children regularly attend some type of religious service (see Figure 8.1).

Additionally, racial/ethnic groups participate frequently in religious activities (see Figure 8.2).

Higher percentages of attendance at religious services were reported by Black non-Hispanic families. For all racial groups responding to the survey, the reported religious service attendance was, for the most part, more frequent for children in

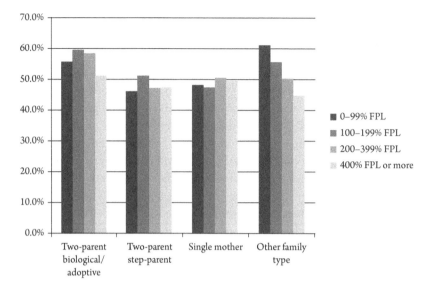

Figure 8.1 WEEKLY RELIGIOUS SERVICE ATTENDANCE BY INCOME AND
FAMILY TYPE. National Survey of Children's Health, NSCH 2007. Maternal and Child Health
Bureau in collaboration with the National Center for Health Statistics. Technical Assistance provided by
the Data Resource Center for Child and Adolescent Health, Child and Adolescent Health Measurement
Initiative, www.childhealthdata.org.

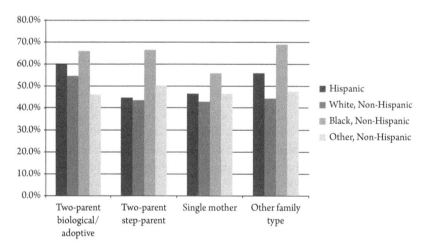

Figure 8.2 WEEKLY RELIGIOUS SERVICE ATTENDANCE BY RACE/ETHNICITY AND
FAMILY TYPE. National Survey of Children's Health, NSCH 2007. Maternal and Child Health
Bureau in collaboration with the National Center for Health Statistics. Technical Assistance provided by
the Data Resource Center for Child and Adolescent Health, Child and Adolescent Health Measurement
Initiative, www.childhealthdata.org.

two-parent biological or adopted families. From these data, one can infer that religious attendance is an important aspect of family life regardless of family structure. In addition to its social benefits, consistent attendance may also be an important means of maintaining structure, orderliness, and family routines. In addition, religious practice has important coping properties and is considered an active approach used as a means to preserve culture, family values, and identity (Roesch et al, 2010).

Notably, the Black church is perceived as the one arena in which African Americans have been able to maintain their cultural traditions in the face of social ostracism, economic deprivation, and political marginality (Peterson, 1990). In Peterson's review of the culture of African American women, they discuss the organization and structure of various churches in the Black community and discuss how these structures allow not only for religious devotion but for the development of leadership skills and the promotion of civic and collective responsibility (Peterson, 1990).

To understand their role in a cultural group's ability to adapt to adversity, it is important to examine the distinctions between religious participation or devotion and spirituality. In a systematic literature review on resilience and indigenous spirituality, Fleming and Ledogar (2008) referred to spirituality as the "the intrinsic human capacity for self-transcendence, in which the self is embedded in something greater than the self, including the sacred," and which motivates "the search for connectedness, meaning, purpose, and contribution"; whereas being religious is defined as "one's relationship with a particular faith tradition or doctrine about a divine other or supernatural power" (Fleming & Ledogar, 2008, p. 49). The motivational properties of spirituality combined with cultural practices may be more protective against the negative effects of acculturative processes and other stressors than religious devotion alone. For indigenous people, spirituality rooted in a cultural framework has been associated with fewer mental health problems, issues with substance abuse, and other behavioral health concerns. An important point that Fleming and Ledogar raise is that the mechanisms of spirituality among indigenous people need to be better understood. More importantly, the researchers admonish that, in treatment and preventive intervention efforts, indigenous spirituality should not be perceived as an antidote to pathologies, but rather as a resource for navigating life and for transcending life's circumstances. Moreover, American Indians view the spiritual and physical beings as inextricably interconnected and foundational to having balance and harmony within and among one's spiritual, relational, emotional, mental, and physical dimensions (Bigfoot, 2010).

For Latina populations, spirituality and adaptation seem to go hand in hand. In my interview with "Ramona," an education coordinator in a local intervention program for immigrant women, spirituality was discussed as a source of resilience:

> I think spirituality plays a huge part in their resiliency. There's this beautiful sentiment in Spanish where everything is in God's hands. So if I say I'll see you tomorrow, your response is "it's in God's hands" and "it's if God allows it." If

God allows it...I'll say over the weekend, "See you on Monday" and "it's if God allows it." My life and my whole being is in God's hands. There is this incredible sense of hope that God is always with me in the worst times in life and the abso- lute best, and God has seen me through. Probably more that God has gotten me here to this spot. Probably without realizing that there's so much within yourself that's gotten you here.

In examining positive outcomes among African Americans, Mattis and colleagues (2003) explored the relationships among social support, everyday racism, religios- ity, and spirituality and dispositional optimism. They found subjective spirituality and relationship with God to be positively correlated with optimism. Notably, an individual's perception of a supportive and loving relationship with God was the sole religiosity variable to emerge as a predictor of optimism (Mattis et al., 2003).

Finally, Spencer (2003) outlined a culturally informed ecological model that includes spirituality and coping as central tenets. Her model, called the Phenomenological Variant of Ecological Systems Theory (PVEST), underscores the importance of including religion, spirituality, and cultural pride as central to developing one's own healthy self-concept and one's sense of self in relation to oth- ers. Using this model as an organizing framework, Spencer (2003) explicitly asked African American youth to indicate whether religion is an important part of a per- son's life, and whether a belief in God can help a person cope through tough life struggles. Her findings showed religion and spirituality to be significantly related to perceived emotional well-being, good feelings about the future, and feeling valued by others. For boys especially, endorsing the importance of religion and spirituality was associated with perceived positive emotional well-being, feeling more valued by others, having more positive feelings about the future, and perceived popular- ity with peers. However, a different set of findings were obtained for the girls in her study. The importance of religion and spirituality was endorsed along with the importance of teaching Black pride. These two values were each significantly related to feeling valued by others. However, these were not related to perceived relation- ship with peers, perceived emotional well-being, or feeling positive about the future, as was the case with the boys. Spencer explained that the different findings for boys and girls may mean that youth engage in different processes of "meaning making" and thus may derive different benefits from the same socialization opportunities. Nonetheless, it appears that spirituality does play an important role in youth's sense of value and worth to self and others.

Racial Socialization and Cultural Identity

In Chapter 4, I discussed parents' socialization practices, defined as the ways that parents transmit to children their values, view of the world, and perceptions regarding their "place" in society in relation to others. I revisit socialization in this chapter, focusing this time on cultural and racial-ethnic socialization—the ways in which parents, and other significant adults in children's lives, transmit information regarding race, ethnicity, and culture as a means of coping and managing the challenges of racial-ethnic discrimination (Hughes, 2003; Hughes et al., 2006).

In addition to experiencing the profound difficulties associated with financial insecurity, disadvantaged families belonging to racial minority groups also experience the stresses of discrimination and perceived threats to their cultural practices and values (Mattis, Fontenot, & Hatcher-Kay, 2003; Scott, 2003). Challenges associated with disadvantage are compounded with these psychological stressors, affecting family functions and exacerbating the risks of poor outcomes for children and adolescents (Brody, Stoneman, & Flor, 1996). However, cultural identity and racial socialization practices within cultural groups have been linked to adaptive behavior and positive outcomes for youth. For example, Hughes and colleagues (2006) reviewed the literature on parents' racial socialization practices to elucidate how families experience and discuss social inequalities and injustices and how they teach children to cope with these challenges. They organize the empirical literature into four categories: cultural socialization, preparation for bias, promotion of mistrust, and egalitarianism. *Cultural socialization* refers to parental practices that teach children about their racial or ethnic heritage and history, promoting cultural, racial, and ethnic pride either deliberately or implicitly (Hughes et al., 2006). These practices include having cultural artifacts in the home, storytelling and oral traditions, wearing of ethnic clothing, eating ethnic meals, and speaking in a native language or cultural dialect, as well as cultural celebrations that perpetuate and reinforce cultural values (Hughes et al., 2006; Gaylord-Harden, Burrow, & Cunningham, 2012; Neblett, Rivas-Drake, & Umaña -Taylor, 2012). These types of socialization practices foster self-esteem in children, as well as a strong racial and ethnic identity. They also promote the use of culturally informed coping strategies that help children interpret and reframe negative messages received about their racial or ethnic group. Most importantly, these practices and associated coping strategies may reduce the psychological distress resulting from discriminatory practices and diminish the likelihood of youth turning to antisocial peer groups or substance abuse to cope with the stress of discrimination (Gaylord-Harden, Burrow, & Cunningham, 2012). In contexts where children may not learn these socialization practices from their nuclear family, it may be possible for community elders, extended family members, churches, natural and formal mentors, and even charter schools that have adopted cultural themes to provide such experiences and to encourage culturally relevant coping strategies. The other socialization practices categorized by Hughes and colleagues—*preparation for bias* (explicit discussions with children about discrimination), *promotion of mistrust* (cautions or warnings about barriers to success), and *egalitarianism* (valuing individual qualities rather than racial group membership and silence about race)—together help to engender a sense of self-worth and cultural awareness among youth.

Cultural identity is also regarded as a protective factor for youth, fortifying them against negative themes about their cultural group and conferring a sense of meaning, purpose, and positive adjustment (Wexler, 2009). Also referred to as racial identity (Neblett et al., 2012; Gaylord-Harden et al., 2012), this protective factor encompasses the attitudes and behaviors that define the significance of race and ethnicity in the lives of youth, as well as the meaning and value they assign to being a member of a particular group.

Gaylord-Harden and colleagues (2012) reported findings suggesting that youth with high levels of racial identity and cultural pride are buffered from the ill effects of discrimination—especially as related to depressive symptoms, perceived stress, psychological distress, academic performance, and motivation. This racial identity is largely a result of parental socialization practices, but it can be developed through other means. For example, my interview with Ashante revealed that cultural identity was the motivating factor for turning his life around. While in jail, he read a book that illuminated his misconceptions about race and his value as an African American male:

> *Everything I was experiencing in gangs, drugs, and all these other things was only a [point] on the timeline of the African narrative. After I understood this, it was like wow, I can't go out and do the same things I always did because I know something now.*
>
> *I understand that when I look in the mirror I'm a physical representation of that African continuity....My world view is my inner understanding reflected outward. I have a sense of peace and a calm and I have a functional understanding of being black. I don't do those things that will be self-destructive to my people. [I] utilize my gifts to help them, instead of utilizing my talents for destruction or to bring shame upon us. That's the thing that a lot of us people in the inner city don't understand because when you're ignorant the only thing you have is your ignorance, so when someone challenges your ignorance, you become violent because it's the only thing you have that's tangible for you to hold on to. When someone challenges that, there are consequences.*

Thus, the process of learning about one's culture is an important resilience factor, especially during middle childhood when youth are becoming aware of cultural differences and their attitudes and perspectives about such differences are being shaped. Zimmerman and colleagues (1998) underscored this point for American Indian children, indicating that cultural identification has positive developmental effects through enhanced self-esteem and conformity to cultural community norms.

Cultural Perspectives on Coping and Resilience

Ungar (2008) studied resilience across cultures and argued that current research is lacking in sensitivity to community and cultural factors. These factors contextualize how resilience is defined by different populations and manifested in everyday practices. The ways that cultural groups respond and adapt to adversity may differ between groups, and their definitions of adversity may differ as well. Along these lines, Clauss-Ehlers and Levi (2002) put forward the term "cultural resilience" to describe the degree to which the strengths of one's culture promote the development of coping. Cultural resilience includes the norms, family structure, and peer relationships of a particular group. In later work, Clauss-Ehlers (2008) concludes that cultural resilience is associated with positive outcomes despite risk status, sustained competence under stress, and recovery from trauma. Examining cultural factors that promote resilience is critically important for understanding the unique processes of adaptation in various groups. This idea is captured in Ramona's description of immigrant women served in her training program and the determination these women have to succeed:

> The women that come here already come with enormous sense of resilience. The word resilience has stuck out over the years. They are alone, isolated, and traumatized. These women have been through so much. Their families have too. It's been generation after generation. But it's their own human psyche that builds resilience from within. There's a great word in Spanish that we use. The word is "coraje." It kinda means this inner like brutal strength that a woman has. She has this really hard, determined "I'm gonna do anything it takes it survive and I'll do what it takes to look after my kids. I've done everything I've had to do to survive. I'm not going to sit in a corner and let you beat me up. I'm not gonna sit in a corner and mistreat my kids or let my kids see that I'm being mistreated. My friends are telling me that the way to get out of this is to go learn English. If I learn English and I really give it a chance that's gonna let me get a job."
>
> They have dreams just like the rest of us. They wanna go to school, they wanna be a nurse, they want to be a psychologist, they want to be a home health aide and it's beautiful. In six months to a year … they're telling me I didn't really think this of myself. And I think they did. It was in them. It was in them that this is what they wanted to do. They're the ones that got themselves here.

It is important to note that Snyder (1994), asserted that hope, as he defined it, is most important for people such as minority adolescents in urban environments, who live in unpredictable, uncontrollable circumstances. As further pointed out by Roesch et al. (2010), these obstacles could potentially be perceived as opportunities for many ethnic minority groups, as reflected in the interview excerpt above.

Scheier and Carver (1992) put forward the idea that people's actions are greatly influenced by their expectations about the consequences of those actions. When people believe that their goals are attainable, they experience positive affect ranging from pride to gratitude and even happiness, depending upon the reasons underlying the expected outcome (Scheier & Carver, 1992). This positive affect may generate effective coping strategies and a sense of personal agency to accomplish those goals. However, cultural groups challenged by discrimination and structural inequality might be less likely to see their goals as attainable. Their actions could appear maladaptive if examined without an understanding of how context and culture interact to influence the resultant coping strategies.

Toward that end, many researchers have studied the varied ways in which people cope with stressful situations (Scheier, Weintraub, & Carver, 1986; McKernon et al., 2001; Lapierre & Allen, 2006; Folkman & Lazarus, 1980). *Problem-focused coping*, discussed earlier in this chapter, has the goal of removing or circumventing the source of the stress. These stressors are deemed to be within an individual's realm of control. Another approach, *emotion-focused coping*, is theorized to reduce or eliminate the emotional distress associated with an adverse circumstance. While problem-focused and emotion-focused coping can co-occur in stressful situations, problem-focused coping is more likely to be applied in situations in which the individual believes something constructive can be done about the stressor (Scheier, Weintraub, & Carver, 1986). In contrast, emotion-focused coping is more likely when people believe that an adverse situation occurring at the greater societal level is something that must be endured. This type of coping may be inherent in cultural groups that have endured historical oppression, racial prejudice, and other challenges stemming from larger societal values. It may be that the strategies deemed most effective by these cultural groups are those allowing them to maintain a sense of cultural integrity despite the presence of seemingly intractable challenges. LaFromboise (2006) referenced a sentiment expressed by a Native American elder on the meaning of resilience and how Native people have traditionally coped with adversity:

> The closest translation of "resilience" is a sacred word that means "resistance"…resisting bad thoughts, bad behaviors. We accept what life gives us, good and bad, as gifts from the Creator. We try to get through hard times, stressful times, with a good heart. The gift [of adversity] is the lesson we learn from overcoming it. (Graham, 2001, cited in LaFromboise, 2006, p. 1)

Cultural Traditions and Practices

Cultural practices and traditions reflect the values, goals, and ideals of a group, its heritage, and its priorities for the future. At the heart of American Indian culture is the value and centrality of children (Bigfoot & Schmidt, 2010). A practice that reflects this value is the naming ceremony as a child is born. As explained in my interview with an American Indian scholar and practitioner to whom I refer as "Sarah," this naming ceremony is an affirming process and places children at the center of the community's hope for the future:

> **Sarah:** *I heard my elders pray for me. In fact I still hear my elders pray for me. If you hear people pray for you and you know those parents, grandparents, great-grandparents, great-great-grandparents—all these people praying for you and know that they anticipated your time here on this earth. And that it was an event that occurred on a regular basis to have someone pray for you and to call you by name. The naming is very important—so using the name and to have someone pray for you, and to have it done generation after generation after generation. So, you do things for more than just your generation. This is where the concept of the seventh generation comes in. You're always a seventh generation person. You think seven generations ahead of you and seven generations behind you. Each generation thinks back. Fourteen generations are there and you think about it. The idea that you do something because it is bigger than you. Because of that, then there's that hope. It's a byproduct of that understanding. That you're part of the multiple circles. By having circles overlapping and interlapping, then there's strength in that. You're doing things that generations that have come before you have done. You're stepping into a circle that's been reinforced by that.*
>
> **Interviewer:** *It seems that these ideas are inculcated in families because it is a part of your ways of being and engaging. Do you expect that there is a forward-looking hope and that you are bringing with you all of the goodwill and blessings of generations that have come before you?*
>
> **Sarah:** *In essence, yes, but also there's generosity, honor, and respect, and patience— all of the principles that go along with that. Most tribes have the concept of the circle and those things that are part of that circle and principles that go along with the teachings.*
>
> **Interviewer:** *The circle signifies unbrokenness. The child is at the heart of a community's ways of being and so child-centeredness is not just a slogan, but a way of life....*
>
> **Sarah:** *Well, if you think of it as the child being the center of the circle—because of the concentric nature of the circle, the total environment is stronger because of it. There's not just one circle but multiple circles. The child is at the center of the circle. It makes an amazing difference in their life. It is affirming to a child to know that they're in the center of generations of support. However, if you take that understanding and take those circles and put big gaps in it because of past injustices, disease, and other things like alcoholism and removal—that's what we're dealing with in our families today. Our hope is in rebuilding so that we can have those circles reconnecting for all children. Our children are in dire straits and that is my work. We need to be able to help our tribal communities reconnect.*

> *The understanding that we have, that children are the center of the circle and that they can continue to be the center. That is the hope—that children can continue to be the center of the circle. [There are] Lots of prophecies about children but it is primarily that "we would return back to teachings that would allow our children to know that they are the center of the circle."*
>
> **Interviewer:** *What do families do in their day-to-day lives that move toward closing this gap?*
>
> **Sarah:** *Various efforts. We're a young population: 50% [are] less than 21 years of age. Adults available to do that for children are limited. Very poor population. Within the capabilities of parents available, there is that attempt—and some parents are successful. High number [of] parents who are teen mothers—they haven't learned those kinds of parenting strategies yet. By the time they get to be grandmothers they might know that, but then we lose a whole generation.... We have gaps and there's an effort with different programs to bridge these gaps, but we have a lot work to do."*

As children come of age, it is important for them to understand and be able to articulate their cultural values and ways of transmitting those values. During middle childhood and emerging adolescence, youth seek to make meaning out of the world they live in; their identities are being formed based on their daily interactions with adults and others in their environment. The time of coming of age is especially important for youth from historically marginalized groups, for whom the strengths and benefits of their traditions and values may be poorly depicted in classrooms and through popular media (Gutiérrez & Rogoff, 2003; Spencer, Fegley, & Harpalani, 2003). As we learned from "Sarah," the benefits of participating in and embracing various cultural traditions include promoting psychological health and well-being and preventing youth from engaging in such health-risk behaviors as substance abuse.

Beauvais (2000) noted, regarding American Indian youth, that adherence to traditional values and pride in one's culture provide a foundation for adolescents as they attempt to take advantage of the strengths of their culture and to blend and connect those strengths with the opportunities of the larger society. Interventions that incorporate cultural values and practices are likely to be perceived more favorably, and the basic components are likely to be adhered to—increasing the likelihood of achieving positive outcomes. Thus, interventionists must be culturally informed, and interventions must be aligned with specific values in order to achieve maximum benefits (Kenyon & Hanson, 2012).

Bigfoot and Schmidt (2010) describe a therapeutic intervention model called *Honoring Children, Mending the Circle* (HC-MC) that reflects the values of American Indian culture. HC-MC has adopted core constructs based on American Indian/ Alaska Native (AI/AN) worldviews: (a) all things are interconnected, (b) all things have a spiritual nature, and (c) existence is dynamic. Central to wellness and healing is the core AI/AN belief that all things, human and earth, have a spiritual nature. The framework for HC-MC is the circle and, according to Bigfoot and Schmidt, the circle is a sacred symbol that has long been used to understand the world. Its symbolism is found in old wisdom transmitted in oral stories, carved into rock formations, sculpted in wood or clay, woven into reed baskets, or painted in colored sand. The circle places spirituality at the core of the individual, and this serves as the foundation for other dimensions of the therapeutic process (Bigfoot & Schmidt, 2010). An example of a spiritual practice that might be used in this intervention is "smudging," a way to cleanse a person, a place, or an object of negative energies, spirits, or influences. Smudging involves the burning of sacred plants and, then, either passing an object through the resulting smoke or fanning the smoke around a person or place (Sanchez-Way & Johnson, 2000).

Children and families are also central in Hispanic and Latin American cultures. Researchers use the term "familism" to describe the centrality of family and family support systems among these groups of people (Sabogal et al., 1987; Schwartz, 2007; LiGrining, 2012). Familism is characterized as a strong identification and attachment of individuals with their families, both nuclear and extended. Essential to this identification are strong feelings of loyalty, reciprocity, and solidarity, making the family a core source of strength, a mechanism for adaptation and resilience, and a buffer against the challenges of acculturation. Moreover, familism emphasizes mutual support and interdependence among members of the family, making it an important adaptive mechanism for these groups (Sabogal et al., 1987; Schwartz, 2007; Li-Grining, 2012). Decades of research have examined ways in which these families protect their members against external physical and emotional stressors, thereby serving as a natural support system that promotes positive mental and emotional health outcomes (Sabogal et al., 1987). In their study of the effects of acculturation on various Hispanic groups (Mexican, Central, and Cuban Americans), Sabogal and colleagues differentiated between the attitudinal aspects of families (beliefs, emotions, feelings) and the behavioral aspects (how individuals act on these beliefs and feelings). Such behaviors, as measured in their study, include a willingness to make sacrifices to guarantee a good education for children and to provide economic support for younger siblings; to consult close relatives on important decisions; to protect and provide for aging parents; to share the home environment with relatives if needed; and to be available to relatives when problems occur.

The findings of their work revealed that the attitudes and behavioral aspects of familism, especially among first-generation immigrants, did not change significantly as they acculturated to mainstream culture in the United States. In fact, the strong sense of solidarity helped to make the acculturation process emotionally manageable, in the sense that families could prepare each other for the possible pitfalls and challenges. Interestingly, perceived support from families, a core component of familism, remained strong across the various groups studied. The reassurance that family is available to solve problems and provide support is protective and helps families to cope with other uncertainties over which they have less control (Sabogal et al., 1987).

These results have been confirmed in contemporary studies as well, showing that familism has an influential role in child outcomes such as self-regulation and prosocial behavior among preschool-aged children in low-income families (Li-Grining, 2012). Familism is believed to moderate the link between parents' warmth and preschoolers' emotional adjustment, in that expressions of warmth may be especially meaningful for children in the context of homes where there are poverty-related risks. The close ties and interdependence of family members may buffer against these risks by allowing children to experience broad-based emotional support (Roosa et al., 2011, cited in LiGrining, 2012).

The principles and basic tenets of familism are also evident among non-Hispanic Black families, including African Americans as well as Caribbean immigrants to the United States. Concepts such as familial honor, respect for familial elders, and familial interdependence (Lugo Steidel & Contreras, 2003) are observed broadly across these cultures and may represent the same type of values in these groups that familism represents in Hispanic and Latin American cultures. For example, the terms "collectivism" or "communalism" are often used to describe the preferences for interdependence over individualism among people of African descent (Boykin, Jagers, Ellison, & Albury, 1997; Schwartz, 2007). These values factor well into the notion of familism. In earlier chapters, the extended family is discussed as a strength for many economically disadvantaged African American families. Aside from its value in terms of providing important social and even financial resources for parents, it may also reflect a fundamental belief in collectivist ways of being.

Schwartz (2007), in a preliminary study, examined the extent to which familism and related concepts were present in non-Hispanic groups. While some differences were observed, Schwartz's findings noted strong correlations on measures that represent respect for and deference to family members and other authority figures, suggesting that familism may indeed take similar forms in both Hispanic and non-Hispanic groups.

In later work, Schwartz and colleagues (2010) examined these concepts more closely to determine the extent to which these collectivist and interdependent factors may be related to psychosocial functioning. Black participants in their study scored highest on communalism and other indices of the primacy of family and family relationships. The researchers noted that collectivist value systems are more strongly observed among African Americans and immigrant Blacks who may acculturate to an African American belief system because of their experiences of historical and structural racism purported to lead to dissolution of the family unit. Cultural practices such as family reunions and Sunday dinners are thought to be outgrowths of these experiences and are a means of promoting family unity and fostering well-being (Dodson & Gilkes, 1995; Sutton, 2004).

However, Schwartz and colleagues (2010) pointed out that putting others, particularly family, before oneself may also be associated with some distress—due to the fact that the United States is a highly individualistic society and promotes values conflicting with those of collectivism and communalism. This may cause some discord within cultural groups as family members strive to adopt American values and live up to American cultural expectations. In addition, this discord may have implications beyond the family context that affect community collective efficacy as well as a community's capacity to leverage its human and material assets. Ashante provides his perspective on this issue:

> Blacks in key positions of power want to emulate White society. They want to be a part of White aristocracy. If they wanted to be a part of something that's Black, they should have reinvested in institutions. There is a narrative that you get paid and you're out of the inner city. Why not stay? But if you leave, [you should] create institutions as an anchor [for your community]. People from the inner city want to see their own make it. [Their] triumphs are something that we can look back and be intoxicated over. However, when [they] take [their] accomplishments as being [their] own [without acknowledging collective inputs], we turn our backs on [them].

Ashante's reflections underscore the importance of a collectivist or interdependent perspective as a strength among cultural groups in helping them overcome adversity. Collective effort among cultural groups can be a source for achieving goals, thereby fostering hope and promoting resilience for individuals and members of the community as whole.

Why Culture Matters

What we learn from insights shared in this chapter is that culture matters. It matters in terms of maintaining the integrity of the heritage of oppressed people, and it matters in terms of its power to transform a life, as we saw with Ashante. The strengths of a culture, such as its focus on spirituality and religion, allow a group to transcend the difficult circumstances of daily life and make meaning out of their situation. Ramona's reflection on the women she serves in her program at The Family Place is an example of the journey toward transcendence. Taken together, strengths and assets that individuals draw upon to manage the day-to-day complexities of their lives are best understood in cultural contexts. From the ways in which parents socialize their children and prepare them to live in the larger society, to family structure and collectivist values—all are influenced by cultural frames of reference. These frames of reference inform the ways in which groups reinterpret adverse situations, giving insight into the particular coping strategies used to overcome adversity.

I recently attended a special viewing of a documentary on the aftermath of the Haiti earthquake of 2010. The filmmaker was careful to allow the authentic voices of people of the affected community to be heard. When the filmmaker asked what it was that allowed the Haitian people to be resilient, their spirituality was the unequivocal response. While formal religion was certainly a critical element of resilience, respondents suggested that by spirituality they referred to the greater good: that there was a greater purpose, even for their suffering, that gave meaning to their suffering, even if that meaning was not readily apparent or understood. *Coraje* is the term that describes how the Latina women served in Ramona's program persevere and strive toward self-actualization. This term has broad applicability to other cultural group experiences as well—especially those with a history of marginalization and oppression. It is the strength of that faith and the belief that there is meaning in a horrific event that will ultimately allow the culture to rebuild, to move beyond mere survival, and to thrive.

Thus, intervention programs must utilize a culturally informed framework as they target specific groups. Honoring traditions and practices, these efforts must aim toward transformation and transcendence rather than remediation. Cultural assets and strengths such as spirituality, racial identity, and familism are useful starting points for building effective programs. Policies must also be culturally appropriate and sensitive to family structure and functioning—allowing families to stay intact as they receive support and services. Sarah's reflections on her culture's naming ceremony remind us why this is important. Children need to be affirmed and valued. Most importantly, they need to know that through our programs and policies, through our words and deeds, they are in the center of our world.

Moreover, as the collectivist or interdependent perspective is often preferred over the individualist view of overcoming the odds, interventions and policies that draw on the wisdom and support of community members and elders may foster better adherence to treatment and program implementation. In addition, having this type of involvement may engender positive emotion among community members and, in so doing, foster confidence and personal agency—allowing members to strive toward their goals and achieve success.

9

Hope in Action

*Case Studies of Motivation, Overcoming,
and Striving toward Well-Being*

> *Real life is not always going to be perfect or go our way, but the recurring
> acknowledgment of what is working in our lives can help us not only survive
> but surmount our difficulties.*
> —Sarah Ban Breathnach, *Simple Abundance* (2008)

I started this volume by introducing family members who have experienced adversity associated with economic disadvantage, and throughout the chapters I've shared their insights along with the insights of the professionals who work with them. While each of the families highlighted has had life experiences that reflect their strengths and assets, their continued struggles remind us that, even when progress is made and some success is achieved, support is still needed to ensure that this progress is sustained. For some individuals, keeping the family together was paramount; for others, maintaining a responsible distance from the family helped them to overcome issues of chaos and dysfunction.

The stories told by each of these families represent the complexities of their lives and the challenges associated with progressing toward success as they have defined it. The lessons learned through their experiences carry very strong implications for designing programs and implementing policies that support families—not only when they are struggling but also as they cross the many thresholds of opportunity and success on the journey toward achieving their full potential. So, in this chapter I'll revisit their stories and frame them as case studies of a particular theme. I'll discuss the elements of their individual journeys in light of the important factors related to hope, optimism, and resilience to understand the processes by which individuals strive toward a state of well-being. I will also describe the research-based elements of the programs that helped to transform their lives and will discuss the necessary resources and support for building skills and competencies to manage and overcome challenges.

Case Studies of Hope in Action

Each of the individuals discussed in this section is at a different place in their journey—some continue to strive for personal success while others, at least at the time of interview, have reached a place of contentment. Nonetheless, their experiences reflect the motivational aspects of hope. As well, they have all shown resilience and are all on their personal journeys toward self-actualization.

The Case for Cultural Identity

"There is a progressive narrative for us. You have to keep perfecting."
—Ashante

Recall my earlier introduction of Ashante. His story sheds light on the power of education and cultural identity to transform a life. His case is an example of the personal awareness that can result from self-reflection and natural mentoring. Notable in this interview is that Ashante defines success as preparing himself academically so that he can focus on the greater good for his community. Having a goal, or even a mission that elevates him from the day-to-day challenges of life, appears to be a potent and motivational force:

> **Interviewer:** *How do you define success?*
> **Ashante:** *Now, success has been coming to graduate school. Being able to obtain education. I know it sounds corny but an individual doesn't understand how those in the inner city are just functioning. How we just exist. It wasn't until I became aware of my cultural identity that I understood how I was misled, how I didn't understand who I was, where I was, and how I got where I was; how I'm living up north and talk with a southern accent and all these other things.*
> **Interviewer:** *What was a motivating or defining factor for you?*
> **Ashante:** *I was in jail. I read a book and, after reading this book, it's like when you watch TV and a movie and you see someone has a revelation or aha moment and you see your whole life flash in front of your eyes that everything I was experiencing in gangs, drugs, and all these other things was only an inkling on the timeline of the African narrative. After I understood this it was like, wow! I can't go out and do the same things I always did because I know something now.*
>
> *From grades 1–5, I was in a gifted school, then I went to junior high in a school in my neighborhood, because my mother she had got on drugs by that time. Instead of sending me to a junior high that was the next level up from the gifted school, she sent me to one in my neighborhood. I can honestly say that was when*

everything changed. That's when I started seeing how the police imposed their will upon everything we did. I would [walk] down the street and we would be stopped. I started seeing drug dealers. I saw everything. Like they say, our parents try to cloak this world up, but in my world the cloak came down sooner for me than it did for a lot of other people.

My mother always sent me to summer school. No matter what, I went to school year round. But she never told me why. I believe if my mother would have told me her motives some of the time—why... You should tell a kid why you're doing something. Cause we live in a society that says fun, fun, fun. So if it's not fun, we don't want to do it. A lot of parents don't tell the kids that. But if you say that the reason I'm sending you to this school is because you're more intelligent than a lot of people you be around. In order for you to have anything in life or to be the best you can be, you need to go to school. School doesn't change you, it refines you. And helps build the qualities you already have 'cause you're a great person. A lot of parents, we don't tell our kids that. We don't tell them our true history. That's where we failing at.

Interviewer: *What continues to be a challenge?*

Ashante: There is a narrative that you get paid and you're out of the inner city. Why not stay?—If you leave, create institutions as an anchor. People from the inner city want to see their own make it. Your triumphs are something that we can look back and be intoxicated over. However, when you take your accomplishments as being your own, we turn our backs on you. That's one of [the] things I do is stay connected.

Interviewer: *What helped you overcome?*

Ashante: Faith and a vision. I see myself happy at the end of some of these doors. I'm constantly walking through opening doors, I'm opening doors. Just keep opening doors. They're all like transparent and they're like glass and at the end I'm happy and I'm waving at myself. I just keep walking and opening doors.

Interviewer: *What hopeful lessons did you learn? What would you tell other young people?*

Ashante: I would let them know that money is not a source, it's a resource. The things that really do matter are the things that are of value, are those things you create yourself. The good name you have, the family that you have, honor that you have, the respect that you have.

It's easy to be destructive, it's easy to be angry, it's easy to lash out. Most of the times, individuals that lash out and are overly aggressive have lots of stuff to say, but they can't convey it themselves.

Everybody's tough. I know people that's dead—that died tough. I know people that are locked up that are tough. Being tough doesn't make you smart. Be happy to be who you are. Me, I'm more content with being myself. 'Cause I can't wake up thinking about being someone else. Thanking God that I'm awake and I can go on into the world to do my endeavors.

The all-too-familiar story of Ashante's early life provides a window into the lives of children and youth who may be following the same path on which he started his life. A child reared in a single-parent-headed household in the inner city, enticed by the temptations of street life and violence, Ashante did what others in his situation did—he sold drugs and participated in the violent gang culture of the streets. To survive meant taking extraordinary risks with his life and the lives of others. By the time Ashante was 15 years old he had spent time in the juvenile justice system and later, at 18, was arrested for drug possession. By age 21, he found himself serving a five-year sentence for sale and distribution of cocaine. The sociological research describes the life trajectories of individuals with similar experiences and underscores the deleterious impact of such experiences. What is less well-documented are the turning points for youth and how they manage to chart out new pathways leading toward more productive lives. As Ashante described in his interview, an experience with a natural mentor in jail marked a turning point for him and the first steps toward a more fulfilling life. He was first introduced to a book titled *The Destruction of Black Civilization: Great Issues of Race from 4500 B.C. to 2000 A.D.,* by Chancellor James Williams. The book focuses on the history of Africans on the African continent, as well as peoples of African descent in the United States and in the African Diaspora. Reading this and other volumes gave Ashante insight into his cultural heritage and helped him develop a cultural identity that led him to earn his high school equivalency diploma while incarcerated and to pursue graduate education and training in African American studies. There was no direct path from jail to college. Ashante entered a community re-entry program that served to provide motivation and accountability (Won, 2011). Re-entry programs that are successful provide mutual benefits—to the formerly incarcerated in terms of educational and vocational retraining, and to the family and community in terms of equipping these individuals with the self-regulatory skills and competencies to contribute to society. Solomon and colleagues (2004) described programs that focused on six core competencies for having success in re-entering the community. These competencies are (1) education and employment, (2) health, (3) housing, (4) family, (5) public safety, and (6) faith. For youth dealing with the consequences of their troubled pasts, these kinds of competencies are essential in helping them gain the skills necessary to prevent recidivism and to have the accountability structures and social support to guide them in the process of transitioning into the broader society.

While cultural identity is obviously not included in community re-entry goals, Ashante was afforded the opportunity to attend college, where he was able to distance himself from the temptations of the streets and minimize the chances of recidivism. The opportunity to learn, in conjunction with caring individuals that guided and challenged him, was an important hallmark of Ashante's transformation.

The Case of the Family That Stays Together

"I thought this is the worst thing that happened to me, but it turned out to be the best thing."

—Josephine

Josephine's wisdom and insights underscore the importance of recognizing the family bond as an asset that should be neither overlooked nor discounted. Rather, it should be valued as a means of inter- and intrapersonal support and strength that families can draw upon, even during their most desperate times. In this case study, assets such as family cohesion and social networks are evident. In addition, elements of both personal and parenting efficacy as well as self-concept will be revealed in Josephine's description of what it felt like for her to have to relocate her family. Despite the challenges Josephine recalls in her interview, a sense of optimism is evident throughout her experiences. While her children were not interviewed for this case study, Josephine's optimism played a role in her ability to adapt and in the ability of her children to adapt to these difficult circumstances. A spiritual strength is clearly evident and, as discussed in the previous chapter, may have contributed to the optimistic outlook as well as the determination to change her circumstances so that she could provide for her children:

> **Interviewer:** *How do you define success?*
> **Josephine:** *One of the things I know from firsthand experience is that when you think everything is gone and when you don't have things and places to live and all of that, if the family can be together then, there's hope. Because the worst thing about being homeless and being all this is that your children are in one place and you're someplace else. The things you did on a natural day-to-day you can't do. Because that structure is no longer there—it's fractured, and so all of a sudden you don't know what you're going to do. You can't plan, you can't dream, you can't think about your future, because all you can focus on is day-to-day, how am I going to make it.*
> **Interviewer:** *What was a motivating factor?*
> **Josephine:** *I came through the shelter system ... We were staying at the hotel and you had to go out every day and take your children. I had five children. I was dragging them down the street because you couldn't stay in. You had to go out in the daytime. I thought that was the worst time in my life. I used to live uptown. Uptown was who I was. Uptown I was respectable. I could accomplish things. I'm working, I've always worked. When I came downtown, I was like ... I want to go back uptown! My identity was tied to where I was. So, you think your house is who you are. That it defines you. You think what you have is who you are. The reality is that people look at you based on who they think you are. I was living in a house before and that's how we wound up being homeless. They said the*

children couldn't be in the house without water. So I finally decided that I couldn't stay there any longer because they were threatening me, so my children couldn't come there at all. It was during the holidays when I came into the shelter. That was really, really discouraging. So I had a lot of thoughts. I felt bad about who I was. I didn't think I was a good mother. I even thought about suicide. But the reason I didn't [was] because I kept thinking, "Who was going to take care of my children? If the world was so cruel to me, what's gonna happen to my children without me?"

Interviewer: *What was (or continues to be) a challenge for you?*

Josephine: *The program helped me with the budget—I hated it at the time. I would ask "How am I going to have a budget when I don't have enough money?" It made me aware of bills. When I pay my bills my emotions were affected. If I couldn't pay bills or feed my children, I felt like I wasn't a good mother. They helped me to prioritize and to understand the importance of having a budget. I purchased a home after that and lost it. The house is not who you are. They gave me what I needed. I was able to go to college. They gave me what I needed to feel that I first had value to myself and then I was valuable to those that I was related to. I always was intelligent, but I never thought I was that smart. I was book smart but I knew nothing about life. I was very naive to life, but coming through the program helped me to understand the world around me and who I was and my purpose in life. It carried me because the most important thing was my family. Because I was able to have my family together and keep my family together, some of the things that I learned I could carry through.*

Interviewer: *What helps/helped you overcome or better manage your situation?*

Josephine: *When I came into the system again, it allowed me to have that structure. Allowed [my children] to go to bed on a regular basis, to go to school every day. I remember somebody asked me: "How do [you] get your children to go to school every day?" I thought that was the weirdest question. I go to work every day, so they go to school every day. People think differently, based on what they think where you are. Because you're homeless, you don't have values, you don't have structure. But a lot of our families do.*

Being in the shelter is something that happened to you—not who you are. The thing I liked about being in transitional housing is that it allowed me to be who I was. I was able to dream and able to pursue those things—a home and school— and continue to keep my family together and get the help I need to go forward. I met friends through the program. I connected with the people who were here. I still connect even after I moved on. We talked and met and communicated after that. It helped me to understand community, and you take that with you and then you can impart that to others...

Interviewer: *What hopeful lessons did you learn?*

Josephine: *Even though there are things that people have done to you, there is a certain amount of responsibility and accountability you have to take for the rest* *of your life, even though bad things have happened and it was horrible that it happened to you. But what are your choices? Do you stay there with the burden of that or do you make other choices? It is important to help people know that doesn't have to hold you. You can go on, you can begin again, and you can start again. There is life after whatever it is.*

Jeremiah 29:11 says: "For I know the plans I have for you, declares the Lord, plans to prosper you and not to harm you, plans to give you hope and a future." For our families, that's what they're looking for. A hope and a future. A life of peace.

It's helpful because if people don't have hope and if you don't have the ability to dream, then all you're doing is living in the moment, and there's no real life to that.

Life is in expectation and hope and dreams and possibilities. I wrote a poem about the walking wounded, and that's what you have in homelessness. You have people who are wounded and walking and just carrying... just like when we were in that place. We had to carry everything out of there. So what do you do? You have to think of what's important to you. What can I keep with me that I don't want to lose?

A takeaway lesson from Josephine's story is the importance of having access to programs that meet basic needs. Maslow's Hierarchy of Needs was discussed in previous chapters in terms of its relevance to hope and its foundational importance to self-actualization. Programs and policies must provide these basic needs in order to lay the groundwork for developing higher-level skills and competencies. Josephine received services from an organization called Hope and a Home (www.hopeandahome.org), a transitional housing program located in the Northeast. The program provides below-market rental units to homeless and low-income families for up to three years. Once the families are enrolled, the staff works with them to "identify and break down personal and external barriers to success and mentor parents and children as they journey from homelessness to permanent housing, from educational failure to success in school, and from instability to a stable and nurturing family life" (www.hopeandahome.org). The program abides by the principles of a creed that all families learn and recite. This creed is displayed prominently in the brownstone that houses the program.

We come together to celebrate ourselves, our families, our community and our relationship to the God of our understanding. We commit ourselves to:

- *good homes for our families*
- *good health, and education for our children, and*
- *good management of our money toward a secure future.*

We build on our strengths, ask for help when we need it, and offer aid to others when we can.

We know that life can be difficult as well as joyous. We are here to learn from each other, to encourage each other, and to create a brighter future for us all. To these ideals we are committed.

The goals of Hope and a Home state that the program brings an intensive, multifaceted response to address the heart of what is perpetuating poverty with each individual family. Using one-on-one coaching and peer support, parents and children build on their aspirations and strengths to achieve permanent housing, higher education, rewarding work, and valuable connections to their community.

As Josephine pointed out in her interview, families may reside in Hope and a Home housing for up to three years, which affords time to plan and develop strategies that will work over the long term to help families get at the source of the problems that place them at high risk for difficult life circumstances. Because this program is comprehensive and offers a longer stay than some other local programs, children have the opportunity to become established in good schools and parents can build strong social networks, learn to parent their children effectively, and acquire the skills that foster long-lasting change.

During the interview, Josephine and a family coordinator referred to the program's *Keys for Change*. These reflect the guiding principles of Hope and a Home's strategic approach to offering low-income families ways to make lifestyle changes that they can sustain and manage over the long term. One of the Keys for Change, a *safe affordable home for all*, was foundational to Josephine's transformation. The aims of this key are to teach competencies related to having a quality home environment and ways to achieve financial stability, including developing a family budget, paying rent and bills on time, and establishing good credit. The ultimate goal of this Key for Change is that the families move to permanent housing, with coaching, training, and mentoring leading families toward this end. Thus, permanent housing serves as a proxy for financial and emotional stability, adaptation, and problem-solving abilities.

The Case of the Parent-Child Attachment Bond

"Hope is going to lead you and faith is going to lead you to doing better. Just believe in yourself because you're all you got."

—Carlton

Carlton's story reflects drive and motivation. In so many ways, his determination to keep his family together and protect his child from experiencing adversity is tantamount to the personal agency and pathways thinking that underlie theories of hope. Equally important, Carlton's story reveals the multiple and interacting challenges that some individuals strive to overcome. His story demonstrates that achieving economic stability is but one aspect of overcoming adversity. Sometimes the stigma and stereotypes projected by society are more difficult barriers to break down, but an attitude of optimism, perseverance, and personal agency go a long way toward helping individuals adapt and show resilience:

Interviewer: How do you define success?

Carlton: *I can't describe it, but I can tell you I'm proud of myself. I'm not big-headed. I'm glad God put people in my life that helped me along the way. A lot of people say I'm humble because I don't talk a lot and say a lot about where I been. I can say profound things...I'm not big-headed, but I'm not stupid either. I been around. I go outside to talk to the guys on the corner and I can go to a dinner party or I can fit right in.*

I can drive different types of trucks. I've answered phones, I've sat [at] a desk. I've been a janitor, I've done insulation. I've done so many different things and I'm comfortable where I'm at, but there's still more to do. There's still more I need to learn. There's more learning to do.

Interviewer: What was a motivating factor for you?

Carlton: *I grew up in a good family. I didn't want for anything. I got what I needed. My father was in the army and my mom was a homemaker. Along the way, family members introduced me to alcohol and, to make a long story short, I became a addict. I got into recovery. And while I was in recovery, my daughter wasn't doing too good with her mother. One time the police came and picked her up from school. That gave me some kind of incentive to make some progress. My recovery stay should have been a little longer. But I had to push things a little bit more and get a place to stay for my daughter.*

I went to different places trying to find myself, I went to Philadelphia, New York, Florida—three different places in Florida. Each place led me to the same thing. They say wherever you go you take yourself.

I found I wasn't getting nowhere. I reached the lowest of the lowest I could get...They say you reach a bottom? I hit a few bottoms. I seemed like I would keep getting help, but I reached another bottom and I would get more help from somebody else and it came to a point where I reached the bottom again and I was homeless. I stayed at the shelter. I had to sleep with my boots under my mattress so nobody would take them at night.

And I knew this is not where I come from. This is not where I should be at. A lady came to me one night and said "God is trying to take the taste of beer out of your mouth". This other man told me: "Take it from one alcoholic to another, you need to slow down." The next day I went where they feed the homeless and a lady turned around and said you better stop playing...and I knew. I knew that this is what I'm supposed to be doing. It was like a path was already laid out for me. And I just took that path.

Interviewer: What continues to be a challenge?

Carlton: She [daughter] knows that I'm an addict and she knows I been out in the streets. I had a friend that came over with a bottle of wine and she was sitting right here and my friend asked me to put it in there and she was like [imitating his daughter watching him and letting him know of her disapproval] (laughter). She's pretty much keeping me in check. She got her eyes on me so…

Interviewer: What helped/ helps you overcome?

Carlton: I believe in God. I believe that everything happens for a reason. He put people in my life that let me know that this is which way to go. It was just a feeling that I had…the faith that I had that God's going to get me out of this. I just knew.

Once I went to [recovery] and learned about the disease of addiction—about myself and why I do what I do. Just wanting to be a part of [wanting to belong]. And me having my daughter—that's a part of. It's just our small little family. It just me and her, but God made it possible for me to get myself together so I can take care of this little girl…

Interviewer: What hopeful lessons did you learn?

Carlton: I would tell most people to just give themselves a chance—give their children a chance. Be open-minded. Be optimistic. There's different ways of doing things and different ways of looking at things.

I would encourage people to go to school because that's where your chance is going to lead you. That's where hope is going to lead you and faith is going to lead you—to doing better. Just believe in yourself, because you're all you got.

I'm not too big on words. I just believe that everybody has a chance to do something in this world—in their life. It's not all about you. Not all the time. It's about helping somebody else, not just yourself.

Carlton's case study gives rise to the importance of self-awareness, self-confidence, and self-efficacy. He recognizes and accepts responsibility for the fact that he is an addict and is in recovery. His openness and candor about his situation reflect that sense of self-awareness. His faith is palpable, even as he describes how he was motivated to improve his life circumstances. In talking with Carlton, I quickly got the sense that this was a man with a plan for himself and his daughter. As we learned in previous chapters, Carlton intervened to ensure that she had the opportunity to learn. Both agency thinking and self-efficacy are evident in his discussions about his professional goals. Carlton aspires to own his own business in the future. His confidence in his ability to take on a higher level of responsibility and the goal-directed strategies used to achieve that goal were striking:

I started taking computer classes on how to do Excel. And I mentioned to my boss the situation I was in. It was a thing about being honest about where

I was at. One day my boss called me in the office and said when I come in tomorrow don't wear my uniform. They took me into the office and gave me a computer, gave me a telephone and told me this is what you gonna be doing. They liked the way I work. I showed them that I wanted to succeed. It's a matter of letting them know this is what I can do. Within me I was tired of moving [and] I wanted something different. Once they gave me this position, I started taking more classes. Once I found out what I needed to do or needed to know, I took more classes. With every new assignment they gave me, I would look online within the job and I would take computer classes. I would take it twice to make sure that I got it. The rest just came to me. The rest is a matter of experience.

As was the case with Josephine, Carlton also receives support from Hope and a Home. At the time of this writing, he had achieved permanent housing with his daughter. The Keys for Change that were transformational in his life were the *affordable home* and *finding rewarding work* goals of the program. Despite his issues with recovery, Carlton maintained a strong work ethic, which worked to his benefit as he progressed along his journey. Through the support of Hope and a Home, Carlton was able to find permanent housing that allowed him to provide a nurturing environment within which to raise his daughter. In addition, he was able to build on his current job position because of his clear and focused career goal of advancing in the company where he worked. He continued to educate himself by taking initiative to advance his knowledge of the technologies and tools needed to be competitive in the workplace, and this initiative was rewarded with a promotion. Carlton's story is also an example of how the strength of the parent-child attachment bond motivates one to strive to overcome adversity. Because of his strong commitment to his daughter, Carlton sought other roles and more responsibility on his job, thus reinforcing Hope and a Home's Key for Change: *rewarding work for good pay.* This key includes having a career goal as opposed to simply having a job. While having fundamental employment is an important starting point, the counseling and career guidance provided by Hope and a Home's job developers help parents to focus on goals that create greater employability as well as the potential for long-term career enhancement. The staff helps families prepare for rewarding work, which may involve keeping and building on the current job (as was the case with Carlton) or improving education and training and learning to network and interview. Helping families to find rewarding work with increased income so that they are able to maintain their housing is an important goal. Other goals are to provide training in the various types of social and communications skills that will lead to success on the job.

The Case of Coping with Family Dysfunction

"Each child needs someone who is irrationally crazy about them—that they're the center of somebody's world."

—Amanda

Amanda's journey is a spiritual one that shows how people can look within, recognize their own strengths, and rely on their faith as a means of achieving happiness and wholeness:

> **Interviewer:** *How do you define success?*
> **Amanda:** *Success to me is fitting into your environment, functioning in your community—in your career. There are individual and communal ways to be successful. Being successful within a community, being a leader, fitting in well with others. More individual definition of success would be having a career aspiration and excelling at that. At the same time you can be within a family—with family members not having similar levels of achievement.*
> **Interviewer:** *What was a motivating factor for you?*
> **Amanda:** *I don't think that I had much hope. I don't remember thinking about that until much later. It was all about survival. I remember being 11 years old and saying I do not want this. I do not want my parents' life. "Seriously, you can't figure this out? You can't balance a checkbook?"*
>
> *I knew what I didn't want—how I didn't want to live. I said I'm going to be a success. I'm working my butt off. I thought I'm going to be a doctor and have a real predictable career. Like working for the government and having something very steady. Maybe I'll work in hotel management.*
>
> *My parents were creative. I wanted anything but that. I wanted something valued in society, something where I can get a paycheck.*
> **Interviewer:** *What continues to be a challenge?*
> **Amanda:** *Siblings can hold you back a lot. It's a constant struggle for me. They know your buttons and everything about you. There's a term called crab bucketing…I feel like I'm being pulled back into the dysfunction. I've had to redefine my sibling relationship on my own. Not involving my parents. We've started having all adult siblings get together and go on a trip together without my parents. That's allowing us to create a new relationship. As much as you can have individual success, if you don't look at your family and if you don't have the strength to figure out what you have around you, you can just fall back into it.*
>
> *I found very little out there on: If you do create a different life for yourself, what's next? How do you live for yourself and for the future? When you come from a dysfunctional family, the family forces you to look backward. Whatever is the latest drama, it's all energy and resources that's sucked backward.*

Interviewer: *What hopeful lessons did you learn?*

Amanda: *One of the things that I've gotten strength through is the 12-step program for dysfunctional families. The cornerstone of that program is recognition of a higher power. I was in the program for about five years. I kind of needed it at the time. It's one of [the] things where I needed it at the time, but grew out of it. It was after college that I got into it. I didn't realize that for enabling family members that this was there.*

I felt desperate, very alone, very unhappy, didn't have many friends, felt very disconnected. I was working at home, didn't have a group of people that I would see regularly.

One of the things I got from it was that every week you go there and speak about how your life is. You could give whatever label you want to use for whatever you're struggling with. The way I described it was that I was showing up for myself. I check in with myself. You do that same practice through journaling or with friends.

For a long time, I filled up my life with things from morning 'til night. I didn't want to be alone with myself.

Success is being a happy person who is well balanced in the major areas of their life—career, family, friends. I'm allowing myself to be happy now. I want my child to grow up feeling she is the most important thing in my life.

Amanda's story reflects the challenges of unstable income and its associated stresses on family life and the long-term impact on a child's developmental trajectory. I discussed in Chapter 4 the impact of parenting behaviors on children's outcomes. In this case, Amanda's experiences not only influenced her educational and career decisions but also affected her sibling relationships as well. Notably, Amanda recognizes how she must manage the interactions with her family members in order to maintain relationships that, despite the fact that they may be stressful, she deems important. The importance of basic needs comes through in Amanda's discussion of wanting to get a job where she can get a steady paycheck. It is important for parents to be cognizant of the fact that children are aware of how family finances affect family functioning. Children need the consistency and stability that comes with a "steady paycheck" and, to the extent possible, family-focused interventions should address budgeting issues and include age-appropriate modules for children. Coping is clearly a theme in Amanda's case. As we learned from her introduction in Chapters 1 and 4, Amanda found other parents in her community to emulate, and she participated in numerous school-based clubs and activities to help her cope and to give her a clearer sense of what her future could potentially be. As a young adult, Amanda chose to seek help to give her tools to continue coping with the adversity she experienced as a child. Amanda benefited from programs like Recoveries Anonymous: The Solution Focused 12 Step Fellowship, which, among other issues, provides support for members of dysfunctional families. Of their signature 12 steps listed below, step 2, which focuses on the belief in and recognition of a higher

power, helped give Amanda a sense of inner peace and provided her with the tools
to grapple with the issues of her family life that caused uncertainty and self-doubt.

1. We admitted we were powerless over our problems and behaviors—that our
    lives had become unmanageable.
2. Came to believe that a Power greater than ourselves could restore us to sanity.
3. Made a decision to turn our will and our lives over to the care of God as we
    understood Him.
4. Made a searching and fearless moral inventory of ourselves.
5. Admitted to God, to ourselves, and to another human being the exact nature of
    our wrongs.
6. Were entirely ready to have God remove all these defects of character.
7. Humbly asked Him to remove our shortcomings.
8. Made a list of all persons we had harmed, and became willing to make amends
    to them all.
9. Made direct amends to such people wherever possible, except when to do so
    would injure them or others.
10. Continued to take personal inventory and when we were wrong promptly
    admitted it.
11. Sought through prayer and meditation to improve our conscious contact with
    God as we understood Him, praying only for knowledge of His will for us and
    the power to carry that out.
12. Having had a spiritual awakening as the result of these steps, we tried to
    carry this message to others, and to practice these principles in all our affairs.
    (Recoveries Anonymous, n.d.)

As Amanda framed it in her interview, the program allowed her to "show up for
herself." In other words, the opportunity to reflect on and put one's life experiences
into perspective fosters a sense of self-worth and value. Having this view allows one
to advocate for oneself and also helps to develop competencies and capacities that
can enable one to create an environment where others feel valued and respected
as well.

Thus, another key point of Amanda's story is that, while group and family interventions are necessary, there are times when an individual in a dysfunctional family
may find success only when they remove themselves from the source of stress and
seek solutions that allow them to build confidence and their own personal identity.
Amanda referred to her family functioning as "organized chaos." While there was
a good deal of structure in terms of having three meals per day and a place to sleep
and do homework, the affection and nurturing were missing from the parent-child
interactions. This contributed to tension and feelings of self-doubt. Programs that
teach parents the importance of creating and sustaining a nurturing environment
are important for helping to create harmony in the home, a harmony that allows

children to feel valued and wanted and that shields them from the external stresses of parental work life that can potentially disrupt family functioning. Such an environment provides the children with the wherewithal to develop important regulatory competencies that will serve them well as they mature and learn to engage with others outside the home. Amanda now has a family of her own. Through her experiences with a 12-step program, as well as in-depth knowledge of child development obtained through her postgraduate studies, Amanda's hope and happiness are now focused on providing the warmth, caring, and nurturance that help her child to feel wanted, loved, and centrally important to her family.

Summary and Conclusion

Together, Ashante, Josephine, Carlton, and Amanda tell an important story about hope, optimism, and resilience. Collectively they tell us that family, employment, housing, parenting, and education matter in helping individuals experiencing adversity to chart a pathway toward positive outcomes. Their stories also reinforce the idea that the path toward success is often nonlinear—instead, there are successes and setbacks along the way. For Ashante, finding work with two felonies on his record was extremely difficult, but having the opportunity to learn—to find an educational home where he could nurture his developing cultural identity and seek guidance for healing the challenges of past life experiences—was of utmost importance.

From Josephine, we learned that policies and programs that allow families to stay together are paramount. In her experience, the shelter system allowed for only nuclear families to be together, while members of an extended family were not permitted stay in the same shelter location. Earlier in this volume, I discussed the importance of the extended family as an asset that can help alleviate some of the pressures and challenges a parent may feel in attempting to rear a child alone. Policies and programs that remove this important resource may thwart the very goal they are attempting to achieve—family stability.

Of course, finding and keeping gainful employment is central to improving the quality of life for any family. For Carlton, this was the means to provide permanent housing for his daughter and have the resources to help strengthen the bond between them. Carlton shows us how economic disadvantage is often complicated by substance abuse, homelessness, and underemployment. His experience also teaches us about the painful stigma associated with these complexities and how that stigma makes it difficult to receive appropriate services for one's family and has the potential to derail the positive steps toward well-being:

I went through an incident when she started going to school. I took her to the doctor to get her shots. The doctor asked her to take her clothes off and asked me to step out. I saw my daughter's face. I said: Hold on—that's not part of the physical. The doctor said that's our normal response. I said no, it's not. You didn't see my daughter's face. We came here to get shots. So they took my daughter down the hall and asked her questions—if I touch her the wrong way or do I hurt her. I didn't know what she asked her at the time.

She wouldn't give me the release forms for her shots. Said I had to come back to get the TB test and all that. When I went back, they still wouldn't give it to me. I called and registered a complaint because I felt offended. I do the best that I can with what I have. Just because I'm a single parent, you single me out. That's how I felt—and for you to insinuate that I'm going to do something to my daughter? I spoke to my (Alcohol Anonymous) sponsor. He said things like this are happening in the homes. I said I'm not talking about that. I'm talking about my house. My parental rights. If I want my daughter to be checked out, I'll find a provider for her. It will be a permanent provider. That's what I need to do. We got into an argument about that because you don't just let anybody check your daughter out. You find a family physician and that person will be the ongoing physician. You just don't take her to any clinic and say oh well I want this person to be her physician. I felt real violated about that.

Through their experiences, both Carlton and Amanda learned to advocate for themselves and their families—to show up for themselves. Parents need to learn how to seek support for their families' needs, as well as have the sense of efficacy and confidence to pursue avenues necessary to receive and benefit from those resources. The most effective programs and policies promote interventions that are comprehensive and help families address the root causes of their adversity. Moreover, these programs need funding and resources to provide support over a long enough period to give families a chance to fully change their behavior. Families that have achieved a level of stability can ultimately serve as models and mentors for others. Both Josephine and Carlton exemplify a Hope and a Home Key for Change that calls for family and community connections. This key encourages families to be self-reflective and to set goals that keep them on track. In so doing, families will reinforce the knowledge and skills obtained while in a supportive environment—recognizing that, when families are on their own once again, they will need to engage in this process to maintain the progress they have made. Notably, the Hope and a Home key also focuses on using community resources as well as giving back to the community. Josephine now works on the family-support staff at Hope and a Home. Having gone through the program herself, she provides a unique firsthand perspective for others struggling with the issues she dealt with in her own time at Hope and a Home.

10

Why Hope (Still) Matters

If you lose hope, somehow you lose the vitality that keeps moving, you lose that courage to be, that quality that helps you go on in spite of it all. And so today I still have a dream.

—Martin Luther King, Jr., *The Trumpet of Conscience* (1968)

I was talking with a group of college students who had spent their spring break volunteering in schools in disadvantaged communities. They were reflecting on their experiences and took note of the stark contrasts between two of the schools they had visited. One of the schools was a high school with a historic legacy of excellence and high achievement. Although in a low-income neighborhood, the school had an established reputation for preparing students for postsecondary education and training. In recent years, however, the school had fallen into disrepair, the academic program was only modestly challenging to students, and the overall school climate was not conducive to learning. Truancy and apathy were pervasive, with students seemingly disinterested and unmotivated and teachers aloof and unsupportive. Some of the high school's students were clearly troubled youth—the volunteers observed one student wearing a house arrest bracelet on his ankle. The other school, also in a low-income community, had a target population of students with a range of social problems such as experiencing abuse and being runaways. The volunteers went to the school expecting to observe the same apathy and disinterest they had seen at the high school. However, despite the challenges, something was different about this environment. What they experienced, a volunteer remarked, was quite surprising: Students there seemed engaged, motivated, and happy to be in school. The teachers were optimistic and upbeat. I asked the volunteers what they thought was the difference. Both schools served students with similar demographics, so why was there such a marked difference between the two schools?

Without hesitation, the volunteers identified the difference: The one high school *tells* students to dream, but the other school helps them work toward their dreams and *shows them how*. The one high school seemed to be just going through the motions of trying to inspire students, while the other school appeared to have novel

173

ways to show they cared so students felt valued and supported. Faculty and staff in the second school advocated for and engaged the community to acquire material resources that gave the students' dreams a sense of reality and possibility. The volunteers saw firsthand the contrast between losing hope and vitality versus having the courage and support to persevere in spite of challenges. Clearly there are many reasons why these contrasts exist—some as obvious as those the students pointed out, others not so evident but nonetheless influential.

That is the aim of this volume—to gain insight into the mechanisms by which individuals are able to go on "in spite of it all" and the processes by which families manage to be resilient in the face of adversity. What are the assets within the family, the community, and the individual that fuel the striving toward self-actualization and well-being? This is a compelling question, especially because recent reports show that an increasing number of children have fallen into poverty due, in part, to the recent economic downturn. In the United States, nearly 16 million children—constituting approximately 22 percent of all U.S. children—live in families with incomes below the federal poverty level. For a family of four this means about $23,000 per year, leaving families well below what they need to provide for their children and meet their household needs (NCCP, 2012).

As mentioned earlier in this book, poverty and economic disadvantage are very serious public health concerns, with long-term consequences for physical and mental health as well as for cognitive and psychosocial functioning. Indeed, poverty is among the greatest threats to children's well-being. Children who experience deep and persistent poverty, especially when they are young, are at the greatest risk for poor outcomes and perpetuating the cycle of poverty (Buckner, Mezzacappa, & Beardslee, 2003; NCCP, 2012). Therefore, while it is important to understand the deleterious effects of economic disadvantage, it is equally important to examine the factors that allow children and families to flourish despite disadvantage. In order to halt the cycle of poverty and ameliorate its effects on children and families, we need more research and resources to illuminate the mechanisms of resilience and *how* it is that some children and families are able to rise above circumstances that would otherwise lead to poor outcomes.

I have explored the role of hope and optimism as important driving forces for some families, and research has revealed important links between hopeful attitudes and well-being. Inasmuch as hope is thought of as a motivational mechanism that involves planning and action, we need to understand its influential role in an individual's ability to overcome adversity: What are the qualities and characteristics of an individual who persists—who seemingly never gives up and has the wherewithal to negotiate the barriers typically thought to hamper one's ability to achieve prosocial goals? We also need to realize that *most* families have some assets and strengths that are best understood in the context of their immediate psychosocial ecology. These collective strengths of families play out in communities, neighborhoods, schools, and other settings where children and youth spend their time. Programs and intervention efforts that tap into these individual qualities and family strengths may increase the likelihood that the ameliorative benefits of the programs will be felt over longer periods of time.

Moreover, mounting evidence demonstrates that cycles of poverty and disadvantage *can* be broken. Studies highlighted in the preceding chapters shed light on some of the processes involved in resilience and adaptation to adversity. This research, along with stories shared by those who participated in the interviews, gives greater insight into the steps that can be taken to advance an agenda that promotes hope and fosters resilience in children and families. To move this agenda forward will require the political and societal will to acknowledge, first, that children and families have strengths and assets that, if cultivated, can be immensely helpful in overcoming adversity; and second, that while overcoming adversity is a necessary goal, it is not sufficient in and of itself to loosen the intergenerational grip of poverty and set families on a path toward thriving and well-being. Ongoing resources and support for education, mental health counseling, job readiness, and financial literacy are needed to keep families from slipping back into self-destructive patterns of behavior as they experience the inevitable setbacks in life. With that in mind, I want to conclude with lessons and recommendations for research, policies, and programs to inform a hopeful agenda on behalf of our society's most precious and valuable resource—our children.

The Promise of Hope

The promise of hope is the well-being of our children. Our collective efforts must focus on promoting family success, however success is defined, so children will thrive and have every possible chance for success in life. Thus, investments in early childhood development are crucial. Research consistently points to the importance of having a nurturing, supportive, and enriched environment early in life, giving children the developmental resources to achieve their highest potential. These early experiences affect children's well-being across the various domains of development—in particular, a stimulating environment helps foster early brain development and gives children a healthy start for learning and engaging in the social world. Programs that help parents and caregivers to understand the importance of their roles in fostering these developmental processes are critical. Home-visiting programs target ineffective parenting practices, teach parents how to create a stimulating environment, and help to redirect behavior that could potentially harm or thwart children's optimal development. Intervention programs containing such evidence-based practices can have long-term, positive effects on children's development. Resources should be directed toward training that prepares qualified health service delivery personnel to engage with these families and implement the interventions with fidelity (Olds, 2007).

Other intervention programs are needed that provide scaffolding and support for parents. However, it is important that these programs have a strong evidentiary base and are disseminated widely so they are readily accessible to communities and families. The National Registry of Evidence-based Programs and Practices (NREPP; http://www.nrepp.samhsa.gov/Index.aspx) is a useful starting point for identifying programs deemed effective and tailoring interventions to the specific needs of parents and families.

As children grow, mature, and engage in the social world beyond the family context, the support of friends can be central to their well-being. Friendships allow children to express their feelings and emotions with a nonjudgmental counterpart. High-quality positive friendships have the potential to ameliorate some of the effects of early adversity in family life, and programs that foster opportunities for children to cultivate these relationships can contribute to their well-being. School improvement efforts that emphasize relationships as the cornerstone for effecting positive outcomes have the potential to cultivate quality and mutually beneficial relationships among peers. Studies focusing on school climate have shown that the relationships between and among a school's students and staff can be transformative, yielding not only positive interpersonal and psychosocial outcomes but also improved academic outcomes (Haynes, 1996). Often, in response to pressures to attain higher levels of academic achievement, schools focus on their academic programs to the exclusion of the social climate. Yet relationships matter for children, especially during the school-age years. School and district-level policies that embrace multiple levers for improvement are more likely to achieve long-term, sustainable results than are schools and districts choosing a unidimensional approach.

Mentors play an important role as well, both within and outside the school context. In communities where resources are limited and prosocial models less available, it is important to have other programs so children have the opportunity to experience appropriate adult guidance and support. Faith-based programs are an important asset in many communities and can play a vital role in providing guidance to vulnerable children for whom resources are sorely needed. Another particularly vulnerable group of youth, children of incarcerated parents, needs a great deal of guidance and support from caring adults. According to the Bureau of Justice Statistics, nearly 1.5 million minor children have a mother or father in prison. In 1999, an estimated 721,500 state and federal prisoners were parents to 1,498,800 children under age 18, and approximately 22 percent of all minor children with a parent in prison were under 5 years old (Mumola, 2000). Further, the nation's prisons held approximately 744,200 fathers and 65,600 mothers at midyear 2007. Parents held in the nation's prisons—52 percent of state inmates and 63 percent of federal inmates—reported having an estimated 1,706,600 minor children, accounting for 2.3 percent of the U.S. population under age 18 (Glaze & Maruschak, 2008). These startling statistics call for intervention on the part of willing individuals to ensure that the children of these parents are cared for. Volunteers within faith-based mentoring programs can often provide a ready source of support, guidance, and encouragement.

Much more needs to be understood about youth in foster care and ways to help them successfully transition from adolescence into adulthood. Mentoring, whether natural or formal, is important for these youth. Research suggests that youth transitioning out of foster care are less likely to interact with the juvenile justice system or to abuse substances if they have supportive adults in their lives (Ahrens et al., 2008). However, to most effectively address the needs of these youth, mentoring relationships need to be sustained over time and resources should be available to ensure adequate training for program volunteers—increasing the likelihood that children and youth will have a chance to flourish and grow into productive adults and contributing members of society.

The Power of Hope

The parent-child attachment bond. Nothing is more powerful and influential than the relationship and bond between parent and child. The parent-child relationship is foundational to child outcomes across nearly all domains of development. The bond helps shape children's capacities for developing social relationships, having healthy emotional functioning, and achieving positive behavioral outcomes. Nearly all the protective and hope-promoting factors discussed in this volume implicate the importance of the attachment bond and underscore its prominent role in resilience. Naturally, a great deal of research has focused on the mother-child bond. However, increasingly more attention is being paid to the role of fathers. As discussed in Chapter 4, we now know that children who have an involved father and an attachment bond are more likely to be emotionally secure and self-confident, and to have better social connections with age-appropriate peers. Notably, when the father has a good relationship with the mother of his children, he is also likely to be more emotionally and psychologically involved with the children, spending quality time and engaging them in ways that help promote the children's psychological and emotional needs (Rosenberg & Wilcox, 2006; Cabrera & Tamis-LeMonda, 2013). A good deal of research has already been devoted to understanding the impact of father absence. Now, more than ever, research is needed to fully understand the impact of the father's presence in the life of a child and the long-term implications for well-being. Family-strengthening programs that include both father and mother are critically important and sorely needed. Indeed, fathers need to understand the processes of development and how their own engagement with their children can promote optimal development and foster competencies that children need for success in life. For example, family-friendly work policies—even in low-wage employment—that allow paternity leave enable fathers to begin the process of bonding early in the life of their child.

Neuroscience literature also supports the importance of this bond and the powerful ameliorating effects of a warm and nurturing relationship, especially during the sensitive period of early brain development (Bernier & Carlson, 2010). Even in the context of extreme stress and adversity, the buffering role of caregivers or supportive adults helps to promote coping and adaptation (National Scientific Council on the Developing Child, 2005). Thus, support for optimal and efficacious parenting is critical for fostering positive youth outcomes. Policies and programs that help provide resources for supporting children during this important developmental period are paramount.

Higher purpose and meaning. We learned, from the stories shared by interviewees and program staff, about the ways in which a higher purpose fueled the drive to persevere. Each, for reasons of his or her own, was compelled to shift from a mentality of merely surviving to one of thriving and well-being. For Carlton, the need to reunite with and take care of his daughter motivated him to go into recovery from alcohol addiction. Josephine needed to fight against the chains of depression and perceived stigma and stay alive to protect her children. Amanda achieved happiness in having a daughter of her own and providing the stability and predictability that make her child feel wanted and loved. Ashante found meaning and purpose through education and learning, and his revelation about the history of his culture fueled a quest for knowledge and truth that he believes can liberate inner-city youth in the same way he was liberated:

> *I tell my son, never look at money as a source. It's a resource. Your source is God, family, your history, your culture, your heritage—because with those things you can get anything material in this world.*

Research supports this conviction and suggests that beliefs are key factors in family resilience. A family's abilities to make meaning of adversity, maintain a positive outlook, and focus on their strengths and potential are important markers of resilience (Walsh, 2006). As Josephine stated, *"I thought this was the worst thing that could have happened, but it turned out to be the best."* Finally, the ability to transcend the impact of the daily stressors gives rise to the kind of personal transformation observed in Ashante. To learn and grow from adversity, as Walsh (2006) posited, empowers families to aspire to achieve goals that they may otherwise have perceived as unattainable.

The Lessons of Hope

Affordable and permanent housing. We learned from Josephine the importance of having a permanent home to promote family cohesion, stability, and structure.

These are important factors that protect against the risks of poor child outcomes and help children build the regulatory capacities associated with resilience. Permanent homes permit routines to be established and other types of family assets to be cultivated and to become normative family processes. Moreover, as Josephine pointed out, permanent housing relieves families of the daily stress of uncertainty and allows them to delay gratification and plan for a bright and hopeful future for themselves and their children:

> *See, you can't really think about anything other than your circumstances if you don't know where you gonna go or where you gonna sleep, or where you gonna be the next day the next night or whatever. Your focus is on survival and that's all you can think about. I've got to survive. How do we keep warm? How do we live from day to day?*
>
> *When you have some type of place…it takes you out of the realm of the emergency and the immediate. And places you back to a place where you can take some steps…if you can begin to take some steps you can begin to dream. You can begin to think about what it is that I want to do. Where do I go from here? There are options that become available to you that don't happen to you when you're constantly moving from place to place.*

Comprehensive and multifaceted housing programs are needed—not only to provide shelter but also to teach parents the essential skills necessary to maintain their housing. These skills include budgeting, paying bills on time, maintaining the residence properly, seeking help, and advocating for family needs. Such skills are often assumed to be present. However, in families with a history of underemployment and inadequate and unstable housing, these skills cannot be assumed but must be directly taught and modeled to prevent families from slipping back into uncertainty. Josephine and Gladys, a family-support person, recount an experience with a resident in their transitional housing program:

> *Sometimes we think people understand…the finances and putting together a budget but people don't understand. What they do is what they know…If your finances have never been a priority, if you were always on welfare and then you start working, it's going to be difficult for you to understand. If you've never paid rent and if you've never paid utilities you don't understand you have to pay them every month. I had one young lady who didn't understand you pay utilities every month. She didn't know; she lived in a family. She never paid bills. She knew she was supposed to pay, but she didn't know she had to pay every month. We take some things for granted.*

Choosing a career versus taking a job. Without question, having employment allows a family to meet some of their basic needs and to provide food, shelter, clothing, and the essential necessities of daily life for their children. However, for many working poor families, the nature of their low-wage employment requires them to work long hours to make ends meet or to take multiple jobs, most of which have very limited or no benefits. Research has examined the relationship between nonstandard parental work schedules and children's development. The findings generally suggest that cognitive, emotional, and social development are negatively affected, inasmuch as child-care arrangements may be less than adequate and may fall short of providing the enrichment and stimulation needed during early stages of development. Moreover, such work arrangements place children at risk for poor mental and physical health outcomes (Dunifon, Ziol-Guest, & Kalil, 2012; Huston, 2012). Research models of family stress call attention to the impact of nonstandard work schedules on parents' levels of stress and well-being and warn that psychological distress affects the ability to provide the warmth, nurturing, and attention that children need (Conger & Donnellan, 2007). Instead, parents may use more punitive and harsh parenting styles, and their ability to monitor their children's activities, supervise homework, and carry out other important responsibilities may be severely hampered (Dunifon, Ziol-Guest, & Kalil, 2012; Huston, 2012). Finally, parents may not have the wherewithal to take preventive health measures due to lack of resources, benefits, and access to care, and as a consequence may attend to only acute health concerns and emergencies.

In light of these challenges, more funding is needed for job development services and employment training, and these programs must help parents transition from a focus on obtaining subsistence jobs to working toward building a career. Of necessity, this shift in focus would require additional education and training, but the benefits of doing so would have a wide-ranging impact on child and family functioning in both the immediate and long term. For example, most career-focused employment opportunities offer a range of benefits that promote health coverage for a family and children. Paid time off allows parents to handle unexpected emergencies or other events without reductions in take-home pay or threats to employment status. Parents are better able to afford quality child care and the early educational experiences essential for promoting important cognitive and regulatory competencies that children need to succeed in life. Notably, parents establish themselves as role models for their children by creating shared learning experiences, taking ownership of their work life, and building relationship networks that foster helpful socialization practices.

One hallmark of Carlton's success was that he educated himself for positions that he aspired to hold. He learned about the competencies needed for the desired position and prepared himself by taking courses online. Carlton's primary motivation for taking these steps was so that he could "step up and take care of my little girl." Doing so enabled him to develop marketable skills and build expertise, which he hopes to someday parlay into his own cleaning business. Programs that teach parents to develop career goals and encourage them to pursue career opportunities are paving the way for long-term and sustained employment. This diminishes the uncertainties of job retention, nonstandard and variable work schedules, and the stresses associated with maintaining a household and providing for children by low-wage employment.

The Quest for Hope

I started this volume by asking whether there is an innate drive toward self-actualization. If there is, what psychological and biological processes fuel that drive? And what social and environmental factors impede one's ability to strive toward the highest potential? I proposed the theory that *hope* is the motivating factor in an individual's journey toward achieving success. Esther Duflo, an award-winning economist, agrees. Her research underscores the facilitating role of hope in promoting competence and confidence in one's ability to achieve. In a recent series of lectures, Duflo points out that:

> ...hope not only works as an enabling capability, but also is a key to the development of other capabilities. Hope can fuel aspirations: for example, a successful role model can change the expectations of what a girl can achieve, and thus affect her own aspirations for herself, or her parents' aspirations for her. In turn, these aspirations can affect behavior. (Duflo, 2012, p. 40)

Duflo and other economists argue that it is the absence of hope that keeps people in poverty because they see their efforts as futile. Feelings of futility engender fear, doubt, and inaction, all of which hamper capability, aspirations, and ultimately behavior, and keep individuals mired in their circumstances with no view of how to bring about change. This situation, according to Duflo and her colleagues, potentially fosters a kind of pathological conservatism, in which people forgo even feasible things with potentially large benefits—such as getting an education, participating in job training, or moving to a different neighborhood—for fear of losing the little they already possess (Hope Springs a Trap, 2012).

Thus, families need a reason to hope. They need to be able to see opportunity— to know that they can walk through its doors and achieve success. The challenges encountered by poor families are often complex and multifaceted, and may often have as much to do with perception and perspective as with economic insecurity. Therefore, multifaceted strategies must be employed to help families rise above their fear and move toward coping and capability.

Chen (2012) described an approach to coping with adversity as a "shift-and-persist" strategy that balances adapting to life stressors with maintaining a focus on the future. *Shifting* involves cognitive reappraisals and emotion regulation, while *persisting* involves enduring life with strength by holding onto hopes for the future. In employing this strategy, individuals strive to change their environment to fit their needs and desires (Chen, 2012). Programs and policies are needed that give families some degree of flexibility to create an environment conducive to this kind of active coping. Families need to play an active role in their own transformation and, with guidance and support, set reasonable goals that can be accomplished. Programs that assume the existence of family strengths, and use those strengths to help families reappraise their circumstances, may foster greater confidence and capability.

Tolan and colleagues (2004) note the existence of large-scale programs that use a strengths-based approach or seek to promote positive youth development. Many of these programs are undergoing extensive and (in some cases) costly evaluations to determine their effectiveness. However, there are also smaller-scale programs in local communities that need funding and impact evaluations to determine what works, why, and for whom. Such efforts would help these programs to better serve children and families. Programs such as Hope and a Home (www.hopeanda-home.org) and The Family Place (http://www.thefamilyplacedc.org/), which were observed in preparing this book, offer individualized and solution-focused training and support for the families they serve. These programs are often understaffed, with the workers serving in multiple capacities and working long hours. They rely on local fundraising efforts and the willingness and commitment of staff to take pay reductions when needed. The value of such local interventions is that they can be quite nimble, with staff responding rapidly to needs. Like Josephine, many program staff had once been clients. This lends authenticity and credibility to the intervention efforts and, importantly, enables families to build social networks that provide additional opportunities for receiving mentored support.

Hope still matters because there are capabilities yet to be discovered within families and children. There is much more to learn from families, and from the professionals who work with them, about the ways we can enable capability and inspire families to find meaning in their experiences so they are able to transcend the daily stresses of their circumstances. *Hope still matters* because we have examples of people like Ashante, Josephine, Carlton, and Amanda, who bring to life Masten's notion of ordinary magic—everyday successes that attest to the possibility of resilient outcomes. *Hope still matters* because embedded deeply in the human spirit is the quest for hope. Our job as a society is to look for the ordinary magic in families and children, and to free their spirits from the encumbrances of poverty, allowing them to soar to their highest potential.

REFERENCES

Aber, J. L., Bennett, N. G., Conley, D. C., & Li, J. (1997). The effects of poverty on child health and development. *Annual Review of Public Health, 18*, 463–483.

Academy of Achievement. (2012). Benjamin S. Carson, MD. Retrieved August 28, 2012, from http://www.achievement.org/autodoc/page/car1bio-1

Ahrens, K. R., DuBois, D. L., Richardson, L. P., Fan, M.-Y., & Lozano, P. (2008). Youth in foster care with adult mentors during adolescence have improved adult outcomes. *Pediatrics, 121*(2), e246–e252.

Ainsworth, M. D. S., Blehar, M. C., Waters, E., & Wall, S. (1978). *Patterns of attachment: A psychological study of the strange situation.* Hillsdale, NJ: Erlbaum.

Amato, P. R. (1994). Father-child relations, mother-child relations, and offspring psychological well-being in early adulthood. *Journal of Marriage and the Family, 56*(4), 1031–1042.

American Academy of Pediatrics. (2003). Family pediatrics: Report of the Task Force on the Family. *Pediatrics, 111*, 1541–1571.

American Psychological Association, Task Force on Resilience and Strength in Black Children and Adolescents. (2008). *Resilience in African American children and adolescents: A vision for optimal development.* Washington, DC: Author. Retrieved from http://www.apa.org/pi/cyf/resilience.html

Ames, C. (1992). Classrooms: Goals, structures, and student motivation. *Journal of Educational Psychology, 84*(3), 261.

Anderson, P. J. (2002). Assessment and development of executive functioning (EF) in childhood. *Child Neuropsychology, 8*(2), 71–82.

Anderson-Moore, K., Redd, Z., Burkhauser, M., Mbwana, K., & Ashleigh, C., (2009). *Children in poverty: Trends, consequences, and policy options.* Washington, DC: Child Trends.

Anglin, R. V. (2004). *Building the organizations that build communities: Strengthening the capacity of faith- and community-based development organizations.* Washington, DC: Department of Housing and Urban Development.

Armenian Medical Network. (2006). *Early deprivation has long-lasting effects.* Retrieved July 20, 2013, from http://www.health.am/ab/more/deprivation-has-long-lasting-effects/#ixzz2ZwBerdvL

Arthur, M. W., Hawkins, J. D., Brown, E. C., Briney, J. S., Oesterle, S., & Abbott, R. D. (2010). Implementation of the Communities That Care prevention system by coalitions in the Community Youth Development Study. *Journal of Community Psychology, 38*(2), 245–258.

Baldwin, A. L., Baldwin, C., & Cole, R. E. (1990). Stress-resistant families and stress-resistant children. In J. E. Rolf (Ed.), *Risk and protective factors in the development of psychopathology* (pp. 257–280). New York, NY: Cambridge University Press.

Bamford, C., & Lagattuta, K. H. (2012). Looking on the bright side: Children's knowledge about the benefits of positive versus negative thinking. *Child Development, 83*(2), 667–682.

Baker, J. A. (1999). Teacher-student interaction in urban at-risk classrooms: Differential behavior, relationship quality, and student satisfaction with school. *The Elementary School Journal, 100*(1), 57–70.

Bandura, A. (1977). Self-efficacy: Toward a unifying theory of behavioral change. *Psychological Review, 84*(2), 191.

Bandura, A., Barbaranelli, C., Caprara, G. V., & Pastorelli, C. (1996). Multifaceted impact of self-efficacy beliefs on academic functioning. *Child Development, 67*(3), 1206–1222.

Barron-McKeagney, T., Woody, J. D., & D Souza, H. J. (2002). Mentoring at-risk Latino children and their parents: Analysis of the parent-child relationship and family strength. *Families in Society, 83*(3), 285–292.

Baumrind, D. (1966). Effects of authoritative parental control on child behavior. *Child Development, 37*(4), 887–907.

Baumrind, D. (1967). Child care practices anteceding three patterns of preschool behavior. *Genetic Psychology Monographs, 75*(1), 43–88.

Baumrind, D. (1971). Current patterns of parental authority. *Development Psychology Monograph, 4*(1, pt.2).

Beauvais, F. (2000). Indian adolescence: Opportunity and challenge. In R. Montmeyer, G. Adams, & T. Gullotta (Eds.), *Adolescent diversity in ethnic, economic, and cultural contexts* (pp. 110–140). Thousand Oaks, CA: Sage.

Beckett, C., Maughan, B., Rutter, M., Castle, J., Colvert, E., Groothues, C., ... Sonuga-Barke, E. J. (2006). Do the effects of early severe deprivation on cognition persist into early adolescence? Findings from the English and Romanian adoptees study. *Child Development, 77*(3), 696–711.

Beier, S. R., Rosenfeld, W. D., Spitalny, K. C., Zansky, S. M., & Bontempo, A. N. (2000). The potential role of an adult mentor in influencing high-risk behaviors in adolescents. *Archives of pediatrics & adolescent medicine, 154*(4), 327.

Bell, T. (1983). *A nation at risk: The imperative for educational reform.* Washington, DC: National Commission on Excellence in Education.

Benzein, E. G., & Berg, A. C. (2005). The level of and relation between hope, hopelessness and fatigue in patients and family members in palliative care. *Palliative Medicine, 19*(3), 234–240.

Berger, L. M., Carlson, M. J., Bzostek, S. H., & Osborne, C. (2008). Parenting practices of resident fathers: The role of marital and biological ties. *Journal of Marriage and Family, 70*(3), 625–639.

Berndt, T. J. (2002). Friendship quality and social development. *Current Directions in Psychological Science, 11*(1), 7–10.

Berndt, T. J., & Keefe, K. (1995). Friends' influence on adolescents' adjustment to school. *Child Development, 66*(5), 1312–1329.

Bernier, A., Carlson, S. M., & Whipple, N. (2010). From external regulation to self-regulation: Early parenting precursors of young children's executive functioning. *Child Development, 81*(1), 326–339.

Betancourt, T. S., & Beardslee, W. (2012). Addressing the consequences of concentrated adversity on child and adolescent mental health. In V. Maholmes & R. B. King (Eds.), *The Oxford handbook of poverty and child development* (pp. 622–639). New York, NY: Oxford University Press.

Beyer, S. (1995). Maternal employment and children's academic achievement: Parenting styles as mediating variable. *Developmental Review, 15*(2), 212–253.

Bigfoot, D. S., & Schmidt, S. R. (2010). Honoring children, mending the circle: Cultural adaptation of trauma-focused cognitive-behavioral therapy for American Indian and Alaska Native children. *Journal of Clinical Psychology, 66*(8), 847–856.

Bigfoot, D. S., & Funderburk, B. W. (2011). Honoring children, making relatives: The cultural translation of parent-child interaction therapy for American Indian and Alaska Native families. *Journal of Psychoactive Drugs, 43*(4), 309–318.

Birch, S. H., & Ladd, G. W. (1997). The teacher-child relationship and children's early school adjustment. *Journal of School Psychology, 35*, 61–79.

Blair, C., Granger, D. A., Willoughby, M., Mills-Koonce, R., Cox, M., Greenberg, M. T., ... Fortunato, C. (2011). Salivary cortisol mediates effects of poverty and parenting on executive functions in early childhood. *Child Development, 82*(6), 1970–1984.

Blair, C., & Raver, C. C. (2012). Child development in the context of adversity: Experiential canalization of brain and behavior. *American Psychologist, 67*(4), 309–318.

Blakemore, S. J., & Choudhury, S. (2006). Development of the adolescent brain: Implications for executive function and social cognition. *Journal of Child Psychology and Psychiatry, 47*(3–4), 296–312.

Bland, R., & Darlington, Y. (2002). The nature and sources of hope: Perspectives of family caregivers of people with serious mental illness. *Perspectives in Psychiatric Care, 38*(2), 61–68.

Blank, M. J., Melaville, A., & Shah, B. P. (2003). *Making the difference: Research and practice in community schools.* Washington, DC: Coalition for Community Schools, Institute for Educational Leadership.

Bodrova, E., & Leong, D. (2007). *Tools of the Mind: The Vygotskian approach to early childhood education* (2nd ed.). New York, NY: Merrill/Prentice Hall.

Bolger, K. E., Patterson, C. J., Thompson, W. W., & Kupersmidt, J. B. (1995). Psychosocial adjustment among children experiencing persistent and intermittent family economic hardship. *Child Development, 66*(4), 1107–1129.

Borrego, J., Anhalt, K., Terao, S. Y., Vargas, E., & Urquiza, A. J. (2006). Parent-child interaction therapy with a Spanish-speaking family. *Cognitive & Behavioral Practice, 13*(2), 121–133.

Bowlby, J. (1969). *Attachment and loss: Vol 1. Attachment.* New York, NY: Basic Books.

Bowlby, J. (1988). *A secure base: Parent-child attachment and healthy human development.* New York, NY: Basic Books.

Boykin, A. W. (1986). The triple quandary and the schooling of Afro-American children. In U. Neisser (Ed.), *The school achievement of minority children: New perspectives* (pp. 57–92). Hillsdale, NJ: Erlbaum.

Boykin, A. W., Jagers, R. J., Ellison, C. M., & Albury, A. (1997). Communalism: Conceptualization and measurement of an Afrocultural social orientation. *Journal of Black Studies, 27*, 409–418.

Bradley, R. H., & Corwyn, R. F. (2002). Socioeconomic status and child development. *Annual Review of Psychology, 53*(1), 371–399.

Branch, A. Y. (2002). *Faith and action: Implementation of the national faith-based initiative for high risk youth.* Philadelphia, PA: Public/Private Ventures and Branch Associates.

Breathnach, S. B. (2008). *Simple abundance: A daybook of comfort and joy.* New York, NY: Grand Central Publishing. Quote retrieved August 2012 from http://www.goodreads.com/quotes/439324-real-life-isn-t-always-going-to-be-perfect-or-go

Bretherton, I. (2010). Fathers in attachment theory and research: A review. *Early Child Development and Care, 180*(1–2), 9–23.

Brody, G. H., Stoneman, Z., & Flor, D. (1996). Parental religiosity, family processes, and youth competence in rural, two-parent African American families. *Developmental Psychology, 32*(4), 696.

Brody, G. H., Flor, D. L., & Gibson, N. M. (1999). Linking maternal efficacy beliefs, developmental goals, parenting practices, and child competence in rural single-parent African American families. *Child Development, 70*(5), 1197–1208.

Bronfenbrenner, U. (1979). *The ecology of human development: Experiments by nature and design.* Cambridge, MA: Harvard University Press

Brooks, R. (2013). The power of parenting. In G. Sam & B. Robert B (Eds.), *Handbook of resilience in children* (pp. 443–458). New York, NY: Springer.

Brown, L. D., Feinberg, M. E., & Greenberg, M. T. (2010). Determinants of community coalition ability to support evidence-based programs. *Prevention Science, 11*(3), 287–297.

Buchanan, G. M. E., & Seligman, M. E. (1995). *Explanatory style.* Hillsdale, NJ: Erlbaum.

Buckner, J. C., Mezzacappa, E., & Beardslee, W. R. (2003). Characteristics of resilient youths living in poverty: The role of self-regulatory processes. *Development and Psychopathology, 15*(1), 139–162.

Buckner, J. C., Mezzacappa, E., & Beardslee, W. R. (2009). Self-regulation and its relations to adaptive functioning in low-income youths. *American Journal of Orthopsychiatry, 79*(1), 19–30.

Bukowski, W. M., Hoza, B., & Boivin, M. (1993). Popularity, friendship, and emotional adjustment during early adolescence. *New Directions for Child and Adolescent Development, 1993*(60), 23–37.

Bukowski, W. M., Newcomb, A. F., & Hartup, W. W. (Eds.). (1998). *The company they keep: Friendship in childhood and adolescence*. Cambridge, England: Cambridge University Press.

Burton, L. M., & Jarrett, R. L. (2000). In the mix, yet on the margins: The place of families in urban neighborhood and child development research. *Journal of Marriage and Family, 62*(4), 1114–1135.

Cabrera, N. J., & Tamis-LeMonda, C. S. (2013). *Handbook of father involvement: Multidisciplinary perspectives* (2nd ed.). New York, NY: Routledge.

Carlson, S. M. (2003). Executive function in context: Development, measurement, theory, and experience. *Monographs of the Society for Research in Child Development, 68*(3), 138–151.

Caspi, A., Henry, B., McGee, R. O., Moffitt, T. E., & Silva, P. A. (1995). Temperamental origins of child and adolescent behavior problems: From age 3 to age 15. *Child Development, 66*, 55–68.

Cattell, V. (2001). Poor people, poor places, and poor health: The mediating role of social networks and social capital. *Social Science & Medicine, 52*(10), 1501–1516.

Caughy, M. O., Hayslett-McCall, K. L., & O'Campo, P. J. (2007). No neighborhood is an island: Incorporating distal neighborhood effects into multilevel studies of child developmental competence. *Health Place, 13*(4), 788–798.

Carver, C. S., & Scheier, M. F. (1999). Optimism. In C. R. Snyder (Ed.), *Coping: The psychology of what works* (pp. 182–204). New York: Oxford University Press.

Carver, C. S., Scheier, M. F., & Segerstrom, S. C. (2010). Optimism. *Clinical Psychology Review, 30*, 879–889.

Chao, R. K. (1994). Beyond parental control and authoritarian parenting style: Understanding Chinese parenting through the cultural notion of training. *Child Development, 65*(4), 1111–1119.

Chavis, D. M., Hogge, J. H., McMillan, D. W., & Wandersman, A. (1986). Sense of community through Brunswick's lens: A first look. *Journal of Community Psychology, 14*(1), 24–40.

Children's Defense Fund. (2009). *Cradle to prison pipeline campaign*. Retrieved July 20, 2013, from http://www.childrensdefense.org/child-research-data publications/data/cradle-prison-pipeline-summary-report.pdf

Child Welfare Information Gateway. (2009). *Understanding the effects of maltreatment on brain development*. Issue Brief: U.S. Department of Health and Human Services: Washington, DC. Retrieved May 30, 2012, from http:// www.childwelfare.gov/pubs/issue_briefs/brain_development/

Child Welfare Information Gateway. (2013). *Parent-child interaction therapy with at-risk families*. Washington, DC: U.S. Department of Health and Human Services, Children's Bureau.

Ceballo, R., & McLoyd, V. C. (2002). Social support and parenting in poor, dangerous neighborhoods. *Child Development, 73*(4), 1310–1321.

Celso, B., Ebener, D., & Burkhead, E. (2003). Humor coping, health status, and life satisfaction among older adults residing in assisted living facilities. *Aging & Mental Health, 7*(6), 438–445.

Centers for Disease Control and Prevention. (n.d.). *Teen pregnancy in the United States*. Retrieved February 20, 2013, from http://www.cdc.gov/TeenPregnancy/AboutTeenPreg.htm#_edn1

Centers for Disease Control and Prevention. (2012). *U.S. teen pregnancy rates by outcome, race, and Hispanic ethnicity 2000–2011*. Retrieved February 20, 2013, from http://www.cdc.gov/TeenPregnancy/AboutTeenPreg.htm#_edn1

Chen, E., & Miller, G. E. (2012). "Shift-and-persist" strategies: Why low socioeconomic status isn't always bad for health. *Perspectives on Psychological Science, 7*(2), 135–158.

Child Trends. (2009). *Results and indicators for children: An analysis to inform discussions about Promise Neighborhoods.* Retrieved January 1, 2013, from http://www.childtrends.org/Files/ Child_Trends-2009_11_06_FR_PromiseNeigh.pdf

Chrisler, A., & Moore, K. A. (2012). *What works for disadvantaged and adolescent parent programs: Lessons from experimental evaluations of social programs and interventions for children.* Fact Sheet. Publication #2012–19. Washington, DC: Child Trends.

Cicchetti, D. (2010). Resilience under conditions of extreme stress: a multilevel perspective. *World Psychiatry, 9*(3), 145–154.

Clark, R. M. (1993). Homework-focused parenting practices that positively affect student achievement. In N. E. Chavkin (Ed.), *Families and schools in a pluralistic society* (pp. 85–105). Albany, NY: State University of New York Press.

Clauss-Ehlers, C. S. (2008). Sociocultural factors, resilience, and coping: Support for a culturally sensitive measure of resilience. *Journal of Applied Developmental Psychology, 29*(3), 197–212.

Clauss-Ehlers, C. S., & Levi, L. L. (2002). Violence and community, terms in conflict: An ecological approach to resilience. *Journal of Social Distress and the Homeless, 11*(4), 265–278.

Coalition for Community Schools. (n.d.). What is a community school? Retrieved November 12, 2012, from http://www.communityschools.org/

Coladarci, T. (1992). Teachers' sense of efficacy and commitment to teaching. *The Journal of experimental education, 60*(4), 323–337.

Coleman, J. S. (1988). Social capital in the creation of human capital. *American Journal of Sociology, 94,* S95–S120.

Coley, R. L. (1998). Children's socialization experiences and functioning in single-mother households: The importance of fathers and other men. *Child Development, 69*(1), 219–230.

Coley, R. L. (2001). (In)visible men: Emerging research on low-income, unmarried, and minority fathers. *American Psychologist, 56*(9), 743.

Collins, W. A., & Steinberg, L. (2008). Adolescent development in interpersonal context. In W. Damon & R. M. Lerner (Eds.), *Child and adolescent development: An advanced course* (pp. 551–578). Hoboken, NJ: Wiley & Sons.

Comer, J. P. (1980). *School power: Implications of an intervention project.* London, England: Free Press.

Comer, J. P. (1988). *Maggie's American dream: The life and times of a Black family.* New York, NY: New American Library.

Comer, J. P., Haynes, N. M., Joyner, E. T., & Ben-Avie, M. (1996). *Rallying the whole village: The Comer Process for change in education.* New York, NY: Teachers College Press.

Conger, R. D., Ge, X., Elder, G. H., Lorenz, F. O., & Simons, R. L. (1994). Economic stress, coercive family process, and developmental problems of adolescents. *Child Development, 65*(2), 541–561.

Conger, R. D., Conger, K. J., Matthews, L. S., & Elder Jr., G. H. (1999). Pathways of economic influence on adolescent adjustment. *American Journal of Community Psychology, 27*(4), 519–541.

Conger, R. D., & Donnellan, M. B. (2007). An interactionist perspective on the socioeconomic context of human development. *Annual Review of Psychology, 58,* 175–199.

Criss, M. M., Pettit, G. S., Bates, J. E., Dodge, K. A., & Lapp, A. L. (2003). Family adversity, positive peer relationships, and children's externalizing behavior: A longitudinal perspective on risk and resilience. *Child Development, 73*(4), 1220–1237.

Crosnoe, R., Johnson, M. K., & Elder, G. H. (2004). Intergenerational bonding in school: The behavioral and contextual correlates of student-teacher relationships. *Sociology of Education, 77*(1), 60–81.

Curry, L. A., Snyder, C. R., & Cook, D. L. (1997). Role of hope in academic and sport achievement. *Journal of Personality and Social Psychology, 73*(6), 1257–1267.

Cutcliffe, J. R. (2006). The principles and processes of inspiring hope in bereavement counselling: A modified grounded theory study—Part one. *Journal of Psychiatric and Mental Health Nursing, 13*(5), 598–603.

Darling, N., & Steinberg, L. (1993). Parenting style as context: An integrative model. *Psychological bulletin, 113*(3), 487–496.

Davis, S., Jenkins, G., & Hunt, R. (2003). *The pact: Three young men make a promise and fulfill a dream*. New York, NY: Riverhead Books, The Berkeley Publishing Group.

Davis-Kean, P. E. (2005). The influence of parent education and family income on child achievement: The indirect role of parental expectations and the home environment. *Journal of Family Psychology, 19*(2), 294.

Davis-Maye, D. (2004). Daddy's little girl. *Journal of Children and Poverty, 10*(1), 53–68.

Dawson, G., Ashman, S. B., & Carver, L. J. (2000). The role of early experience in shaping behavioral and brain development and its implications for social policy. *Development and Psychopathology, 12*(04), 695–712.

DeAngelis, T. (2008). The two faces of oxytocin: Why does the "tend and befriend" hormone come into play at the best and worst of times? *APA Monitor, 39*(2), 30. Retrieved from http://www.apa.org/monitor/feb08/oxytocin.aspx

De Luca, C. R., & Leventer, R. J. (2008). Developmental trajectories of executive functions across the lifespan. In V. Anderson, R. Jacobs, & P. Anderson (Eds), *Executive functions and the frontal lobes: A lifespan perspective* (pp. 3–21). Washington, DC: Taylor & Francis.

Diamond, A., Barnett, W. S., Thomas, J., & Munro, S. (2007). Preschool program improves cognitive control. *Science, 318*, 1387–1388.

Dionne, E. J., & Chen, M. H. (Eds.). (2001). *Sacred places, civic purposes: Should government help faith-based charity?* Washington, DC: Brookings Institution Press.

Dodson, J. E., & Gilkes, C. T. (1995). "There's nothing like church food": Food and the US Afro-Christian tradition: Re-membering community and feeding the embodied S/spirit(s). *Journal of the American Academy of Religion, 63*(3), 519–538.

Dorsey, S., & Forehand, R. (2003). The relation of social capital to child psychosocial adjustment difficulties: The role of positive parenting and neighborhood dangerousness. *Journal of Psychopathology and Behavioral Assessment, 25*(1), 11–23.

Dryfoos, J. G. (1994). Full-service schools: *A revolution in health and social services for children, youth, and families*. San Francisco, CA: Jossey-Bass.

Dryfoos, J., & Maguire, S. (2002). *Inside full-service community schools*. Thousand Oaks, CA: Corwin Press.

DuBois, D. L., & Silverthorn, N. (2005). Natural mentoring relationships and adolescent health: Evidence from a national study. *American Journal of Public Health, 95*(3), 518.

DuBois, D. L., & Rhodes, J. E. (2006). Introduction to the special issue: Youth mentoring: Bridging science with practice. *Journal of Community Psychology, 34*(6), 647–655.

Duflo, E. (2012) Tanner lectures. Retrieved December 5, 2102, from http://economics.mit.edu/files/7904

Duncan, G. J., Yeung, W. J., Brooks-Gunn, J., & Smith, J. R. (1998). How much does childhood poverty affect the life chances of children? *American Sociological Review, 63*(3) 406–423.

Dunifon, R. E., Ziol-Guest, K. M., & Kalil, A. (2012). Non-standard work schedules and child development. In V. Maholmes & R. B. King (Eds.), *Oxford handbook of child development and poverty* (pp. 260–277). New York, NY: Oxford University Press.

Dweck, C. (2006). *Mindset: The new psychology of success*. New York, NY: Random House.

Eccles, J., & Harold, R. (1993). Parent-school involvement during the early adolescent years. *The Teachers College Record, 94*(3), 568–587.

Eccles, J. S. (1999). The development of children ages 6–14. *The Future of Children, 9*(2), 30–43.

Education Law Center. (n.d.). *The history of Abbott v. Burke*. Retrieved November 8, 2012, from http://www.edlawcenter.org/cases/abbott-v-burke/abbott-history.html

Elder, G. H., & Caspi, A. (1988). Economic stress in lives: Developmental perspectives. *Journal of Social Issues, 44*(4), 25–45.

Eliot, G. (1887). *Daniel Deronda*. Boston: Estes and Lauriat. Quote retrieved November 2012 from http://www.goodreads.com/quotes/100874-let-my-body-dwell-in-poverty-and-my-hands-be

Encyclopedia of World Biography. (n.d.). Bill Clinton biography. Retrieved August 28, 2012, from http://www.notablebiographies.com/Ch-Co/Clinton-Bill.html#ixzz27YF2Zjkd

Ennis, S. R., Ríos-Vargas, M., & Albert, N. G. (2011). *The Hispanic population: 2010.* 2010 Census Briefs. Retrieved March 25, 2013, from http://www.census.gov/prod/cen2010/briefs/c2010br-04.pdf

Epstein, J. L. (2001). *School, family, and community partnerships: Preparing educators and improving schools.* Bolder, CO: Westview Press.

Erikson, E. H. (1968). *Identity, youth and crisis.* New York, NY: W.W. Norton and Company.

Evans, G. W. (2004). The environment of childhood poverty. *American Psychologist,* 59(2), 77–92.

Evans, G. W., Gonnella, C., Marcynyszyn, L. A., Gentile, L., & Salpekar, N. (2005). The role of chaos in poverty and children's socioemotional adjustment. *Psychological Science,* 16(7), 560–565.

Feeney, J. A., Noller, P., Roberts, N. (2000). Attachment and close relationships. In C. Hendrick & S. S. Hendrick (Eds.), *Close relationships: A sourcebook* (pp. 185–201). Thousand Oaks, CA, US: Sage Publications.

Feinberg, M. E., Jones, D., Greenberg, M. T., Osgood, D. W., & Bontempo, D. (2010). Effects of the Communities That Care model in Pennsylvania on change in adolescent risk and problem behaviors. *Prevention Science,* 11(2), 163–171.

Fernandez, M. A., Butler, A. M., & Eyberg, S. M. (2011). Treatment outcome for low socioeconomic status African American families in Parent-Child Interaction Therapy: A pilot study. *Child and Family Behavior Therapy,* 33(1), 32–48.

Fletcher, A. C., Walls, J. K., Cook, E. C., Madison, K. J., & Bridges, T. H. (2008). Parenting style as a moderator of associations between maternal disciplinary strategies and child well-being. *Journal of Family Issues,* 29, 1724–1744.

Fleming, J., & Ledogar, R. J. (2008). Resilience and indigenous spirituality: A literature review. *Pimatisiwin,* 6(2), 47–64.

Folkman, S., & Lazarus, R. S. (1980). An analysis of coping in a middle-aged community sample. *Journal of Health and Social Behavior,* 21(3) 219–239.

Fordham, S., & Ogbu, J. U. (1986). Black students' school success: Coping with the "burden of 'acting white.'" *The Urban Review,* 18(3), 176–206.

Fox, E. (2012). *Optimism and pessimism: What makes us who we are?* Retrieved November 12, 2012, from http://wellcometrust.wordpress.com/2012/09/10/optimism-and-pessimism-what-makes-us-who-we-are/

Fox, N. A., & Rutter, M. (2010). Introduction to the special section on the effects of early experience on development. *Child Development,* 81(1), 23–27.

Fox, S. E., Levitt, P., & Nelson III, C. A. (2010). How the timing and quality of early experiences influence the development of brain architecture. *Child Development,* 81(1), 28–40.

French, S., & Joseph, S. (1999). Religiosity and its association with happiness, purpose in life, and self-actualisation. *Mental Health, Religion & Culture,* 2(2), 117–120.

Furman, W., Brown, B. B., & Feiring, C. (Eds.). (1999). *The development of romantic relationships in adolescence.* New York, NY: Cambridge University Press.

Funderburk, B. W., & Eyberg, S. (2010). History of parent-child interaction therapy. In J. C. Norcross & D. K. Freedheim (Eds.), *History of psychotherapy: Continuity and change* (2nd ed., pp. 415–420). Washington, DC: American Psychological Association.

Garmezy, N., & Rutter, M. (1983). *Stress, coping, and development in children.* New York, NY: McGraw-Hill.

Garmezy, N. (1991). Resilience and vulnerability to adverse developmental outcomes associated with poverty. *American Behavioral Scientist,* 34(4), 416–430.

Garmezy, N. (1993). Children in poverty: Resilience despite risk. *Psychiatry: Interpersonal and Biological Processes,* 56(1), 127–136.

Garmezy, N., Masten, A. S., & Tellegen, A. (1984). The study of stress and competence in children: A building block for developmental psychopathology. *Child Development,* 55(1), 97–111.

Gaylord-Harden, N. K., Burrow, A. L., & Cunningham, J. A. (2012). A cultural-asset framework for investigating successful adaptation to stress in African American youth. *Child Development Perspectives,* 6(3), 264–271.

Gilchrest, A., & Kyprianou, P. (2011). *Social networks, poverty and ethnicity*. York, United Kingdom: Joseph Roundtree Foundation. Retrieved July 7, 2013, from http://www.jrf.org. uk/sites/files/jrf/poverty-ethnicity-social-networks-full.pdf

Gillham, J., & Reivich, K. (2004). Cultivating optimism in childhood and adolescence. *The Annals of the American Academy of Political and Social Science, 591*(1), 146–163.

Gifford-Smith, M. E., & Brownell, C. A. (2003). Childhood peer relationships: Social acceptance, friendships, and peer networks. *Journal of School Psychology, 41*(4), 235–284.

Glaze, L. E., & Maruschak, L. M. (2008). *Parents in prison and their minor children*. NCJ 222984. Bureau of Justice Statistics. U.S. Department of Justice. Office of Justice Programs. Retrieved March 13, 2013, from http://www.bjs.gov/index.cfm?ty=pbdetail&iid=823

Goldschein, E., & Eisenberg, D. (2011). 15 inspirational rags-to-riches stories. *Business Insider*. Retrieved August, 28, 2012, from http://www.businessinsider.com/rags-to-riches-stories-2 011-11?op=1#ixzz27YA50AKK

Gone, J. P. (2004). Mental health services for Native Americans in the 21st century United States. *Professional Psychology Research and Practice, 35*(1), 10–18.

Gordon, M. B. (2003). *Making the match: Law enforcement, the faith community and the value-based initiative*. Washington, DC: U.S. Dept. of Justice, Office of Community Oriented Policing Services.

Gortmaker, S. L. (1979). The effects of prenatal care upon the health of the newborn. *American Journal of Public Health, 69*(7), 653–660.

Graham, B. L. (2001). Resilience among American Indian youth: First Nations' youth resilience study. Published Dissertation, University of Minnesota, Minneapolis, MN.

Graham, C. (2011). Adaptation amidst prosperity and adversity: Insights from happiness studies from around the world. *The World Bank Research Observer, 26*(1), 105–137.

Gray, R. M., & Steinberg, L. (1999). Unpacking authoritative parenting: Reassessing a multi-dimensional construct. *Journal of Marriage and Family, 61*(3), 574–587.

Green, C. S., & Bavelier, D. (2008). Exercising your brain: A review of human brain plasticity and training-induced learning. *Psychology and Aging, 23*(4), 692.

Greenberg, M. T. (2006). Promoting resilience in children and youth preventive interventions and their interface with neuroscience. *Annals of the New York Academy of Sciences, 1094*, 139–50.

Greenberger, E., & Goldberg, W. A. (1989). Work, parenting, and the socialization of children. *Developmental Psychology, 25*(1), 22.

Greenfield, E. A., & Marks, N. F. (2010). Sense of community as a protective factor against long-term psychological effects of childhood violence. *The Social Service Review, 84*(1), 129.

Gunnar, M. R., & Donzella, B. (2002). Social regulation of the cortisol levels in early human development. *Psychoneuroendocrinology, 27*(1), 199–220.

Guthrie, D. D. A. (2011). Hope is the ticket to life: Insights from disadvantaged African American youth. Published Dissertation. Loyola University Chicago.

Gutiérrez, K. D., & Rogoff, B. (2003). Cultural ways of learning: Individual traits or repertoires of practice. *Educational Researcher, 32*(5), 19–25.

Hamre, B. K., & Pianta, R. C. (2001). Early teacher-child relationships and the trajectory of children's school outcomes through eighth grade. *Child Development, 72*(2), 625–638.

Hardaway, C. R., & McLoyd, V. C. (2009). Escaping poverty and securing middle class status: How race and socioeconomic status shape mobility prospects for African Americans during the transition to adulthood. *Journal of Youth and Adolescence, 38*(2), 242–256.

Hardaway, C. R., McLoyd, V. C., & Wood, D. (2012). Exposure to violence and socioemotional adjustment in low-income youth: An examination of protective factors. *American Journal of Community Psychology, 49*(1–2), 112–126.

Harding, D. J. (2009). Collateral consequences of violence in disadvantaged neighborhoods. *Social Forces, 88*(2), 757–784.

Harley, D. M. (2011). *Perceptions of hope and hopelessness among low-income African Americans* (Doctoral dissertation). Ohio State University, Columbus, Ohio.

Harrell, M. C., & Bradley, M. (2009). *Data collection methods: Semi-structured interviews and focus groups*. Santa Monica, CA: RAND Corporation. Retrieved from http://www.rand.org/pubs/technical_reports/TR718

Harris, K. M., Furstenberg, F. F., & Marmer, J. K. (1998). Paternal involvement with adolescents in intact families: The influence of fathers over the life course. *Demography, 35*(2), 201–216.

Hart, B., & Risley, T. R. (1995). *Meaningful differences in the everyday experience of young American children*. Baltimore, MD: Brookes Publishing.

Hartman, T. A. (2002). *Moving beyond the walls: Faith and justice partnerships working for high risk youth*. Philadelphia, PA: Public/Private Ventures.

Hartup, W. W. (1989). Social relationships and their developmental significance. *American Psychologist, 44*(2), 120–126.

Hartup, W. W., & Stevens, N. (1999). Friendships and adaptation across the life span. *Current Directions in Psychological Science, 8*(3), 76–79.

Hawkins, J. D., Brown, E. C., Oesterle, S., Arthur, M. W., Abbott, R. D., & Catalano, R. F. (2008). Early effects of communities that care on targeted risks and initiation of delinquent behavior and substance use. *The Journal of Adolescent Health, 43*(1), 15–22.

Hawkins, J. D., Oesterle, S., Brown, E. C., Arthur, M. W., Abbott, R. D., Fagan, A. A., & Catalano, R. F. (2009). Results of a type 2 translational research trial to prevent adolescent drug use and delinquency: A test of Communities That Care. *Archives of Pediatrics & Adolescent Medicine, 163*(9), 789.

Hawley, T., with Gunnar, M. (2000). *Starting smart: How early experiences influence brain development* (2nd ed.). Washington, DC: Zero to Three.

Haynes, N. M. (1996). Creating safe and caring school communities: Comer School Development Program schools. *Journal of Negro Education, 65*(3), 308–314.

Heckman, J. J. (2006). Skill formation and the economics of investing in disadvantaged children. *Science, 312*(5782), 1900–1902.

Heckman, J. J. (2007). The economics, technology, and neuroscience of human capability formation. *Proceedings of the National Academy of Sciences, 104*(33), 13250–13255.

Heckman, J. J. (2008). Schools, skills, and synapses. *Economic Inquiry, 46*(3), 289–324.

Helland, M. R., & Winston, B. E. (2005). Towards a deeper understanding of hope and leadership. *Journal of Leadership and Organizational Studies, 12*(2), 42–54.

Herrera, C., Sipe, C. L., McClanahan, W. S., & Arbreton, A. J. A. (2000). *Relationship development in community-based and school-based programs*. New York, NY: Public/Private Ventures.

Hickman, C. W., Greenwood, G., & Miller, M. D. (1995). High school parent involvement: Relationships with achievement, grade level, SES, and gender. *Journal of Research & Development in Education, 28*(3), 125–134.

Hill, N. E., Castellino, D. R., Lansford, J. E., Nowlin, P., Dodge, K. A., Bates, J. E., & Pettit, G. S. (2004). Parent academic involvement as related to school behavior, achievement, and aspirations: Demographic variations across adolescence. *Child Development, 75*(5), 1491–1509.

Hill, N., & Tyson, D. F. (2009). Parental involvement in middle school: A meta-analytic assessment of the strategies that promote achievement. *Developmental Psychology, 45*(3) 740–763.

Hofer, M. A. (1995). Hidden regulators. *Attachment theory: Social, developmental and clinical perspectives*, 203–230.

Hoover-Dempsey, K. V., & Sandler, H. M. (1997). Why do parents become involved in their children's education? *Review of Educational Research, 67*(1), 3–42.

Hoover-Dempsey, K. V., Walker, J. M., Sandler, H. M., Whetsel, D., Green, C. L., Wilkins, A. S., & Closson, K. (2005). Why do parents become involved? Research findings and implications. *The Elementary School Journal, 106*(2), 105–130.

Hope Springs a Trap: An absence of optimism keeps people trapped in poverty. (2012). Retrieved March 17, 2013, from http://www.economist.com/node/21554506

Hopson, L. M., & Lee, E. (2011). Mitigating the effect of family poverty on academic and behavioral outcomes: The role of school climate in middle and high school. *Children and Youth Services Review, 33*(11), 2221–2229.

Howard, D. E. (1996). Searching for resilience among African-American youth exposed to community violence: Theoretical issues. *Journal of Adolescent Health, 18*(4), 254–262.

Howes, C. (1989). Friendships in very young children: Definition and functions. In B. H. Schneider et al. (Eds), *Social competence in developmental perspective* (pp. 127–129). Dordrecht: The Netherlands: Springer.

Hughes, D., & Chen, L. (1997). When and what parents tell children about race: An examination of race-related socialization among African American families. *Applied Developmental Science, 1*(4), 200–214.

Hughes, D. (2003). Correlates of African American and Latino parents' messages to children about ethnicity and race: A comparative study of racial socialization. *American Journal of Community Psychology, 31*(1), 15–33.

Hughes, D., Rodriguez, J., Smith, E. P., Johnson, D. J., Stevenson, H. C., & Spicer, P. (2006). Parents' ethnic-racial socialization practices: A review of research and directions for future study. *Developmental Psychology, 42*(5), 747–770.

Hughes, J. N., & Kwok, O. M. (2006). Classroom engagement mediates the effect of teacher-student support on elementary students' peer acceptance: A prospective analysis. *Journal of School Psychology, 43*(6), 465–480.

Hughes, J., & Kwok, O. M. (2007). Influence of student-teacher and parent-teacher relationships on lower achieving readers' engagement and achievement in the primary grades. *Journal of Educational Psychology, 99*(1), 39.

Hughes, L. (1994). *Dreams. The collected poems of Langston Hughes.* New York, NY: Knopf Doubleday Publishing Group. Quote retrieved November 2012 from http://www.goodreads.com/quotes/12030-hold-fast-to-dreams-for-if-dreams-die-life-is

Hurd, N., & Zimmerman, M. (2010). Natural mentors, mental health, and risk behaviors: A longitudinal analysis of African American adolescents transitioning into adulthood. *American Journal of Community Psychology, 46*(1), 36–48.

Hurd, N., Sánchez, B., Zimmerman, M., & Caldwell, C. (2012). Natural mentors, racial identity, and educational attainment among African American adolescents: Exploring pathways to success. *Child Development, 83*(4), 1196–1212.

Huston, A. (2012). How welfare and employment policies influence children's development. In V. Maholmes & R. B. King (Eds.), *Oxford handbook of child development & poverty* (pp. 278–293). New York, NY: Oxford University Press.

Ingoldsby, E. M., & Shaw, D. S. (2002). Neighborhood contextual factors and early-starting antisocial pathways. *Clinical Child and Family Psychology Review, 5*(1), 21–55.

Jackson, L. M., Pratt, M. W., Hunsberger, B., & Pancer, S. M. (2005). Optimism as a mediator of the relation between perceived parental authoritativeness and adjustment among adolescents: Finding the sunny side of the street. *Social Development, 14*(2), 273–304.

Jackson-Newsom, J., Buchanan, C. M., & McDonald, R. M. (2008). Parenting and perceived maternal warmth in European American and African American adolescents. *Journal of Marriage and Family, 70*(1), 62–75.

Jarrett, R. L. (1995). Growing up poor: The family experiences of socially mobile youth in low-income African American neighborhoods. *Journal of Adolescent Research, 10*(1), 111–135.

Jarrett, R. L. (1999). Successful parenting in high-risk neighborhoods. *The Future of Children, 9*(2) 45–50.

Jekielek, S., Moore, K. A., & Hair, E. C. (2002b). *Mentoring programs and youth development: A synthesis.* Washington, DC: Child Trends.

Jekielek, S., Moore, K. A., Hair, E. C., & Scarupa, H. (2002a). *Mentoring: A promising strategy for youth development.* Washington, DC: Child Trends.

Johnson, M. H. (1997). *Developmental cognitive neuroscience.* Cambridge, MA: Blackwell.

Jones, D. J., Forehand, R., Brody, G. H., & Armistead, L. (2002). Positive parenting and child psychosocial adjustment in inner-city single-parent African American families: The role of maternal optimism. *Behavior Modification, 26*(4), 464–481.

Kalil, A. (2003). *Family resilience and good child outcomes. A review of the literature*. Wellington, New Zealand: Centre for Social Research and Evaluation, Ministry of Social Development, Te Manatu- Whakahiato Ora.

Kaufman, J., Plotsky, P. M., Nemeroff, C. B., & Charney, D. S. (2000). Effects of early adverse experiences on brain structure and function: Clinical implications. *Biological Psychiatry, 48*(8), 778–790.

Keller, H. (1903). *Optimism: An essay*. Retrieved August 2012 from http://www.afb.org/section.aspx?FolderID=1&SectionID=1&TopicID=193&SubTopicID=22&DocumentID=1208

Kenny, M. E., Walsh-Blair, L. Y., Blustein, D. L., Bempechat, J., & Seltzer, J. (2010). Achievement motivation among urban adolescents: Work hope, autonomy support, and achievement-related beliefs. *Journal of Vocational Behavior, 77*(2), 205–212.

Kenyon, D. B., & Hanson, J. D. (2012). Incorporating traditional culture into positive youth development programs with American Indian/Alaska Native youth. *Child Development Perspectives, 6*(3), 272–279.

King, M. L. (1968). *The trumpet of conscience*. New York, NY: Harper & Row. Quote retrieved December 2012 from http://www.goodreads.com/quotes/79713-if-you-lose-hope-so mehow-you-lose-the-vitality-that

Klaw, E. L., Rhodes, J. E., & Fitzgerald, L. F. (2003). Natural mentors in the lives of African American adolescent mothers: Tracking relationships over time. *Journal of Youth and Adolescence, 32*(3), 223–232.

Kerensky, V. (1975). The educative community. *National Elementary Principal, 54*(3), 43–47.

Klem, A. M., & Connell, J. P. (2004). Relationships matter: Linking teacher support to student engagement and achievement. *Journal of School Health, 74*(7), 262–273.

Knight, G. P., Berkel, C., Umana-Taylor, A. J., Gonzales, N. A., Ettekal, I., Jaconis, M., & Boyd, B. M. (2011). The familial socialization of culturally related values in Mexican American families. *Journal of Marriage & Family, 73*(5), 913–925.

Knudsen, E. I. (2004). Sensitive periods in the development of the brain and behavior. *Journal of Cognitive Neuroscience, 16*(8), 1412–1425.

Knudsen, E. I., Heckman, J. J., Cameron, J. L., & Shonkoff, J. P. (2006). Economic, neurobiological, and behavioral perspectives on building America's future workforce. *Proceedings of the National Academy of Sciences, 103*(27), 10155–10162.

Kochanska, G., Aksan, N., & Joy, M. E. (2007). Children's fearfulness as a moderator of parenting in early socialization: Two longitudinal studies. *Developmental Psychology, 43*(1), 222.

Kochanska, G., Aksan, N., Penney, S. J., & Boldt, L. J. (2007). Parental personality as an inner resource that moderates the impact of ecological adversity on parenting. *Journal of Personality and Social Psychology, 92*(1), 136.

Kohman, R. A., & Rhodes, J. S. (2013). Neurogenesis, inflammation and behavior. *Brain, Behavior, and Immunity, 27*, 22–32.

Komro, K. A., Flay, B. R., & Biglan, A. (2011). Creating nurturing environments: A science-based framework for promoting child health and development within high-poverty neighborhoods. *Clinical Child and Family Psychology Review, 14*(2), 111–134.

Kopp, C. B. (1982). Antecedents of self-regulation: a developmental perspective. *Developmental Psychology, 18*(2), 199–214.

Koratamaddi, N. P. (2012). Stroke rehabilitation and neuroplasticity: Efficacy and methods available. *Student Pulse, 4*(5). Retrieved November 12, 2012, from http://www.studentpulse.com/articles/644/2/stroke-rehabilitation-and-neuroplasticity-efficacy-and-methods-available

Korenman, S., Miller, J. E., & Sjaastad, J. E. (1995). Long-term poverty and child development in the United States: Results from the NLSY. *Children and Youth Services Review, 17*(1), 127–155.

Kozol, J. (1991). *Savage inequalities: Children in America's schools*. New York, NY: Crown.

Krause, N. (1992). Stress, religiosity, and psychological well-being among older blacks. *Journal of Aging and Health, 4*(3), 412–439.

Kretzmann, J., & McKnight, J. P. (1996). Assets-based community development. *National Civic Review, 85*(4), 23–29.

Kumpfer, K. L., Alvarado, R., Tait, C., & Whiteside, H. O. (2007). The strengthening families program: An evidence-based, multicultural family skills training program. In P. Tolan, J. Szapocznik, & S. Sambrano (Eds.), *Preventing youth substance abuse: Science-based programs for children and adolescents* (pp. 159–181). Washington, DC: American Psychological Association.

Ladson-Billings, G. (2006). From the achievement gap to the education debt: Understanding achievement in US schools. *Educational Researcher, 35*(7), 3–12.

LaFromboise, T. D., Coleman, H. C., & Gerton, J. (1993). Psychological impact of biculturalism: Evidence and theory. *Psychological Bulletin, 114*, 395–412.

LaFromboise, T. D., & Dizon, M. (2003). American Indian children and adolescents. In J. T. Gibbs & L. N. Huang (Eds.), *Children of color: Psychological interventions with culturally diverse youth* (pp. 45–90). San Francisco, CA: Jossey-Bass.

LaFromboise, T. D., Hoyt, D. R., Oliver, L., & Whitbeck, L. B. (2006). Family, community, and school influences on resilience among American Indian adolescents in the upper Midwest. *Journal of Community Psychology, 34*(2), 193–209.

La Greca, A. M., & Harrison, H. M. (2005). Adolescent peer relations, friendships, and romantic relationships: Do they predict social anxiety and depression? *Journal of Clinical Child and Adolescent Psychology, 34*(1), 49–61.

Lamb-Parker, F., Piotrkowski, C. S., Baker, A. J., Kessler-Sklar, S., Clark, B., & Peay, L. (2001). Understanding barriers to parent involvement in Head Start: A research-community partnership. *Early Childhood Research Quarterly, 16*(1), 35–51.

Langhout, R. D., Rhodes, J. E., & Osborne, L. N. (2004). An exploratory study of youth mentoring in an urban context: Adolescents' perceptions of relationship styles. *Journal of Youth and Adolescence, 33*(4), 293–306.

Lapierre, L. M., & Allen, T. D. (2006). Work-supportive family, family-supportive supervision, use of organizational benefits, and problem-focused coping: Implications for work-family conflict and employee well-being. *Journal of Occupational Health Psychology, 11*(2), 169.

Lee, T. Y., Cheung, C. K., & Kwong, W. M. (2012). Resilience as a positive youth development construct: A conceptual review. *The Scientific World Journal,* 2012. doi:10.1100/2012/390450

Lengua, L. J. (2012). Poverty, the development of effortful control, and children's academic, social and emotional adjustment. In V. Maholmes & R. King (Eds.), *The Oxford Handbook of Poverty and Child Development.* New York, NY: Oxford University Press.

Lerner, R. M., Lerner, J. V., Almerigi, J. B., Theokas, C., Phelps, E., Gestsdottir, S., . . . Ma, L. (2005). Positive youth development, participation in community youth development programs, and community contributions of fifth-grade adolescents: Findings from the first wave of the 4-H Study of Positive Youth Development. *Journal of Early Adolescence, 25*(1), 17–71.

Lerner, R. M., von Eye, A., Lerner, J. V., Lewin-Bizan, S., & Bowers, E. P. (2010). Special issue introduction: The meaning and measurement of thriving: A view of the issues. *Journal of Youth and Adolescence, 39*(7), 707–719.

Letiecq, B. L., & Koblinsky, S. A. (2004). Parenting in violent neighborhoods: African American fathers share strategies for keeping children safe. *Journal of Family Issues, 25*(6), 715–734.

Leventhal, T., & Brooks-Gunn, J. (2000). The neighborhoods they live in: The effects of neighborhood residence on child and adolescent outcomes. *Psychological Bulletin, 126*(2), 309–337.

Li-Grining, C. P. (2012). The role of cultural factors in the development of Latino preschoolers' self-regulation. *Child Development Perspectives, 6*(3), 210–217.

Lopez, S. J., Rose, S., Robinson, C., Marques, S. C., & Pais-Ribeiro, J. (2009). Measuring and promoting hope in schoolchildren. In R. Gilman, E. S. Huebner, & M. J. Furlong (Eds), *Handbook of positive psychology in schools* (pp. 37–50). New York, NY: Routledge.

Luthar, S. S., Cicchetti, D., & Becker, B. (2000). The construct of resilience: A critical evaluation and guidelines for future work. *Child Development, 71*(3), 543–562.

Luthar, S. S., & Zelazo, L. B. (2003). Research on resilience: An integrative review. In S. S. Luthar (Ed), *Resilience and vulnerability: Adaptation in the context of childhood adversities* (pp. 510–549). New York, NY: Cambridge University Press.

Luthar, S. S. (2006). Resilience in development: A synthesis of research across five decades. In D. Cichetti & D. J. Cohen (Eds), *Developmental psychopathology: Risk, disorder and adaptation* (pp. 740–795). New York, NY: Wiley.

Maccoby, E. E., & Martin, J. A. (1983). Socialization in the context of the family: Parent-child interaction. In P. Mussen (Ed.), *Handbook of child psychology* (pp. 1–101). New York, NY: Wiley.

Maccoby, E. E. (1992). The role of parents in the socialization of children: An historical overview. *Developmental Psychology, 28*(6), 1006.

MacQueen, K. M., McLellan, E., Metzger, D. S., Kegeles, S., Strauss, R. P., Scotti, R., … Trotter, R. T. (2001). What is community? An evidence-based definition for participatory public health. *American Journal of Public Health, 91*(12), 1929–1938.

Maddi, S. (1996). *Personality theories: A comparative analysis* (6th ed.). Pacific Grove, CA: Brooks/Cole Publishing Company.

Maholmes, V., & King, R. B. (2012). *The Oxford handbook of poverty and child development.* New York, NY: Oxford University Press.

Mandela, N. (1995). *Long walk to freedom: The autobiography of Nelson Mandela.* New York, NY: Little Brown & Co. Quote retrieved July 2012 from http://www.goodreads.com/author/quotes/367338.Nelson_Mandela

Martins, C., & Gaffan, E. A. (2000). Effects of early maternal depression on patterns of infant-mother attachment: A meta-analytic investigation. *Journal of Child Psychology and Psychiatry, 41,* 737–746.

Martin, R. A. (2008). Humor and health. *The Primer of Humor Research, 8,* 479.

Martin, R. A., & Lefcourt, H. (2004). Sense of humor and physical health: Theoretical issues, recent findings, and future directions. *Humor, 17*(1/2), 1–20.

Mattis, J. S., Fontenot, D. L., & Hatcher-Kay, C. A. (2003). Religiosity, racism, and dispositional optimism among African Americans. *Personality and Individual Differences, 34*(6), 1025–1038.

Mayer, S. E. (1997). *What money can't buy: Family income and children's life chances.* Cambridge, MA: Harvard University Press.

Maslow, A. H. (1943). A theory of human motivation. *Psychological Review, 50*(4), 370.

Masten, A. S., Hubbard, J. J., Gest, S. D., Tellegen, A., Garmezy, N., & Ramirez, M. (1999). Competence in the context of adversity: Pathways to resilience and maladaptation from childhood to late adolescence. *Development and Psychopathology, 11*(1), 143–169.

Masten, A. S. (2001). Ordinary magic: Resilience processes in development. *American Psychologist, 56*(3), 227–238.

Masten, A. S. (2012). Resilience in children: Vintage Rutter and beyond. In A. M. Slater & P. C. Quinn (Eds.), *Developmental psychology: Revisiting the classic studies* (pp. 204–222). Thousand Oaks, CA: Sage Publications.

Masten, A. S., & Tellegen, A. (2012). Resilience in developmental psychopathology: Contributions of the Project Competence Longitudinal Study. *Development and Psychopathology, 24*(2), 345–361.

Masten, A. S., & Reed, M.-G. J. (2002). Resilience in development. In C. R. Synder & S. J. Lopez (Eds.), *Handbook of positive psychology* (pp. 74–88). New York, NY: Oxford University Press.

Masten, A. S. (2010). Ordinary magic: Lessons from research on resilience in human development. *Education Canada, 49*(3), 28–32. Retrieved November 2012 from http://www.cea-ace.ca/sites/cea-ace.ca/files/EdCan-2009-v49-n3-Masten.pdf

Mathie, A., & Cunningham, G. (2003). From clients to citizens: Asset-based community development as a strategy for community-driven development. *Development in Practice, 13*(5), 474–486.

McCabe, K. M., & Clark, R. (1999). Family protective factors among urban African American youth. *Journal of Clinical Child Psychology, 28*(2), 137–150.

McGhee, P. E. (2010). *Humor: The lighter path to resilience and health*. Bloomington, IN: AuthorHouse Publishers.

McKernon, W. L., Holmbeck, G. N., Colder, C. R., Hommeyer, J. S., Shapera, W., & Westhoven, V. (2001). Longitudinal study of observed and perceived family influences on problem-focused coping behaviors of preadolescents with spina bifida. *Journal of Pediatric Psychology, 26*(1), 41–54.

McLoyd, V. C. (1990). The impact of economic hardship on black families and children: Psychological distress, parenting, and socioemotional development. *Child development, 61*(2), 311–346.

McLoyd, V. C., & Wilson, L. (1991). The strain of living poor: Parenting, social support, and child mental health. In A. C. Huston (Ed.), *Children in poverty* (pp. 105–135). New York, NY: Cambridge University Press.

McLoyd, V. C. (1998). Socioeconomic disadvantage and child development. *American Psychologist, 53*(2), 185–204.

McLoyd, V. C., Kaplan, R., Purtell, K. M., & Huston, A. C. (2011). Assessing the effects of a work-based antipoverty program for parents on youth's future orientation and employment experiences. *Child Development, 82*(1), 113–132.

McMahon, S. D., Parnes, A. L., Keys, C. B., & Viola, J. J. (2008). School belonging among low-income urban youth with disabilities: Testing a theoretical model. *Psychology in the Schools, 45*(5), 387–401.

McMillan, D., & Chavis, D. (1986). Sense of community: A definition and theory. *Journal of Community Psychology, 14*, 6–23.

McRoberts, O. M. (2001). *Black churches, community and development*. National Housing Institute. Shelterforce Online. Retrieved March 22, 2013, from http://www.shelterforce.com/online/issues/115/McRoberts.html

Menninger, K. (1959). The academic lecture: Hope. *The American Journal of Psychiatry 116*, 481–491.

Middlebrooks, J. S., & Audage, N. C. (2008). *The effects of childhood stress on health across the lifespan*. Atlanta, GA: Centers for Disease Control and Prevention, National Center for Injury Prevention and Control.

Miller, J. F., & Powers, M. J. (1988). Development of an instrument to measure hope. *Nursing Research, 37*(1), 6–10.

Molgaard, V. K., Spoth, R. L., & Redmond, C. (2000). *Competency training: The Strengthening Families Program, for Parents and Youth 10–14*. Washington, DC: U.S. Department of Justice, Office of Justice Programs, Office of Juvenile Justice and Delinquency Prevention.

Montgomery County Public Schools. (2009). *Beyond "heroes and sheroes": The success of Montgomery County Schools*. Retrieved September 5, 2012, from http://www.learningfirst.org/stories/MontgomeryCounty

Morenoff, J. D., Sampson, R. J., & Raudenbush, S. W. (2001). Neighborhood inequality, collective efficacy, and the spatial dynamics of urban violence. *Criminology, 39*(3), 517–558.

Morris, A. S., Silk, J. S., Steinberg, L., Myers, S. S., & Robinson, L. R. (2007). The role of the family context in the development of emotion regulation. *Social Development, 16*(2), 361–388.

Muller, C. (2001). The role of caring in the teacher-student relationship for at-risk students. *Sociological Inquiry, 71*(2), 241–255.

Mumola, C. J. (2000). *Incarcerated parents and their children*. NCJ 182335. Bureau of Justice Statistics. U.S. Department of Justice. Office of Justice Programs. Retrieved March 13, 2013, from http://www.bjs.gov/index.cfm?ty=pbdetail&iid=586

Munson, M. R., & McMillen, J. C. (2009). Natural mentoring and psychosocial outcomes among older youth transitioning from foster care. *Children and Youth Services Review, 31*(1), 104–111.

Murberg, T. A. (2012). The influence of optimistic expectations and negative life events on somatic symptoms among adolescents: A one-year prospective study. *Psychology, 3*(2), 123–127.

Murphy, D. (2012). *The Child Indicator: The Child, Youth, and Family Indicators Newsletter, 13*(1). Publication #2012-35. Washington, DC: Child Trends.

National Center for Children in Poverty (NCCP). (2012). *Child poverty.* Mailman School of Public Health. Columbia University. Retrieved March 13, 2013, from http://www.nccp.org/topics/childpoverty.html

National Council of Teachers of English. (1996). *Opportunity-to-learn standards, statement of principles.* Retrieved October 5, 2012, from http://www.ncte.org/positions/statements/opptolearnstandards

National Education Association. (2011). *Family-school-community partnerships 2.0: Collaborative strategies to advance student learning.* Retrieved August 7, 2013, from http://www.nea.org/assets/docs/Family-School-Community-Partnerships-2.0.pdf

National Public Radio. (2010). *How important is economic diversity in schools?* Retrieved September 5, 2012, from http://www.npr.org/templates/story/story.php?storyId=130647610

National Scientific Council on the Developing Child. (2005). *Excessive stress disrupts the architecture of the developing brain.* Working Paper No. 3. Retrieved May 2012 from www.developingchild.harvard.edu

National Scientific Council on the Developing Child. (2007a). *The timing and quality of early experiences combine to shape brain architecture.* Working Paper No. 5. Retrieved May 2012 from www.developingchild.harvard.edu

National Scientific Council on the Developing Child. (2007b). *The science of early childhood development.* Retrieved May 2012 from http://www.developingchild.net

National Survey of Children's Health. (2007). *Data query from the Child and Adolescent Health Measurement Initiative.* Data Resource Center for Child and Adolescent Health. Retrieved October 10, 2012, from www.childhealthdata.org

Neblett, E. W., Rivas-Drake, D., & Umaña-Taylor, A. J. (2012). The promise of racial and ethnic protective factors in promoting ethnic minority youth development. *Child Development Perspectives, 6*(3), 295–303.

Nelson, C. A. (1999a). Neural plasticity and human development. *Current Directions in Psychological Science, 8*(2), 42–45.

Nelson, C. A. (1999b). Change and continuity in neurobehavioral development: Lessons from the study of neurobiology and neural plasticity. *Infant Behavior and Development, 22*(4), 415–429.

Nelson, C. A. (2000). The neurobiological bases of early intervention. *Handbook of Early Childhood Intervention, 2,* 204–227.

Nelson, C. A., Zeanah, C. H., Fox, N. A., Marshall, P. J., Smyke, A. T., & Guthrie, D. (2007). Cognitive recovery in socially deprived young children: The Bucharest early intervention project. *Science, 318*(5858), 1937–1940.

Neblett, E. W., Rivas-Drake, D., & Umaña-Taylor, A. J. (2012). The promise of racial and ethnic protective factors in promoting ethnic minority youth development. *Child Development Perspectives, 6*(3), 295–303.

Nes, L. S., & Segerstrom, S. C. (2006). Dispositional optimism and coping: A meta-analytic review. *Personality and Social Psychology Review, 10*(3), 235–251.

Newcomb, A. F., & Bagwell, C. L. (1995). Children's friendship relations: A meta-analytic review. *Psychological Bulletin, 117*(2), 306.

Noddings, N. (2003). *Happiness and education.* Cambridge, England: Cambridge University Press.

Obst, P. L., Smith, S. G., & Zinkiewicz, L. (2001). An exploration of sense of community, part 3: Dimensions and predictors of psychological sense of community in geographical communities. *Journal of Community Psychology, 30*(1), 119–133.

Oettingen, G. (1995). Explanatory style in the context of culture. In G. M. Buchanan & M. E. P. Seligman (Eds.), *Explanatory style* (pp. 209–224). Hillsdale, NJ: Erlbaum.

Ogbu, J. U. (1994). From cultural differences to differences in cultural frame of reference. In P. M. Greenfield & R. R. Cocking (Eds.), *Cross-cultural roots of minority child development* (pp. 365–391). Hillsdale, NJ: Erlbaum.

Olds, D. L. (2006). The nurse-family partnership: An evidence-based preventive intervention. *Infant Mental Health Journal, 27*(1), 5–25.

Olds, D. L., Henderson, C. R., Tatelbaum, R., & Chamberlin, R. (1986). Improving the delivery of prenatal care and outcomes of pregnancy: A randomized trial of nurse home visitation. *Pediatrics, 77*(1), 16–28.

Olds, D. L., Henderson Jr., C. R., Tatelbaum, R., & Chamberlin, R. (1988). Improving the life-course development of socially disadvantaged mothers: A randomized trial of nurse home visitation. *American Journal of Public Health, 78*(11), 1436–1445.

Olds, D. L., & Kitzman, H. (1990). Can home visitation improve the health of women and children at environmental risk? *Pediatrics, 86*(1), 108–116.

Olds, D. L., Kitzman, H., Hanks, C., Cole, R., Anson, E., Sidora-Arcoleo, K., ... Bondy, J. (2007). Effects of nurse home visiting on maternal and child functioning: age-9 follow-up of a randomized trial. *Pediatrics, 120*(4), e832–845.

Ong, A., Edwards, L. M., & Bergemon, C. S. (2006). Hope as a source of resilience in later adulthood. *Personality and Individual Differences, 41*(7), 1263–1273.

Owens, M. L. (2004). Capacity building: The case of faith-based organizations. In R. V. Anglin (Ed.), *Building the organizations that build communities: Strengthening the capacity of faith- and community-based development organizations* (pp. 127–163). Washington, DC: U.S. Department of Housing and Urban Development. Office of Policy Development and Research.

Page, E. E., & Stone, A. M. (2010). *From Harlem Children's Zone to Promise Neighborhoods: Creating the tipping point for success.* Washington, DC: Georgetown Public Policy Institute.

Pan, R. J., Littlefield, D., Valladolid, S. G., Tapping, P. J., & West, D. C. (2005). Building healthier communities for children and families: Applying asset-based community development to community pediatrics. *Pediatrics, 115*(Supp 3), 1185–1187.

Panter-Brick, C., & Eggerman, M. (2012). Understanding culture, resilience, and mental health: The production of hope. In M. Ungar (Ed.), *The social ecology of resilience. A handbook of theory and practice* (pp. 369–386). New York, NY: Springer.

Perkins, D. D., & Long, D. A. (2002). Neighborhood sense of community and social capital: A multi-level analysis. In A. Fisher, C. Sonn, & B. Bishop (Eds.), *Psychological sense of community: Research, applications, and implications* (pp. 291–318). New York, NY: Plenum.

Perry, B. D. (2001). The neurodevelopmental impact of violence in childhood. In D. Schetky & E. P. Benedek (Eds.), *Textbook of child and adolescent forensic psychiatry* (pp. 221–238). Washington, DC: American Psychiatric Press.

Perry, B. D. (2002). Childhood experience and the expression of genetic potential: What childhood neglect tells us about nature and nurture. *Brain and Mind, 3*(1), 79–100.

Perry, B. D. (2006). Applying principles of neurodevelopment to clinical work with maltreated and traumatized children: The neurosequential model of therapeutics. In N. B. Webb (Ed.), *Working with traumatized youth in child welfare* (pp. 27–52). New York: The Guilford Press.

Pescitelli, D. (1996). An analysis of Carl Rogers' theory of personality. Retrieved October 15, 2013, from http://pandc.ca/?cat=carl_rogers&page=rogerian_theory

Peterson, C. (1991). The meaning and measurement of explanatory style. *Psychological Inquiry, 2*(1), 1–10.

Peterson, C. (2000). The future of optimism. *American Psychologist, 55*(1), 44.

Peterson, C., & Steen, T. (2009). Optimistic explanatory style. In C. R. Snyder & S. Lopez (Eds), *Oxford handbook of positive psychology* (2nd ed., pp. 313–322). New York, NY: Oxford University Press.

Peterson, J. W. (1990). Age of wisdom: Elderly Black women in family and church. In J. Sokolowsky (Ed.), *The cultural context of aging* (pp. 213–228). New York, NY: Bergin and Garvey.

Pinderhughes, E. E., Nix, R., Foster, E. M., & Jones, D. (2001). Parenting in context: Impact of neighborhood poverty, residential stability, public services, social networks, and danger on parental behaviors. *Journal of Marriage and Family, 63*(4), 941–953.

Pines, M. (1975, December). In praise of "invulnerables." *APA Monitor,* p. 7.

Pope, A. (1733). *An essay on man: Epistle I.* Retrieved May 2012 from http://allpoetry.com/poem/8448567-An_Essay_on_Man_Epistle_1-by-Alexander_Pope

Pulvers, J. N., Schenk, J., Arai, Y., Fei, J. F., Saito, K., & Huttner, W. B. (2007). On the origin of neurons. *Genome Biology, 8*(7), 311.

Rabipour, S., & Raz, A. (2012). Training the brain: Fact and fad in cognitive and behavioral reme-diation. *Brain and Cognition, 79*(2), 159–179.

Recoveries Anonymous: The Solution Focused Twelve Step Fellowship. (n.d.). Retrieved March, 2013 from http://www.r-a.org/i-dysfunctional-families.htm

Redd, Z., Sanchez Karver, T., Murphey, D., Anderson Moore, K., & Knewstub, D. (2011). *Two gen-erations in poverty: Status and trends among parents and children in the United States, 2000-2010*. Child Trends: Washington, DC

Repetti, R. L., Taylor, S. E., & Seeman, T. E. (2002). Risky families: Family social environ-ments and the mental and physical health of offspring. *Psychological Bulletin, 128*(2), 330–366.

Rhodes, J. E., Bogat, G. A., Roffman, J., Edelman, P., & Galasso, L. (2002). Youth mentoring in per-spective: Introduction to the special issue. *American Journal of Community Psychology, 30*(2), 149–155.

Rhodes, J. E., & Chan, C. S. (2008). Youth mentoring and spiritual development. *New Directions for Youth Development, 2008*(118), 85–89.

Rhodes, J. E., Grossman, J. B., & Resch, N. L. (2000). Agents of change: Pathways through which mentoring relationships influence adolescents' academic adjustment. *Child Development, 71*(6), 1662–1671.

Rhodes, J. E., Grossman, J. B., & Resch, N. L. (2003). Agents of change: Pathways through which mentoring relationships influence adolescents' academic adjustment. *Child Development, 71*(6), 1662–1671.

Rhodes, J. E., Spencer, R., Keller, T. E., Liang, B., & Noam, G. (2006). A model for the influence of mentoring relationships on youth development. *Journal of Community Psychology, 34*(6), 691–707.

Riegle-Crumb, C., Farkas, G., & Muller, C. (2006). The role of gender and friendship in advanced course taking. *Sociology of Education, 79*(3), 206–228.

Roche, K. M., Ensminger, M. E., & Cherlin, A. J. (2007). Variations in parenting and adolescent out-comes among African American and Latino families living in low-income, urban areas. *Journal of Family Issues, 28*(7), 882–909.

Roesch, S. C., Duangado, K. M., Vaughn, A. A., Aldridge, A. A., & Villodas, F. (2010). Dispositional hope and the propensity to cope: A daily diary assessment of minority adolescents. *Cultural Diversity and Ethnic Minority Psychology, 16*(2), 191.

Rockett, H. R. (2007). Family dinner: More than just a meal. *Journal of the American Dietary Association, 107*(9), 1498–1501.

Rogers, C. (1961). *On Becoming a Person: A therapist's view of psychotherapy*. London: Constable.

Rogers, C. (1995). *On becoming a person: A therapist's view of psychotherapy*. New York: NY Houghton Mifflin Harcourt.

Rogers, C. R. (1977). *Carl Rogers on personal power*. Delacorte Press: New York.

Rogoff, B., & Wertsch, J. V. (1984). *Children's learning in the "zone of proximal development."* San Francisco: Jossey-Bass.

Rosenberg, J., & Wilcox, W. B. (2006). *The importance of fathers in the healthy development of children*. Washington, DC: U.S. Department Health and Human Services, Administration for Children and Families, Administration on Children, Youth and Families, Children's Bureau, Office of Child Abuse and Neglect.

Rubin, K. H., Dwyer, K. M., Booth-LaForce, C., Kim, A. H., Burgess, K. B., & Rose-Krasnor, L. (2004). Attachment, friendship, and psychosocial functioning in early adolescence. *Journal of Early Adolescence, 24*(4), 326–356.

Rubin, K. H., Bukowski, W., Parker, J., & Bowker, J. C. (2008). Peer interactions, relationships, and groups. In W. Damon & R. Lerner (Eds.), *Child and adolescent development: An advanced course* (pp. 141–180). Hoboken, NJ: Wiley & Sons.

Runyan, D. K., Hunter, W. M., Socolar, R. R., Amaya-Jackson, L., English, D., Landsverk, J., ... & Mathew, R. M. (1998). Children who prosper in unfavorable environments: The relationship to social capital. *Pediatrics, 101*(1), 12–18.

Rutter, M. (2000). Resilience reconsidered: Conceptual considerations, empirical findings, and policy implications. In J. P. Shonkoff & S. J. Meisels (Eds.), *Handbook of early childhood intervention* (pp. 651–682). New York: Cambridge University Press.

Sabogal, F., Marín, G., Otero-Sabogal, R., Marín, B. V., & Perez-Stable, E. J. (1987). Hispanic familism and acculturation: What changes and what doesn't? *Hispanic Journal of Behavioral Sciences, 9*(4), 397–412.

Sameroff, A. J., & Rosenblum, K. L. (2007). Psychosocial constraints on the development of resilience. *Annals of the New York Academy of Sciences, 1094*(1), 116–124.

Sampson, R. J., Raudenbush, S. W., & Earls, F. (1997). Neighborhoods and violent crime: A multilevel study of collective efficacy. *Science, 277*(5328), 918–924.

Sampson, R. J., Raudenbush, S. W., & Earls, F. (1998). *Neighborhood collective efficacy—does it help reduce violence?* Retrieved December 24, 2012, from http://www.nij.gov/pubs-sum/fs000203.htm

Sampson, R. J., Morenoff, J. D., & Earls, F. (1999). Beyond social capital: Spatial dynamics of collective efficacy for children. *American Sociological Review, 64*, 633–660.

Sampson, R. J., Morenoff, J. D., & Gannon-Rowley, T. (2002). Assessing "neighborhood effects": Social processes and new directions in research. *Annual Review of Sociology, 28*, 443–478.

Sanchez-Way, R., & Johnson, S. (2000). Cultural practices in American Indian prevention programs. *Juvenile Justice, 7*(2), 20–30.

Sanders, M. R., Markie-Dadds, C., & Turner, K. M. (2003). *Theoretical, scientific and clinical foundations of the Triple P-Positive Parenting Program: A population approach to the promotion of parenting competence* (Vol. 1). Queensland: Parenting and Family Support Centre, The University of Queensland.

Sanders, A. E., Lim, S., & Sohn, W. (2008). Resilience to urban poverty: Theoretical and empirical considerations for population health. *American Journal of Public Health, 98*(6), 1101–1106.

Saphire-Bernstein, S., Way, B. M., Kim, H. S., Sherman, D. K., & Taylor, S. E. (2011). Oxytocin receptor gene (OXTR) is related to psychological resources. *Proceedings of the National Academy of Sciences, 108*(37), 15118–15122.

Sapienza, J., & Masten, A. S. (2011). Understanding and promoting resilience in children and youth. *Current Opinion in Psychiatry, 24*, 267–273.

Sarason, S. B. (1977). *The psychological sense of community: Prospects for a community psychology.* London, England: Jossey-Bass.

Scales, P. (1999). Reducing risk and building developmental assets. *Journal of School Health, 69*, 113–119.

Scales, P. C., Benson, P. L., Roehlkepartain, E. C., Sesma, A., Jr., & van Dulmen, M. (2006). The role of developmental assets in predicting academic achievement: A longitudinal study. *Journal of Adolescence, 29*(5), 691–708.

Schargel, F. P., & Smink, J. (2001). *Strategies to help solve our school dropout problem.* Larchmont, NY: Eye on Education.

Scheier, M. F., Weintraub, J. K., & Carver, C. S. (1986). Coping with stress: Divergent strategies of optimists and pessimists. *Journal of Personality and Social Psychology, 51*(6), 1257.

Scheier, M. F., & Carver, C. S. (1987). Dispositional optimism and physical well-being: The influence of generalized outcome expectancies on health. *Journal of Personality, 55*, 169–210.

Scheier, M. F., & Carver, C. S. (1992). Effects of optimism on psychological well-being: Theoretical overview and empirical update. *Cognitive Therapy and Research, 16*, 201–228.

Schulman, P., Castellon, C., & Seligman, M. E. (1989). Assessing explanatory style: The content analysis of verbatim explanations and the attributional style questionnaire. *Behaviour Research and Therapy, 27*(5), 505–509.

Schunk, D. H. (1991). Self-efficacy and academic motivation. *Educational Psychologist, 26*, 207–231.

Schunk, D. H., & Pajares, F. (2002). The development of academic self-efficacy. In A. Wigfield & J. Eccles (Eds.), *Development of achievement motivation* (pp. 16–31). San Diego, CA: Academic Press.

Schwartz, D., Dodge, K. A., Pettit, G. S., & Bates, J. E. (2000). Friendship as a moderating factor in the pathway between early harsh home environment and later victimization in the peer group. *Developmental Psychology, 36*(5), 646.

Schwartz, S. J. (2007). The applicability of familism to diverse ethnic groups: A preliminary study. *The Journal of Social Psychology, 147*(2), 101–118.

Schwartz, S. J., Weisskirch, R. S., Hurley, E. A., Zamboanga, B. L., Park, I. J. K., Kim, S. Y.,…Greene, A. D. (2010). Communalism, familism, and filial piety: Are they birds of a collectivist feather? *Cultural Diversity and Ethnic Minority Psychology, 16*(4), 548.

ScienceDaily. (2011). *Poverty-related stress affects readiness for school.* Retrieved November 12, 2012, from http://www.sciencedaily.com/releases/2011/10/111026091218.htm

Scott, L. D. (2003). Cultural orientation and coping with perceived discrimination among African American youth. *Journal of Black Psychology, 29*(3), 235–256.

Seccombe, K. (2002). "Beating the odds" versus "changing the odds": Poverty, resilience, and family policy. *Journal of Marriage and Family, 64*(2), 384–394.

Segerstrom, S. C. (2005). Optimism and immunity: Do positive thoughts always lead to positive effects? *Brain, Behavior, and Immunity, 19*(3), 195–200.

Segerstrom, S. C. (2007). Optimism and resources: Effects on each other and on health over 10 years. *Journal of Research in Personality, 41*(4), 772–786.

Sharot, T., Riccardi, A. M., Raio, C. M., & Phelps E. A. (2007). Neural mechanisms mediating optimism bias. *Nature, 450*(7166), 102–105.

Sharot, T. (2011). *The optimism bias. Time: Health & Family.* Retrieved November 12, 2012, from http://www.time.com/time/health/article/0,8599,2074067-2,00.html

Shaw, E., Levitt, C., Wong, S., & Kaczorowski, J. (2006). Systematic review of the literature on postpartum care: Effectiveness of postpartum support to improve maternal parenting, mental health, quality of life, and physical health. *Birth, 33*(3), 210–220.

Shonkoff, J. P., & Phillips, D. (2000). *From neurons to neighborhoods: The science of early childhood development.* Washington, DC: National Academies Press.

Shonkoff, J. P., Garner, A. S., Siegel, B. S., Dobbins, M. I., Earls, M. F., McGuinn, L.,…& Wood, D. L. (2012). The lifelong effects of early childhood adversity and toxic stress. *Pediatrics, 129*(1), e232–e246.

Sheldon, S. B. (2002). Parents' social networks and beliefs as predictors of parent involvement. *The Elementary School Journal, 102*(4), 301–316.

Silverstein, S. (1974). *Where the sidewalk ends.* New York, NY: HarperCollins Publishers. Quote retrieved November 2012 from http://www.poetrysociety.org/psa/poetry/poetry_in_motion/atlas/portland/listen_to_the_mustn/

Simons, L. G., & Conger, R. D. (2007). Linking mother-father differences in parenting to a typology of family parenting styles and adolescent outcomes. *Journal of Family Issues, 28*(2), 212–241.

Sipe, C. L. (2002). Mentoring programs for adolescents: A research summary. *Journal of Adolescent Health, 31*(6), 251–260.

Slavin, R. E., & Madden, N. A. (1989). What works for students at risk: A research synthesis. *Educational Leadership, 46*(5), 4–13.

Snyder, C. R. (1994). *The psychology of hope: You can get there from here.* New York, NY: The Free Press.

Snyder, C., Feldman, D., Shorey, H., & Rand, K. (2002). Hopeful choices: A school counselor's guide to hope theory. *Journal of Personality and Social Psychology, 65*, 1061–1070.

Snyder, C., Rand, K. L., & Sigmon, D. R. (2002). Hope theory: A member of the positive psychology family. In C. R. Snyder & S. J. Lopez (Eds.), *Handbook of positive psychology* (pp. 257–276). New York, NY: Oxford University Press.

Snyder, C. R., Lehman, K. A., Kluck, B., & Monsson, Y. (2006). Hope for rehabilitation and vice versa. *Rehabilitation Psychology, 51*(2), 89.

Solomon, A. L., Waul, M., Van Ness, A., & Travis, J. (2004). Outside the walls: A national snapshot of community-based prisoner reentry programs. Washington, DC: Urban Institute.

Southwick, S. M., Vythilingam, M., & Charney, D. S. (2005). The psychobiology of depression and resilience to stress: Implications for prevention and treatment. *Annual Review of Clinical Psychology, 1*, 255–291.

Southwick, S. M., Morgan, C. A., Vythilingam, M., & Charney, D. (2007). Mentors enhance resilience in at-risk children and adolescents. *Psychoanalytic Inquiry, 26*(4), 577–584.

Spaulding K. (2008). *Exercise, humor, music, and the brain: The positive effects of these three things on mental health.* Retrieved October 8, 2012, from http://ksspaulding.wordpress.com/article/exercise-humor-music-and-the-brain-3smazt4fj02nv-19/

Spencer, M. B., Fegley, S. G., & Harpalani, V. (2003). A theoretical and empirical examination of identity as coping: Linking coping resources to the self processes of African American youth. *Applied Developmental Science, 7*(3), 181–188.

Spera, C. (2005). A review of the relationship among parenting practices, parenting styles, and adolescent school achievement. *Educational Psychology Review, 17*(2), 125–146.

Sroufe, L. A. (2005). Attachment and development: A prospective, longitudinal study from birth to adulthood. *Attachment & Human Development, 7*(4), 349–367.

Steele, C. M. (1997). A threat in the air: How stereotypes shape intellectual identity and performance. *American Psychologist, 52*(6), 613.

Steidel, A. G. L., & Contreras, J. M. (2003). A new familism scale for use with Latino populations. *Hispanic Journal of Behavioral Sciences, 25*(3), 312–330.

Steinberg, L., Lamborn, S. D., Dornbusch, S. M., & Darling, N. (1992). Impact of parenting practices on adolescent achievement: Authoritative parenting, school involvement, and encouragement to succeed. *Child Development, 63*(5), 1266–1281.

Steinberg, L. (2001). We know some things: Parent-adolescent relationships on retrospect and prospect. *Journal of Research on Adolescence, 11*(1), 1–19.

Steinberg, L. (2007). Risk taking in adolescence: New perspectives from brain and behavioral science. *Current Directions in Psychological Science, 16*(2), 55–59.

Stephanou, G. (2011). Children friendship: The role of hope in attributions, emotions and expectations. *Psychology, 2*(8), 875–888.

Stevens, F. I., & Grymes, J. (1993). Opportunity to learn: Issues of equity for poor and minority students. Washington, DC: U.S. Dept. of Education, Office of Educational Research and Improvement, National Center for Education Statistics.

Stiles, J. (2000). Neural plasticity and cognitive development. *Developmental Neuropsychology, 18*(2), 237–272.

Sutton, C. R. (2004). Celebrating ourselves: The family reunion rituals of African-Caribbean transnational families. *Global Networks, 4*(3), 243–257.

Taylor, L. C., Clayton, J. D., & Rowley, S. J. (2004). Academic socialization: Understanding parental influences on children's school-related development in the early years. *Review of General Psychology, 8*(3), 163–178.

Taylor, R. D., & Roberts, D. (1995). Kinship support and maternal and adolescent well-being in economically disadvantaged African-American families. *Child Development, 66*(6), 1585–1597.

Taylor, R. D. (2010). Risk and resilience in low-income African American families: Moderating effects of kinship social support. *Cultural Diversity and Ethnic Minority Psychology, 16*(3), 344.

Taylor, S. E., Repetti, R. L., & Seeman, T. (1997). Health psychology: What is an unhealthy environment and how does it get under the skin? *Annual Review of Psychology, 48*(1), 411–447.

Taylor, Z. E., Larsen-Rife, D., Conger, R. D., Widaman, K. F., & Cutrona, C. E. (2010). Life stress, maternal optimism, and adolescent competence in single mother, African American families. *Journal of Family Psychology, 24*(4), 468–477.

Taylor, Z. E., Widaman, K. F., Robins, R. W., Jochem, R., Early, D. R., & Conger, R. D. (2012). Dispositional optimism: A psychological resource for Mexican-origin mothers experiencing economic stress. *Journal of Family Psychology, 26*(1), 133.

Teti, M., Martin, A. E., Ranade, R., Massie, J., Malebranche, D. J., Tschann, J. M., & Bowleg, L. (2012). "I'm a keep rising. I'm a keep going forward, regardless": Exploring Black men's resilience amid sociostructural challenges and stressors. *Qualitative Health Research, 22*, 524–533.

The National Commission on Excellence in Education. (1983). *A nation at risk: The imperative for educational reform.* Washington, DC: U.S. Department of Education.

Theokas, C. L., & Lerner, R. M. (2006). Observed ecological assets in families, schools, and neighborhoods: Conceptualization, measurement, and relations with positive and negative developmental outcomes. *Applied Developmental Science, 10*(2), 61–74.

Thompson, L. A., & Kelly-Vance, L. (2001). The impact of mentoring on academic achievement of at-risk youth. *Children and Youth Services Review, 23*(3), 227–242.

Thompson, R. A., & Nelson, C. A. (2001). Developmental science and the media: Early brain development. *American Psychologist, 56*(1), 5.

Tiger, L. (1979). *Optimism: The biology of hope.* New York: Simon and Schuster.

Till, C., Ghassemi, R., Aubert-Broche, B., Kerbrat, A., Collins, D. L., Narayanan, S., … Banwell, B. L. (2011). MRI correlates of cognitive impairment in childhood-onset multiple sclerosis. *Neuropsychology, 25*(3), 319–332.

Tolan, P. H., Sherrod, L. R., Gorman-Smith, D., & Henry, D. B. (2004). Building protection, support, and opportunity for inner-city children and youth and their families. In K. Maton, C. J. Schellenbach, B. J. Leadbeater, & A. L. Solarz (Eds.), *Investing in children, youth, families, and communities: Strengths-based research and policy* (pp. 193–211). Washington, DC: American Psychological Association.

Toldson, I. A. (2008). *Breaking barriers: Plotting the path to academic success for school-age African-American males.* Washington, DC: Congressional Black Caucus Foundation.

Toldson, I. A. (2011). *Breaking barriers 2: Plotting the path away from juvenile detention and toward academic success for school-age African American males.* Washington, DC: Congressional Black Caucus Foundation.

Tong, E. M. W., Fredrickson, B. L., Chang, W., & Lim, Z. X. (2010). Re-examining hope: The roles of agency thinking and pathways thinking. *Cognition & Emotion, 24*(7), 1207–1215.

Tschannen-Moran, M., & Hoy, A. W. (2001). Teacher efficacy: Capturing an elusive construct. *Teaching and Teacher Education, 17*(7), 783–805.

Tsujimoto, S. (2008). The prefrontal cortex: Functional neural development during early childhood. *The Neuroscientist, 14*(4), 345–358.

Tyson, K., Darity, W., & Castellino, D. R. (2005). It's not "a black thing": Understanding the burden of acting white and other dilemmas of high achievement. *American Sociological Review, 70*(4), 582–605.

Ungar, M. (2008). Resilience across cultures. *British Journal of Social Work, 38*(2), 218–235. doi:10.1093/bjsw/bcl343

Urban, J. B., Lewin-Bizan, S., & Lerner, R. M. (2009). The role of neighborhood ecological assets and activity involvement in youth developmental outcomes: Differential impacts of asset poor and asset rich neighborhoods. *Journal of Applied Developmental Psychology, 30*(5), 601–614.

Urbig, D., & Monsen, E. (2012). The structure of optimism: "Controllability affects the extent to which efficacy beliefs shape outcome expectancies." *Journal of Economic Psychology, 33*(4), 854–867.

United States Department of Education. (2013). Promise neighborhoods. Retrieved January, 1, 2013, from http://www2.ed.gov/programs/promiseneighborhoods/index.html

U.S. Department of Health and Human Services. (2012). *HHS poverty guidelines.* Retrieved September 2012 from http://aspe.hhs.gov/poverty/12poverty.shtml

Utsey, S. O., Bolden, M. A., Lanier, Y., & Williams, O. (2007). Examining the role of culture-specific coping as a predictor of resilient outcomes in African Americans from high risk urban communities. *Journal of Black Psychology, 33*, 75–93.

Valladares, S., & Anderson Moore, K. (2009). *The strengths of poor families.* Washington, DC: Child Trends.

Vanderbilt-Adriance, E., & Shaw, D. S. (2008). Conceptualizing and re-evaluating resilience across levels of risk, time, and domains of competence. *Clinical Child and Family Psychology Review, 11*(1), 30–58.

Van Roekel, D. (2008). Parent, family, community involvement in education. Policy Brief. Washington, DC: National Education Association.

Vygotsky, L. S. (1978). *Mind in society: The development of higher psychological processes.* Cambridge, MA: Harvard University Press.

Wagmiller, R. L., & Adelman, R. M. (2009). *Childhood and intergenerational poverty: The long-term consequences of growing up poor.* New York: National Center for Children in Poverty. Columbia University, Mailman School of Public Health.

Walsh, F. (2006). *Strengthening family resilience* (2nd ed.). New York, NY: Guilford Press.

Wang, M. T. (2009). School climate support for behavioral and psychological adjustment: Testing the mediating effect of social competence. *School Psychology Quarterly, 24*(4), 240–251.

Weis, R., & Speridakos, E. C. (2011). A meta-analysis of hope enhancement strategies in clinical and community settings. *Psychology of Well-Being: Theory, Research and Practice, 1*(1), 1–16, 5.

Weisel, Elie (1986). Adapted from Nobel lecture: Hope, despair and memory. Retrieved March 2013 from http://www.nobelprize.org/nobel_prizes/peace/laureates/1986/wiesel-lecture.html

Werner, E. (1990). Protective factors and individual resilience. In S. J. Meisels J. P. & Shonkoff (Eds.), *Handbook of early childhood intervention* (pp. 97–116). New York, NY: Cambridge University Press.

Werner, E. E. (1993). Risk, resilience, and recovery: Perspectives from the Kauai Longitudinal Study. *Development and Psychopathology, 5,* 503–503.

Wexler, L. (2009). The importance of identity, history, and culture in the wellbeing of indigenous youth. *The Journal of the History of Childhood and Youth, 2*(2), 267–276.

Wheeler, M. E., Keller, T. E., & DuBois, D. L. (2010). Review of three recent randomized trials of school-based mentoring. *Social Policy Report, 24*(3).

Williams, C. J. (1987). *Destruction of black civilization: Great issues of a race from 4500 B.C. to 2000 A.D.* (3rd ed.). Chicago, IL: Third World Press.

Wolpert, S. (2011). *Psychologists discover a gene's link to optimism, self-esteem.* UCLA Newsroom. Retrieved November 12, 2012, from http://newsroom.ucla.edu/portal/ucla/ucla-life-scientists-discover-215259.aspx

Won, C. (2011). From gang life to grad school—*"I would've never seen myself in this position."* Journaltimes.com. Retrieved December 21, 2012, from http://www.journaltimes.com/news/local/from-gang-life-to-grad-school

Xue, Y., Leventhal, T., Brooks-Gunn, J., & Earls, F. J. (2005). Neighborhood residence and mental health problems of 5- to 11-year-olds. *Archives of General Psychiatry, 62*(5), 554–563.

Zeanah, C. H., Nelson, C. A., Fox, N. A., Smyke, A. T., Marshall, P., Parker, S. W., & Koga, S. (2003). Designing research to study the effects of institutionalization on brain and behavioral development: The Bucharest Early Intervention Project. *Development and Psychopathology, 15*(4), 885–907.

Zimmerman, B. J. (2000). Self-efficacy: An essential motive to learn. *Contemporary Educational Psychology, 25*(1), 82–91.

Zimmerman, M. A., Ramirez, J., Washienko, K. M., Walter, B., & Dyer, S. (1998). Enculturation hypothesis: Exploring direct and protective effects among Native American youth. In H. I. McCubbin, E. A. Thompson, A. I. Thompson, & J. E. Fromer (Eds.), *Resiliency in Native American and immigrant families* (pp. 199–220). Thousand Oaks, CA: Sage Publications.

INDEX

Page numbers followed by "t" indicate a reference to a table on the specified page.
Italicized page numbers indicate a figure on the specified page.